CIRCLE OF THE ONE

Transcendent Healing Stories

Through Divine Guidance

for Soul Activation

Visionary Author

Dolly Alessandra Mayenzet

Presented by

Blue Limits DGG Holdings

CIRCLE OF THE ONE
Volume I

Book Cover Design
Troy R. Chadwick, Doe Renée, and Traydon Inspires

Art and Card Design
Troy R. Chadwick and Doe Renée

Interior Book Design and Formatting
Kathy White and Troy R. Chadwick

Published By: Blue Limits DGG Holdings - USA

Printed in China

ISBN: 979-8-988-99900-3

Dedication

To my cherished sons, Gabriel and Gavin,

In the pages of this book, Circle of The One, I offer a heartfelt dedication to both of you, my greatest treasures. You are the guiding lights that illuminate my path and the driving force behind my unwavering pursuit of becoming the best version of myself.

Gabriel, as your name represents, you are a warrior angel, embodying incredible courage, strength, and resilience. From the moment you came into this world, you have shown me the true meaning of bravery. Your unwavering determination to face challenges head-on inspires me to summon the warrior within me. Your presence in my life fills every moment with awe and pride. You are my guiding star, my source of inspiration, and the embodiment of unconditional love.

Gavin, as your name represents, you are a Godsend, a white hawk soaring gracefully through the skies of my life. Your gentle spirit, wisdom beyond your years, and innate ability to bring comfort and joy to those around you fill my heart with profound gratitude. You are a constant reminder of divine guidance and the miraculous ways in which life unfolds. Your presence in my life is a precious gift, reminding me to embrace the magic that surrounds us. You are my guardian, my teacher, and the purest embodiment of love.

Both of you hold an irreplaceable place in my heart, and it is through your unwavering love and support that I find the strength to pursue this journey of self-discovery and transformation.

Your belief in me, your boundless love, and the joy you bring to my world are the greatest blessings I could ever receive.

Gabriel and Gavin, I dedicate this book to you as a testament to the profound impact you have had on my life. May its pages remind you of the boundless potential that resides within you and inspire you to embrace your own unique paths. As you navigate the ever-changing landscapes of life, may the stories within these pages ignite the flames of courage, resilience, and purpose within your souls.

Know that my love for you knows no boundaries. You are my guiding stars, my pillars of strength, and the purest expressions of love in my life. Thank you for blessing my world with your presence and for teaching me the true meaning of unconditional love.

With all my love,

Mom

(Dolly Alessandra)

Table of Contents

Acknowledgements

With utmost gratitude and a heart brimming with love, I humbly offer my acknowledgment to God, the Universe, and the divine forces that orchestrate the symphony of life. It is through your boundless grace and guidance that Circle of The One has come to fruition, becoming a vessel of transformation, wisdom, and inspiration.

To my dear dad thank you for always allowing me to be free in who I wanted to be. You always saw strength in me. Your unwavering faith that I would find my way. I love you.

To my mom thank you for guiding me. I miss you. I love you.

To the master teachers who have illuminated my path and expanded my consciousness, I extend my deepest appreciation. Neville Goddard, Thomas Troward, Genevieve Behrend, Wayne Dyer, Abraham Hicks, Bob Proctor, Bruce Lipton, Michael Beckwith, Don Green, Ernest Holmes, Robert Collier, Louis Hayes, Dr. Joe Dispenza, Genevieve Behrend, Arndrea King, Florence Shinn, Omar Gomez, Gerard Powell, and others who have ignited my inner flame, your teachings have shaped my journey and set my soul ablaze. Your wisdom has opened the doors of possibility, empowering me to step into my true purpose and live a life of authenticity.

I now turn my gratitude towards the remarkable authors who have shared their transformative stories within the pages of Circle of The One. You are the embodiment of Gods and Goddesses, light workers who illuminate the path for others. Without your courageous vulnerability, unwavering dedication, and willingness to share your personal journeys, this book would be but an empty vessel. Together, we create a harmonious symphony of resilience, hope, and enlightenment, reminding the world of its inherent magnificence.

To those who have played a pivotal role in helping me recognize the Goddess within and step into the life I was designed to live, I offer a heartfelt acknowledgement.

To Troy Chadwick, thank you for your unwavering belief in me and for helping me hold the vision of this project. Your support and encouragement have been the guiding light in moments of doubt.

To Kathy White, your amazing discipline and organizational skills have been a cornerstone of this project. Your meticulous attention to detail and commitment to excellence have ensured its success.

To Naqiya Taha, your exceptional service and support have touched the lives of everyone involved in this endeavor. Your dedication and kindness have made a lasting impact.

To Doe Renée, you are a beacon of light and creativity, infusing this project with beauty and inspiration. Your contributions have elevated the collective spirit of Circle of The One.

To Yashica Mack, your unwavering presence and dedication to doing what needed to be done have been invaluable. Your selfless commitment has propelled this project forward.

I would like to thank our chief editor Jackie Raymond for the amazing editing job on many of our authors.

I would also like to extend my gratitude to Karem Zafra-Vera, Victoria Vera-Zafra, and Gregg Gonzales.

To anyone whom I may have unintentionally omitted, please know that your contribution has not gone unnoticed. Each person involved in this journey has brought their unique gifts and energy, weaving a tapestry of beauty and wisdom. Your presence has enriched the essence of Circle of The One, and for that, I am eternally grateful.

In closing, I wish to acknowledge the profound beauty that resides within each and every soul who has contributed to this book. Together, we have created a world where transformation thrives, hearts heal, and spirits' soar. With heartfelt appreciation and boundless love, I honor each and every one of you.

Forever united in light,

Dolly Alessandra

Thank You
Arndrea Waters King!

A few years ago, I found myself standing on the precipice of one of the most intimidating moments of my life. It was a chilling echo of the time I met Bob Proctor seven years prior. I found myself in a quiet plea with the universe, yearning for the opportunity to learn from the great leaders of the world. My heart whispered the name, Yoda, as a metaphor for wisdom and strength.

The illustrious Martin Luther King Jr. held a unique spot in my heart, ever since I was a child, a bond inexplicably interwoven with my birthday. To the world, it was a national holiday, but to me, it felt like a personal gift, an extended celebration of my existence. I used to think, as a child, that I owed this small joy to him. This gratitude blossomed into a deep respect for his charismatic aura and powerful persona.

Even as a child, I sensed that there was something captivating about Dr. King, something that moved people, that sparked change. I marveled at this force, this ability to influence and inspire. I often wondered, could it be mere coincidence that our lives would intertwine in such an extraordinary way years later?

Indeed, just a few years ago, I found myself in the grip of fear. But somehow, the universe conspired, and the paths of our destinies crossed once more. A testament, perhaps, to the truth that we are all interconnected in this vast tapestry of life, bound by threads of love, respect, gratitude, and the undying pursuit of justice.

I was consumed by a fear that ran bone-deep. I was a mother of two, balancing the tender love for my children with the fiery pursuit of an entrepreneurial dream.

In 2021, I had discovered what I believed would be my golden ticket to freedom, but like a mirage in the desert, it wasn't as it seemed.

Let's travel a little further back in time, to 2018, my path led me to a sanctuary of healing in Costa Rica, a place called Rythmia. This journey was not merely a change of location, but a profound shift within my very soul. It was there that I encountered a book of cards, the only oracle deck in sight, nestled amidst the bookshelf.

I was raised in a tradition that branded oracle cards as tools of evil, convincing me that no one could foresee the future. Yet these cards whispered to my curiosity, beckoning me to challenge the beliefs I had held for so long.

Adjacent to the bookshelf stood an enchanting depiction of the goddess Isis. It was a sight so mesmerizing that it became a magnet for photographs. As I indulged in my meals, my gaze would invariably be drawn to her image, a picture brimming with poise and mystique. I found myself lost in her eyes, wondering about the life she led, yearning for the strength and grace she personified.

The oracle cards, calling out to me from the corner of my eye, became increasingly hard to ignore. After a particularly intense experience, I found myself drawn towards them, breaking the chains of my upbringing. I reached out, my fingers grazing the deck, and I allowed myself to plunge into the unknown, just to see...

What I discovered within those cards was a profound awakening, a prism of understanding refracting wisdom gleaned from the narratives of others. These were not merely stories of strangers but echoes of my own existence. The cards stirred something deep within me, activating dormant cells, instigating a transformation from within.

In this oasis of self-discovery, I encountered a soul whose energy was as formidable as it was gentle, as powerful as it was kind. We shared a meal, our conversations intertwining with the soft caress of the evening breeze. There was a sense of familiarity, a feeling of having met in a forgotten past. A soul sister, a mirror to my own spirit.

I had always harbored the belief that I was destined for something greater, that I was born to transcend the ordinary. And in braving the tempest of fear, I found myself crossing paths with Arndrea Waters King, the daughter-in-law of the legendary Martin Luther King Jr.

Arndrea had devoted over three decades to the pursuit of becoming a beacon of love and light. She was the embodiment of the wisdom and strength I had yearned for; the Yoda I had invoked in my prayers before venturing into this vibrant blue zone of life and transformation. From the moment our paths intertwined, we have been exploring life's mysteries together, week after week.

To know Arndrea and her family is a privilege, an honor beyond words. Their legacy is a testament to the power of love, the strength of conviction, and the resilience of the human spirit. My journey with them continues, a journey that transcends time and space, grounded in love, light, and the shared pursuit of a world bound by the ties of compassion and understanding.

I am forever grateful.

I embody her resilience when fear seeks to cripple me. I remember the first time she revealed to me the profound sensation of spiritual warfare, a battle waged not in the physical realm but within the heart and soul. It was a revelation that shook me to my core, yet in the same breath, it fortified me with a newfound strength.

"Surround yourself with the Dreamers"

- Arndrea Waters King

Foreword From
Arndrea Waters King

Dolly Alessandra's 'Circle of One: Transcendent Healing Stories Through Divine Guidance for Soul Activation," provides a wonderful collection of testimonial tributes to the power of faith, hope and courage in the pursuit of self-actualization. The stories told here by 33 diverse individuals shed new light on the varieties of spiritual and psychological qualities, including: perseverance; wisdom; grace; optimism; self-love; reflection; mercy, rebirth, empowerment and many other deeply-human concerns as we seek to excavate the authentic self in our troubled times.

Tapping into the teachings of great educators and ideas, including Bob Proctor, Napolean Hill and the law of attraction, these essays explore the dynamic power of love in dispelling fear and discouragement. As my father-in-law, Martin Luther King, Jr. once said, "Hatred and bitterness can never cure the disease of fear; only love can do that. Hatred paralyzes life; love releases it. Hatred confuses life; love harmonizes it. Hatred darkens life; love illumines it."

These stories also recall the phenomenal wisdom and insight of my mother-in-law, Coretta Scott King, who said that "The true greatness of a community is most accurately measured by the compassionate acts of its citizens." As we join together to dispel fear and build community, these extraordinary stories show us the wondrous compassion of people who have experienced unique forms of personal suffering, oppression and struggle. With great courage and determination, however, they overcame debilitating neuroses and fears to unlock their full potential as caring human beings.

In our highly-polarized and divided society, we too often succumb to the siren songs of scarcity, distrust and bitter negativity. But the essays in "Circle of One" do indeed show us more creative approaches to healing and personal transformation through love and all-inclusive goodwill toward all people. Yes, we can build the Beloved Community of Dr. King's dream for our nation, if we answer the call to community with faith, courage and commitment.

The creative, transcendent power of love in overcoming adversity is the golden thread that runs through these moving stories of struggle and hope. I commend them to you with the assurance that they will illuminate your path, lighten your load and help you find the way to a better future.

Arndrea Waters King

Introduction

"What you seek, seeks you" -Rumi

Welcome to the epic tale of 33 heroic warriors, revered as deities of our time. As they recount their brave exploits and share their wisdom and experiences.

Their journeys and adventures will transport you to different dimensional realities, activating cells within you to raise awareness and expand your consciousness. Through their relatable stories, you will discover the power of transformation, trusting your intuition to guide you.

Join us on a quest to find the most powerful healers of this era, as we use the intentional laws of the universe to manifest our desires and embody our true essence.

Remember, why we do this… we do this to remember.

You Are The One!

Dolly Alessandra

~ Enlightenment ~

Bathed in the radiant glow of her inner wisdom, the enlightenment Goddess illuminates the path of truth, guiding souls towards awakening and liberation

Unleash Your Soul

by Dolly Alessandra

What does it truly mean to possess an awakened imagination, to unleash your soul? Down the rabbit hole we go. I recall as a child feeling the wonder and magic of life and sensing my future held great promise that would be a manifestation of my vivid imagination. But, as time passed, those hopes and dreams of a fairytale life seemed to elude me. At 36 years old, I found myself yearning for more in life.

The glossy pages of magazines and the silver screen portrayed a life I dreamed of having, but with entry-level jobs and an impending divorce, the reality of my situation was daunting. How would I support my young children financially? I had always believed that a happy family with a husband, two kids, and a dog would lead to the amazing life I desired, but now, in March 2017, I was on my knees, having hit rock bottom.

My relationship with God was already rocky due to my mother's death when she was 49, and my belief that He failed to save her. I had no one else to turn to and felt that my children would be better off without me. The fear of the world consumed me, and I was labeled as codependent, feeling completely lost. With tears streaming down my face, I called out to the heavens and begged for guidance. I was on my hands and knees, my heart aching with unbearable pain and smothering fear. In that moment, I was willing to do anything to escape the suffocating grip of my suffering. I cried out with all my might, pleading for a sign, a glimmer of hope. "Please show me the way," I shouted into the void, "and I promise to tell the world it was you!"

The universe works in mysterious ways, and I was about to experience its magic firsthand. In a moment of divine timing, a video appeared before me, featuring a man who looked like a run-of-the-mill salesman. But something within urged me to click "play". And thank the stars I did, for in that instant, my world was forever changed.

The man on the screen spoke of profound truths, truths that resonated deep within my soul. He proclaimed we are not mere mortals, but rather, eternal spirits having a fleeting human experience. His words were like a catalyst, igniting a fire within me I never knew existed. I hungered for more, and thirsted for knowledge that would help me grow and evolve beyond my wildest dreams. I was completely captivated.

I devoured every piece of content I could find. I delved into his books, his speeches, his teachings, and I was awestruck by the sheer amount of wisdom and knowledge he possessed. With his guidance, and within a mere month, I had transformed so much. I gave up smoking — a habit that had once held me captive — and I began to prioritize my health and wellbeing like never before. The transformation was so rapid, so profound, that those around me doubted it would last. But I knew, deep down in my soul, this was different. I felt a power within me I had never known before, a drive and a determination that couldn't be extinguished.

My loved ones didn't understand my newfound passion, leaving me feeling isolated and alone. But I refused to let fear hold me back. I made a vow to meet my mentor in person, to learn from him and show him the impact he'd had on my life. I made a decision, a bold and daring choice that would change the course of my life forever. I vowed to seek out the alchemists, the visionaries, the leaders of the New World, even if it meant risking everything I had. I had no money, no resources, no connections.

But that didn't stop me. I was driven by a burning desire to find something greater than myself, a purpose that would give my life meaning.

There was this courage I had never felt inside of me before (I was borrowing his belief). I set my sights on Toronto, Canada, where one of these alchemists lived. The journey was long and treacherous, and the cost was 25 times more than what my humble vehicle was worth. But I didn't let that deter me. I did exactly what I was coached to do and manifested what I needed to.

I had two young children to support, and finding a job seemed like the responsible thing to do. But, deep down, I knew there was something more out there for me — and I was willing to risk all to find it. This man, this alchemist, offered me a chance to pursue my dreams, to follow my heart wherever it may lead. He gave me permission to explore the depths of my soul and to discover my true purpose in life. And so I embarked on a journey of self-discovery, a quest for truth.

I still remember the moment he walked into the room. The air crackled with electricity, and every head turned to see him. He was a force of nature, commanding attention and respect with every step he took. He was dressed in a white gray suit — a symbol of purity and light — and he spoke with a sharp clarity that cut through the noise and confusion of the world. It was as if he were a modern-day Merlin, wielding a magic that was both ancient and new. I couldn't believe my luck. I was sitting in a room where he was teaching, absorbing every word like a sponge. And then, in a flash, we were in his home, surrounded by his books, his studio, his family.

I saw firsthand what it took to be a true leader, to live a life of purpose and meaning. It was like I had been transported to the land of Oz, following the yellow brick road to the Emerald City.

But, instead of a wizard, I'd found a man who embodied the very essence of what it meant to be a spiritual human being. In his presence, I felt a deep sense of awe and reverence. He showed me what was possible, what I could achieve if I only had the courage to follow my dreams. And I knew, without a shadow of a doubt, my life would never be the same again. The problem was, I had never really known what I wanted to do in life. I was actually quite lost.

He then said he could show and teach me how he did what he did. I knew right away this was what I was meant to do!!! I felt my soul had been set alight. But what exactly did it mean to be my higher self, to remember who I really was? I was breathing in life. As I said, I knew as a young girl there was more to life. I was shown that if I leaned into this world — the one I saw in my imagination — then more of that world would be revealed to me.

I love movies like "Labyrinth", and I love the movie, "The Princess Bride" — anything with fantasy that allows us to travel to a world of magic, dragons, superheroes, etc. What if we could…? Imagine a world where everything we dreamed of could become a reality! A world where we could create our own movie, feel every emotion, and live every moment. This is the power of being player one, the power to co-create our own destiny. It may seem crazy to believe in such a world, but the more we open ourselves up to it, the more it reveals its wonders to us.

It's like discovering a whole new world, a world beyond conformity and limitations. But to truly unlock this power, we must surround ourselves with dreamers, those who see the possibilities beyond what others consider impossible. As the saying goes, we become the five people we surround ourselves with, and when we surround ourselves with dreamers, we become unstoppable. This book holds great power for you. In the six short years I have discovered this truth — and I have still barely scratched the surface — my life has completely changed. I now realize how movies are inspired, and how books and TV series are inspired. They are inspired by true life stories. By following a leader of love and light, I was given a blueprint of how we could change, and by doing certain things in a certain way, we could completely change our reality. This wasn't just fantasies. This truly was a reality, and that reality is…we become what we think about.

So let us dare to dream, let us embrace the power of being player one, and let us surround ourselves with those who believe in the impossible. For in doing so, we unleash a force more powerful than we could ever imagine: the force of love, the force that can change the world. Remember why we do this. We do this to remember.

Divine Beloved

by Dolly Alessandra

Dear Divine Beloved,

Heart full of grace and beauty. I am in awe of the exquisite elegance that surrounds me, and I am grateful for the power that flows through me in every moment.

I am filled with a divine radiance, knowing that my beauty shines forth from within. I embrace my unique essence, knowing that it is what makes me truly beautiful. I move through the world with grace and poise, touching others with my gentle spirit and compassionate heart.

My elegance is a reflection of my inner strength and wisdom. I am confident in my abilities, knowing that I have the courage to overcome any obstacle that comes my way. I trust in my intuition, knowing that it is a powerful source of guidance and support.

I am committed to living a life of abundance and love. I am grateful for the blessings that flow into my life with ease and grace, and I share my abundance freely with those around me. I am surrounded by love, knowing that it is the most powerful force in the universe and that it flows to me effortlessly.

Thank you, Divine Beloved, for the exquisite beauty and elegance that surrounds me. May I continue to embody these qualities, serving as a vessel of love and light for all those around me.

With love and gratitude.

About

Dolly Alessandra

Dolly Alessandra is a highly accomplished entrepreneur, esteemed CEO, and Founder of Blue Limits Academy. In addition, she holds the position of Vice President of Global Master Coaches at the Napoleon Hill Institute, where she has made significant contributions to the world of coaching and personal development. She was also a certified Proctor Gallagher Consultant, having honed her skills under the guidance of the legendary Bob Proctor. Her expertise in coaching and personal development has earned her the opportunity to work with many luminaries of the world, leveraging her deep knowledge and experience to help transform their lives and businesses.

As a devoted mother of two remarkable boys, Gabriel and Gavin, Dolly is deeply committed to balancing her personal and professional life with grace and finesse.

Dolly's unwavering passion and commitment to her destiny have driven her to seek out all the deities of this century, remaining steadfastly behind the scenes to learn and share the stories of the leaders of the new earth. Her journey is marked by a profound reverence for the transformative power of knowledge and an unyielding determination to make a positive impact on the world.

Dolly's deep spiritual connection and mastery of manifestation have allowed her to unlock the secrets of the universe, helping people to tap into their true potential and achieve their wildest dreams. Her passion for personal growth and self-discovery has led her to go to the ends of the earth in search of the truth, driven by a deep desire to know thyself and help others do the same.

In her relentless pursuit of excellence, Dolly Alessandra has become a living embodiment of the very principles she teaches, demonstrating that with passion, dedication, and an unshakable belief in oneself, anything is possible. Her extraordinary journey serves as an inspiration to all who cross her path, leaving an indelible mark on the hearts and minds of those fortunate enough to learn from her wisdom and experience.

dollyalessandra.com

www.circleoftheone.com

Troy R Chadwick

2

~ Providence ~

With profound wisdom and unwavering grace, this divine architect orchestrates the threads of our lives, intricately crafting each moment and purpose with divine precision. "Trust in the grand design of the universe, for even in the darkest hour, the seeds of transformation are sown."

Run From Safety

by Troy R Chadwick

"It must happen to us all… We pack up what we've learned so far and leave the familiar behind. No fun, that shearing separation, but somewhere within, we must dimly know that saying goodbye to safety brings the only security we'll ever know." ~ Richard Bach

Music is amazing. I love to write music and I love the way I feel when I listen to a song I have created. I remember a time when I was in my mid 20s. There were four of us in the band: Mike played drums; Gerald played bass; Eric played keyboards; and I played guitar and sang. We were so good. We practiced countless hours in the studio, perfecting our songs. It felt incredible.

One day Mike approached me with something I wasn't expecting. "We need to talk…" he said. Hmm, I thought. What's this about? He continued, "I love how great we sound, and I love the feeling of our sound, but I don't want to practice anymore." I was perplexed. I mean, what the heck? We had just finished a great practice session — better than all the other practice sessions — and he doesn't want to practice anymore? Before I could ask him why, he spoke up. "I want to go out on the stage. I stood there for a moment, staring at him, thinking about what I was going to say. I was uncomfortable.

The dominant thought in my mind was that we weren't ready. I snapped out of that moment and followed up with great enthusiasm and concern. "I hear you, but we're not ready and need to practice more to make it perfect. We only have one chance to make a first impression." Mike stood there. The awkward silence between us was deafening. That moment was a turning point for us. Not much was said after that. We packed up our gear and within a few days, the band was dissolved. Mike and Gerald left. Eric and I both agreed we would find a way to make it work, so we moved forward without them.

A few months passed. Eric and I were writing more songs together as a duo. Out of the blue, I received a phone call from Mike. Curious, I answered the phone. "Hey, Mike, what's up?" He answered, "Hey Troy. It's good to hear you… Um… me and Gerald are opening at Madame Wong's in Hollywood on Thursday night. You and Eric should come." I thought, Oh my God, are you kidding me? Madame Wong's was a popular club where a lot of great bands played. I couldn't understand how this was possible. How were they ready to go on stage in only two months? I mean, seriously, our other band practiced for almost two years. That's a heck of a lot longer than that and we weren't ready. I was intrigued, so I told him that Eric and I would be there.

Thursday came. We arrived at the club early that evening. They were scheduled to go on at 9 p.m. as the opening act. When we walked into the room they were scheduled to perform in, there were only 10 people, including them. Mike's mom and dad were there too. We walked around and greeted them, wishing them luck, then sat down at our table. My mind was spinning. I was so curious about what I was about to hear. Within a few moments, they stepped on stage. There were three of them: drummer (Mike), bass (Gerald), and the guitar player (I don't remember his name). Gerald and the guitar player plugged in their guitars, sending out the scratching sounds of the guitars through the speakers. They proceeded with the mic checks as feedback echoed throughout the room. Mike sat on his drum seat, delivering a quick run on his drum kit with his sticks. The suspense was killing me.

They all looked at each other to signal their readiness, then Mike clicked his drumsticks for the countdown to begin the first song. Before I knew it, they were playing. As the song progressed, I couldn't believe what I was hearing. My stomach started to cringe. My jaw dropped. They sucked so bad! It was horrible. I was so embarrassed for them. All I wanted to do was hide because I didn't want to face them to tell them the truth about how bad they really were. It took all of me not to cover my face. I didn't want them to see my disappointment. All I kept thinking about was how much better we were in the previous band, that we would have been a thousand times better on that stage than they were. I did the best I could to hide how I was feeling with a smile, but obviously, my smile was fake.

The first song ended — but not soon enough — then they started another song, and then another one and another one. I was hoping they would get better as the night went on, but the opposite happened. It was either more of the same or even worse. By the time they'd got to the fifth song, something strange started to happen inside of me. I began to feel even more uncomfortable, but not because they weren't getting better. They were doing what I really wanted to do. They were doing something I didn't have the guts to do, which was to go up on that stage. I was jealous and full of self-pity. How they sounded became 100% irrelevant. The more they played, the worse I felt. Unfortunately, that realization wasn't enough to shift me to act because the story in my head was, "This is who I am". It was what I believed. The real story behind that was the fear I had inside. "What if I mess up in front of everyone?" "What if I'm not as good as I think I am?" "What if we aren't as good as we think we are?" "What if someone criticizes us?" "What if they hate us?" "What if I fail?" "What if I …?" and so the list went on. It was sad.

Alibi after alibi kept popping up. Unfortunately, I didn't have the me I am today saying to me, "If you were as good as you believe you are, get your band back together NOW and book a date for next week!" I didn't understand that, for me to achieve something I have never achieved, I had to become someone I have never been. Even though I understood the reasons for practice, I didn't realize it was the same thing for the stage. I didn't understand that it was OK to suck in the beginning, just as it did when we first started practicing in the studio, and that over time I would get better. I didn't associate practice in a room with practice on a stage, that even though they were different, the growing process was the same. I'd played it "safe".

From here, you would think that I would be sharing with you how I overcame playing it safe at that time, but I'm not going to do that, because that's not what happened. I'm going to share with you how not understanding that pattern of playing it safe keeps you stuck without knowing it. Did you notice how I used the word "pattern"? I'm referring to habits. That wonderful power each one of us has embedded within us, that enables us to live our lives effortlessly. Habits are wonderful. Think about how difficult your life would be if you didn't have the ability to form habits. Habits are God's gift to us to make our lives easy. Habits enable us to do things without thinking. It isn't an issue as to whether habits are good for us. The issue is that we have bad habits, thinking patterns, that are not in harmony with how we would love our lives to be.

Fast forward 20-something years from that band experience to about 10 years ago. I was sitting in my home office, staring at my beautiful Tacoma guitar. It's a beautiful sounding guitar. I was broken inside regarding my dreams as a creative songwriter. Most of my working life up to that point had been spent in businesses not related to music in any way. For more than 20 years I worked in the mortgage industry with my mom. The main reason I did it was to help her, and it was safe. What she didn't know was that I hated the business.

Although I made a lot of money and helped her to make a lot of money, I was miserable. There was no connection. Fortunately, I got to choose what I wanted to do within the business. I always gravitated towards the creative side, which was marketing, operations, and branding. Even though I learned and grew a lot, the many years of working in a business I had no desire to be in took its toll on me. I had to get out. I started planning my exit sometime around 2002. I knew I wanted a change, but I didn't know what that change was going to be.

Around that time, I ran into a Cold Stone Creamery. What I saw was amazing. Lines out the door, selling one of my favorite foods: ice cream. I saw it and said to myself, "That. I could do that." Right there and then I decided I was going to sell ice cream, and I went further and added cookies. From mortgages to ice cream! That should give you a good idea about how much I hated the mortgage business. Selling ice cream and cookies sounded fun and exciting. How hard could it be? All I needed was the right product and the right location.

Once I'd made the decision, I obtained a franchise license and what I thought was a home-run location. Everything was in alignment. The location I ended up landing was a brand new 600,000-square-foot development being built across the street from Disneyland. Ice cream and Disneyland traffic! How could I lose? Done! The franchise agreement was in place and the lease agreement was secured. The mall was scheduled to open in 2004. Unfortunately, the developer ran into delays. They ended up breaking ground in 2006. Soon after, the building process for my store began. After spending almost half a million dollars on this store, we opened in June of 2008.

It was a lot of hard work. Having said that, even though there were tremendous challenges, I found it was easy to do because of the belief I had inside me, knowing I could do it. It turned out beautifully! We had the best-looking store for the entire franchise. Have you heard that phrase, "Location, location, location"? An important piece that phrase left out is "timing". December arrived and we all know what happened then. The real estate market crashed. This drastically changed everything for this mall and for everyone attached to it. A small percentage of the tenants were able to finish. The rest halted. The mall's occupancy never rose above 30 percent. It was a disaster.

I lasted as long as I could, which was two years. Unfortunately, I had put everything I had into this and ended up losing everything. Out of that disaster came the idea to open an online store selling nothing but dinosaur-themed merchandise from toys, games, shirts, shoes to plushes. If it had a dinosaur on it, I was going to sell it. The idea came from a seed that was inadvertently planted in my mind three years prior. I was in Texas, training for the ice cream franchise, and on the way home I stopped by the museum. They had a large dinosaur exhibit which was awesome. I was a little kid again. The store in the museum had lots of dinosaur-themed merchandise. What really caught my eye were these dinosaur shoes they were selling. As I was there, I remembered how much time and money I spent getting dinosaur stuff for my oldest son. My youngest son was also starting to like dinosaurs and he ended up getting a pair of those shoes.

That moment was etched into my mind, but my focus shifted back to what I was preparing to do at that moment, which was to open my ice cream store. The name of the site ended up being called Nothing But Dinosaurs. Out of the gate it was successful. It was created at a time when e-commerce was booming. Amazon was rooted, but not a factor yet. I remember, when I was in only my third month online, generating over $28,000 in sales in one month. Over the life of this e-commerce business, I would end up selling over $2.5 million dollars-worth of dinosaur-themed merchandise. After several years of doing that, I felt empty inside. My creativity was stagnant. My identity wasn't exciting to me. From that moment, another idea surfaced. The idea was dinosaur humanoid creatures. They were something I could sell on my site on shirts and possibly as toys. I spun the idea on the toy reps I was close to for their feedback.

One of them got back to me with a peculiar and quiet excitement. She loved what she saw and said these four words that piqued my interest. This was my introduction into the world of storytelling. She said, "I see a story." Inside I was puzzled. I didn't know what she meant so I proceeded to ask her. It turned out she had a degree in film, specializing in screenwriting. Now I had to address the elephant in the room. She had a master's degree in filmmaking from USC, yet she was selling toys. "What the hell are you selling toys for?" I blurted out. "Are you crazy?!"

She then started to share how she needed a job to offset the difficult nature of the film business and found a job as a toy rep. It turned out that it paid well. She basically said, "Life happened." Now that her background was out of the bag, I was both intrigued and excited. Turns out she was also a sci-fi nut. The stars were aligned. A story! How cool was that? We quickly began collaborating. The chemistry was great. The more we dug into it, the more we realized how much we needed each other to do this. Our feelings were mutual, so we decided to officially partner up to do this crazy creative thing.

We started a production company, but we needed a name for our company and the story. For the company, we came up with a great name. For the story, we came up with Dinosaurians. That was perfect! After the name of our story was determined, I found myself in my home office, staring at my beautiful and dusty Tacoma guitar. I was humming a melody I'd created with words that described the story we were developing. It was like my guitar was calling me by name to pick her up and play her, so I did just that. Something amazing happened. I ended up writing the theme song in about 30 minutes, lyrics and all. To top it off, it wasn't just good, it was great! I couldn't believe it!

In my mind I heard a rock band with a lead singer that sounded somewhere between Chris Cornell and Bon Jovi. I recorded it on my iPhone then quickly shared the result with my business partner. Her response confirmed my feelings about it. She loved it too. It worked! Soon after, I wrote more songs, and they were getting even better. The inspiration of this venture unleashed something I didn't know I had inside of me. As I was enjoying what was happening, I found myself reflecting on just a few months prior, when I was focusing on how I was in my mid 40s with four kids and graying hair, thinking about how the music hadn't worked out. I remembered the stories I was repeatedly telling myself: "Time to stop and change course." "You have four kids. This dream isn't responsible." "Time to let go. After all, who wants to hear music from a graying man with four kids anyways?" "Today, music is all about the young or established people and you aren't either one of those." "You tried everything." It scared me. All I could think about was that these songs almost didn't happen because of the stories I'd been telling myself.

As I dug deeper, I saw those stories were all made up, especially the one about me having tried "everything". What a load of crap! Isn't that what a lot of us do? We try a few things and call them "everything". The truth was I only tried what didn't work. If I had tried everything, I'd have what I wanted because the solution is included in everything.

The big question that emerged from this was, "What other stories was I telling myself that I wasn't aware of?" From there, we moved forward with developing the story. Our goal was a movie. To start, we decided on delivering it in the form of a graphic novel. It seemed like the best steppingstone, considering the resources we had available and that we were still working in the toy business. How hard could it be? Next, we had to figure out a way to transition into our production company full time. As we were brainstorming for a way to fund our production company, an idea surfaced from something I was already working on.

In my e-commerce business, there was demand for high-quality dinosaur backpacks. My customers were asking for them, but I couldn't find a manufacturer that made what I was looking for. Everything available in the marketplace was cheap and cheesy so I decided to design one myself. During the prototype process, the amazing idea of interchangeable flaps surfaced. We solved a problem we didn't even know was there. The excitement was huge. Since both of us were already in the business of selling products for kids, both of us decided it would be a good strategy to move forward with this backpack company to fund the production company. Now think about that. That was normal for us. It was something we were acclimated to.

We ended up raising over $220,000 to bring in 10,000 units. We even filed for a patent and were granted one. Sales began and we were successful. The customer reviews were exceptional, but we needed some help with marketing. I decided to take a marketing course from Chalene Johnson, called The Marketing Impact Academy. It changed a lot for me. As amazing as the course was, and as awesome as Chalene is, the change I am referring to wasn't because of the course content overall. What changed everything for me was a small module within the course that was only five minutes long, where she focused on helping me to clearly see how the world sees me, so I could refine the content to be specific for the vision I had for myself. It was something I had never paid close attention to. This was crucial.

Chalene instructed us to look at everything we post on social media and everything we talk about with other people. With that information, we will be able to clearly see how others see us. I did the exercise and what I saw crushed me. I was the e-commerce guy. I was the dinosaur toy store guy. I was the backpack guy. Even though I knew I was doing these things, none of them were how I wanted to be remembered. What's scary is that I didn't even know I was doing it. How did this happen? I then dug deeper into my past to apply this same exercise. The results were astonishing. I was the ice cream guy. I was the guy who stayed in a working environment I disliked for over 20 years.

I analyzed them more, feeling there was something strangely familiar with all of them. I saw it. All these ventures and business decisions were safe to me, except the production company. I realized that the ice cream store, e-commerce store and backpack company were all safe things I knew I could do; none of them were ventures that really stretched me. To compound things, I had just raised — and spent — over $220,000 on a backpack company. This is something I knew I could do, but it wasn't something I needed to do to fund the production company. What I ended up doing was adding something into my life that took my attention away from what I really wanted to do.

Now sit with that for a moment. Big questions arose from deep within me, which led to one main puzzling one: Why didn't I have enough belief in myself to raise the money to invest directly into the production company? The pattern was clear. The backpack company was the practice. The production company was the stage. I realized most of what I had accomplished were things I knew I could do, rather than the things I truly desired to do. Even though the things I knew I could do had some risk elements, to me they were safe. I never left the rehearsal studio!

I share this story to help you see how deeply rooted patterns can affect your life in big ways, over a long period of time, without you being aware of it. I also share this story to help you identify patterns that are not serving you. One of the most common patterns I have seen in most people, including myself, is the pattern of staying with what's safe, staying in your comfort zone. This brings me to share with you a wonderful jewel of wisdom written by Bob Riggs. It's worth studying many times over.

"THE COMFORT ZONE — Many of us have established a comfort zone in our lives. We're just coasting along, taking the path of least resistance, and just getting by. This is a very common and understandable attitude. We've all worked hard to get where we are and it may seem a good place to be. The problem with this is that once we stop reaching, stretching, seeking, and risking, we actually stop growing. The comfort zone frame of mind is settling for what we are TODAY. That may be fine today, but without continued growth, WE ARE NOW ALL WE ARE EVER GOING TO BE. If you're in a comfort zone, BEWARE – the danger of a comfort zone is that it doesn't hurt, and it may even feel good."

The Comfort Zone is the Safety Zone. If you stay in the comfort zone, you will never realize your true potential. As Neville Goddard says, "Everything depends on your attitude towards yourself. That which you will not affirm as true of yourself can never be realized by you."

Today my story is very different. I am working on developing movies, and I am also working with other highly successful people who live extraordinary lives, one of which is a beautiful man named Ramy El-Batrawi. Ramy went from homeless to billionaire in six years. He wrote a fantastic book about how he did it called, "Can You Really Think and Grow Rich?" I recommend that all you purchase that book and study it. I also created and lead a powerful daily study program called "Master

Your Mind" that helps people to remove the deeply rooted beliefs and habits that don't serve them and replace them with powerful positive beliefs and habits that are in harmony with the good that they desire. Everyone who uses it as it's intended to be used experiences the change they seek.

All these results are happening in my life BECAUSE I CHANGED MY MINDSET.

I changed what I believed to be true and the habits I had by studying from the best teachers in the world and applying their way of thinking to my life. I weeded out most of the deeply rooted limitations that had been planted either by me or the race and replaced them with new powerful ideas that are in harmony with the philosophy that "Impossible is just an opinion". This is an important bit of wisdom to absorb. Whenever people share with you how long it took them to get to where they are, they aren't sharing with you how long it took them to get there; they are sharing with you how long it took them to figure it out.

Through the experiences of others, you can get there faster if you will just learn from their lessons. It is my hope that you will see it doesn't have to take you as long to figure this out as it did me, that through my story and the stories of others, you will be able to speed up your journey to enlightenment, awareness, understanding, and bliss. Study who you truly are and how your marvelous, miraculous, incredible mind works. Those are the only two things you need to study to understand in your life to deliver a life of freedom, fulfillment, and joy.

Providence

Providence represents the divine guidance, protection, and foresight that shapes our lives. It encompasses the idea of a higher power orchestrating events and providing for our needs. Providence is linked to powerful and righteous thoughts, as it inspires individuals to trust in divine wisdom, have faith in the greater plan, and make choices aligned with moral principles and virtuous actions. Through embracing the concept of providence, one can cultivate a mindset that acknowledges the interconnectedness of events, embraces gratitude, and seeks to act in harmony with the greater good.

Divine Providence Prayer

By Troy R Chadwick

Divine Providence, the source of all creation and infinite abundance, I humbly come before you with a heart filled with profound gratitude. I recognize that in this present moment, I am aligned with the power and wisdom that guides the universe.

I am deeply grateful for the extraordinary life that unfolds before me. I am a magnet for boundless prosperity and financial freedom. Every day, I am blessed with abundant opportunities to create wealth and financial success. Money flows effortlessly into my life, allowing me to experience the joy of financial independence and the freedom to live a life of purpose and generosity.

In this sacred moment, I affirm that my body is a temple of vibrant health and vitality. Every cell radiates with optimal well-being and vitality. I am a beacon of energy and strength, effortlessly maintaining a state of balance and harmony. I am grateful for the abundance of health and vitality that permeates every aspect of my being.

With immense gratitude, I embrace happiness as my natural state of being. I am a vessel of joy, embracing each day with enthusiasm and a positive outlook. I radiate love, kindness, and compassion, creating harmonious relationships and attracting like-minded souls into my life. I am grateful for the overflowing happiness and contentment that fills my heart.

I express my deepest gratitude for the power of my thoughts and beliefs. I am the conscious creator of my reality, and I choose thoughts that empower and uplift me. I release all limiting beliefs and replace them with empowering beliefs that align with my highest potential. I am worthy of all the blessings and abundance that the universe has to offer.

In this present moment, I surrender any doubts or fears to your divine wisdom. I trust that everything unfolds perfectly and in divine timing. I release the need for control, knowing that I am supported by the infinite intelligence that governs all creation. I am open and receptive to divine guidance, and I follow the path that leads to my highest good.

Thank you, Divine Providence, for the limitless blessings bestowed upon me. I am eternally grateful for the extraordinary life of financial freedom, health, and happiness that is my birthright. I live in a state of profound gratitude, fully aware of the abundance that surrounds me. I embrace this powerful, extraordinary life with open arms and a grateful heart.

In deepest gratitude, I affirm that this is my reality now and always. And so it is.

About
Troy R Chadwick

Troy Chadwick's story is one of transformation. For many decades, he thrived in the mortgage industry, earning a comfortable income. However, deep down, he felt a restless spirit, knowing that he was neglecting his true purpose. Driven by safety and security, he remained in that industry for far too long, until he finally reached his breaking point.

In 2008, Troy took a courageous leap into a new venture—an ice cream franchise. With unwavering determination, he invested everything he had, both financially and emotionally, into building this dream. Unfortunately, the Recession of 2010 hit with unyielding force, causing him to lose not only his house but also every penny he had poured into the franchise.

During that tumultuous time, Troy's mental state was shattered. Anxiety consumed him, panic attacks gripped his being, and he found himself in the hospital numerous times, convinced that death was imminent. Fear became an unwelcome companion, to the point where he even purchased a cell phone in his thirties solely out of dread for a potential heart attack.

A few years later, Troy ventured into a unique online business, immersing himself in the world of selling dinosaur-themed merchandise. From there, he founded a successful backpack company, earning a patent for his creation. Despite these accomplishments, a lingering sense of unfulfillment persisted, driving him to search for answers and understand the process behind his achievements.

It was in the realm of personal development that Troy discovered the true catalyst for lasting change—a revelation bestowed upon him by one of the greatest minds of the past half-century, Bob Proctor. Bob Proctor, a legendary figure impacting the lives of millions, became Troy's beacon of wisdom. Despite the financial barrier, Troy yearned for Bob to be his mentor and found a way to make it happen. This decision forever altered the trajectory of his life.

It was the most profound and impactful choice Troy had ever made, not just for himself but also for his family and those around him. Despite the fear and discomfort, he wholeheartedly committed to shattering the barriers that held him back, ultimately forging the person he is today.

Bob Proctor's words resonated deeply with Troy: "If you can hold it in your mind, you can hold it in your hand." Through relentless study, Troy unlocked the immense power behind those words. He realized that everything we perceive in the material world is the manifestation of thoughts and corresponding actions. Troy discovered that who he was at any given moment was merely the effect—a reflection of his thoughts acting as the cause. By mastering the art of thinking, he witnessed profound shifts in his external reality that directly correlated with the changes he cultivated within himself.

Today, Troy's life stands as a testament to this profound transformation. He finds himself collaborating with an Academy Award-winning film producer, passionately developing impactful movies. Moreover, he works alongside highly successful individuals who lead extraordinary lives, including the remarkable Ramy El-Batrawi. Ramy, having triumphed over homelessness to become a billionaire in just six years, authored an extraordinary book titled "Can You Really Think and Grow Rich?"—a transformative resource Troy wholeheartedly recommends.

Additionally, Troy created and leads a powerful daily study

program called "Master Your Mind!" This program, when used correctly, empowers individuals to shed deeply rooted beliefs and habits that hinder their progress, replacing them with powerful positive beliefs and habits aligned with their desires. Those who wholeheartedly embrace this program experience the transformative change they seek.

Troy's approach is rooted in simplicity. He believes in breaking things down to their simplest form, making them easily understandable. This enables him to effectively communicate complex concepts to those seeking a deep understanding of mindset and how to change it.

Troy's talent lies in his ability to explain these ideas in a clear and relatable manner, earning him admiration from many. He emphasizes the principle of autosuggestion, harnessing the power of repetitive positive affirmations to reprogram the mind and bring about transformative change. Through his eloquence and insightful teachings, Troy has helped countless individuals grasp the essence of mindset and unlock their potential for personal growth.

These exceptional outcomes have manifested in Troy's life because he dared to change his mindset. He firmly believes that if he, Troy Chadwick, could undergo such a profound transformation, the power to change resides within each and every one of us.

www.TroyRChadwick.com

TroyRChadwick@gmail.com

TikTok @troyrchadwick

John Corbellini

~ Rebirth ~

With boundless grace, this divine orchestrator breathes life into the decaying remnants of what once was, summoning from the ashes a triumphant resurgence of hope and renewal. "Arise, for you are not defined by your past but by the infinite possibilities that lie ahead."

No One Dies Alone

by John Corbellini

John Edward said, "When a baby is born, it is the most traumatic experience of that baby's life, but there are people on the other side, here, waiting and happily anticipating that child's arrival. When we die, there will be family and friends on the other side, waiting to greet us again."

Let's get away from dying for a minute. When we grow, a part of us has to die in order to grow into the next stage of our life. There is a fear of letting go of our "old" self to become and grow into the "new" self. It is scary and it can be debilitating to accept that in order to grow, part of us has to die. This is the "comfort zone" everybody is talking about. It is a very traumatic experience, especially when those around you see you changing, and they don't understand the "why" behind it.

Sometimes, you know in your heart, that "something" has to change: ending a relationship, leaving a job, leaving home, starting over. All these things can stop you from growing into who you were always meant to be. However, as soon as you make the decision to change and move forward, you are reborn. The old version of you is gone. Some friends you had in the past will not be joining you on your journey because they can't. It's not their journey, it's your journey. Can you find the strength to leave behind what was "safe" and "known", and "comfortable" to go and see what you are truly capable of?

If you did choose to change, did you notice the new room of people you walked into? There are new friends here, on the other side of your emotional and spiritual birth, waiting to greet you. No one dies alone. There is always someone on the other side waiting for you.

No one is born alone.

I was somewhere around 6 or 7 years old when I found out I was adopted. The fact that my adoptive parents, who raised me and gave me a home, loved me, didn't matter. I knew they loved me because that's what parents are supposed to say, but my biological parents got rid of me. At least that's what I thought back then. All I could think was "If my own parents didn't want me, what good am I?" That story I'd created stayed with me throughout my teenage years and well into my adult life. I was wrong about quite a lot of things. I assigned my worth to not being enough for my biological parents. I was the 98lb weakling. I was the one who got beat up almost every day. I was too small and too scared to defend myself and everyone around me took advantage of that. No matter what I did, I couldn't get away from the bullies. I never asked out any girls. I didn't apply myself in school, and I didn't try out for sports. I didn't go to school dances, I never went to the prom, and I didn't care. "Why bother?" I thought. All I wanted was to be invisible, to be left alone. I never felt important, so I never put myself in a position to be acknowledged. I can't tell you how many times I asked God to take me home. I didn't understand why I was here on earth. To me, I had no reasons. There was no "life" in my life. I was just existing. God didn't listen. Sometimes the greatest blessings are unanswered prayers.

When my wife and I got divorced, I was devastated. She wanted it. I didn't. Part of me died that day. I was a husband, now I was an ex-husband. I lost my identity and didn't like the new one assigned to me. Now what? I did what most hurting people do: I got depressed, I got angry, I wasn't suicidal, but the thought popped into my head. "I don't have a family anymore, what's the point?" I thought. That wasn't true at all, but I couldn't see past my pain at that moment. "Moment" isn't the right word; "months" — even "years" — is more accurate.

In time, I accepted that fact that I was divorced. I no longer lived with my children. I was moving forward alone, but I realized I was still moving forward. I didn't like the man I had become. I was miserable. But in time, I woke up and realized I am responsible for my life. Every decision I ever made had brought me to where I was. Now, for the record, there was never any infidelity, I never raised a hand to her, none of that. We simply went our separate ways. We weren't present for each other. We just weren't there. I started to understand why she wanted the divorce. I took a hard look at myself. I wasn't the man she needed me to be. She had married a boy. It took the divorce for me to realize this.

The divorce is what had to happen for me to grow into the man I am proud to be today. As I mentioned above, it was painful, but it was worth it. Divorce is never fun, but that part of me HAD to die in order for me to grow, and I wasn't alone after all. I knew other friends who were divorced, so I leaned on them because they knew exactly where I was. As grateful as I am to them for building a safety net underneath me while I had my own emotional funeral, I knew there was more. I just didn't know how much more.

The truth is, I was living an average life. One where I did what was demanded of me without ever asking any internal questions. I was mad at the world and never thought to ask myself why, let alone how do I change. I had to let that version of myself die. I had to be reborn. An average life is one without questions. Average is a sad word. It's boring, lifeless, plain. But "exceptional" is a powerful word! It has life, energy, and purpose! People pay attention to those who are exceptional. They want to be around people who are exceptional. You can be like everyone else: average, going through motions, getting by. Or you can DECIDE to live an exceptional life. I had to decide to live exceptionally. That meant making decisions that were difficult. I had to choose. Those success stories aren't because those people were better than anyone else. It's because they made a decision, a choice, to change in order to step into who they were meant to be. They chose to make a difference. They chose their playing field. They decided they were going to live life on their terms. They had a definiteness of purpose. They knew exactly what they wanted, and they had a burning desire to have it!

Just like the hot air balloon that wants to rise, my spirit wants to rise and grow. If that's true, then why was I stuck in the same place? Why wasn't I growing? Because I hadn't stepped into my power yet. I had no idea what that even meant, but something greater was calling me.

Before my divorce, my definiteness of purpose was just to get through the day. The external world had complete and utter control. I was just existing. External motivation is just that - external. It is the "want" of things. Money, cars, the girl, the guy, the house, the respect, the being noticed, the being appreciated and feeling valued. The people around you and society in general told us that these "things" are important. Maybe they are, but it is a learned habit. Just like learning to read and write, the value of "things" is learned as well. What I learned is that all the "stuff" doesn't matter. I had the stuff: the house, a wife, a family. I thought I'd arrived! I thought I'd made it. That "old" version of me, the husband, was a "thing" too! I was hanging on to an identity that no longer existed. That was tough to let go of, but that "thing" was making me miserable. I had to let that die too.

After the divorce, I realized the one thing I didn't have. Love. Not external love, but internal love. I never loved ME. I was never "good enough" in my own mind. Just like the ropes on the hot air balloon that hold it down, my beliefs about myself were holding me down. All the "I AM" statements, like "I'm not good enough"; "I can't do this or that"; "I'll never be able to afford the things I want"; "I'll never find love again"... This is what was holding me down. I

46

had to learn to let go of those beliefs. I had to learn to forgive myself. So many people misunderstand the meaning of the word "forgiveness". Most people think that forgiveness is about letting someone else off the hook. That's not the case at all. Forgiveness is about letting YOURSELF off the hook. Loving YOURSELF enough to say, "OK, this event happened, but it does not own me, it does not define me, and I will not carry it into my future!"

We, all of us, hear with our ears, but we listen with our feelings and our emotions. When our feelings are about "not being enough" and our emotion is anger, what we receive is more of not being good enough and more anger. When we surrender and we learn to listen to our true feelings and emotions, those of love and forgiveness, we receive more love and forgiveness. Interesting how that works, right? Because, at the end of the day, the single greatest blessing of forgiveness is inner peace. I had to forgive myself for not knowing any better. I thought I had to forgive my biological parents for "getting rid of me", but what they really did was to roll the dice in the hope that another couple would be able to give me the life they couldn't. They gambled, and they won! So did I! When you can listen from a place of inner peace, knowing that God has your back, you get to ask better questions and you'll get better answers. You'll be able to make better decisions and choices, and you'll get a better result!

I am learning to see — to "see" my value, my worth as a human being, God's highest form of creation. It's a "knowing" that I AM more than what I currently was. I used to think that God gave me life and I was here to figure it out, that I was on my own. What I didn't realize was that God already had it "figured out", all I had to do was be open to receive. God took the time to CREATE you, He gave you the free will to BE you, now your job is to FIND you! So, the question now becomes "Who Are You?" John 1.0 wasn't ready to receive. That version of me was nothing short of oblivious. John 2.0 is ready to receive, open to learning, willing to shut up and listen. Once I did that internal work, John 2.0 began to emerge. I was empowered and free. A weight had been lifted off my shoulders and my spirit, my true self, was finally free to come out and play. My divorce is what had to happen for the real me to show up. I died the day my ex and I got divorced, but ultimately, I was reborn. Through the healing, the boy had become a man.

What happened, the specifics, don't really matter anymore, because the past is "back there", and I don't live back there anymore. I don't live in the future, in some fantasy land, either. I live in the now because "now" is all I'm ever going to have. I learned that if you're not having fun, you're doing it wrong. If you're worried about anything, you're not being present for YOU. I mentioned earlier that my ex and I weren't "present" for each other, and it's true. But I had to be present for me, in order to be present for her. I had to heal and accept myself, in order to show up the way I needed to.

There's a real power in letting go. There's rebirth. A caterpillar goes into a cocoon and comes out a butterfly. A snake sheds its skin. Your rebirth comes when you let go of your old self. Whenever I find myself in an uncomfortable place, not knowing which choice is the right one, I remember how I had to go through struggles and heartache to grow into the next version of myself. That little inner voice will tell you what to do. You'll know. If you just listen. God already figured it out for you, too. If you don't CHANGE anything, you don't change ANYTHING. There are people on the other side waiting for you. No one is born alone.

God of Rebirth Prayer

by John Corbellini

Dear God,

You created me and gave me the free will to be me. Please help me to find me. The "me" that you created, not the one I and the outside world created.

Help me to fully believe that You already have a plan in place to help me get there.

Teach me how to love myself enough to let go and trust.

Help me to set the example for others, to live IN Your heart and love FROM mine.

Allow me to be the light that shines on those who haven't found theirs yet.

You gave me my gifts for Your reasons. Please teach me how to find them and how to use them.

Amen

About

John A. Corbellini

John is an Empowerment coach, a Foundational Coach, and a Professional Speaker. He studied in the Robbins Madanes Coaching Program established by Tony Robbins and Chloe Madanes and has graduated from Unleash the Power Within and Date with Destiny. He is the host of InnerVisions Podcast, a published author in Write and Shine Magazine, a co-author of "Which Leader to Follow", and "Everything You Need to Know about becoming a Coach", and is currently writing his own book, "Life As You Know It, Is Over"

He recently graduated from the Tony Robbins Coaching Academy and is also a founding member and Ambassador of the Napoleon Hill Institute, where he is working to become a Think And Grow Rich coach for Napoleon Hill Institute.

John is a Board-Certified NLP Practitioner, Board Certified NLP Coach and Certified in Time-Line Therapy ™ and certified by the American Board of Hypnotherapy.

John is a divorced father of 4 who had to rebuild himself from the ground up and now, using a transformational approach, helps other men and women to do the same. He also works with men and women from around the world to improve the quality of their lives after divorce.

John lives in Naples, Florida.

Jaccoaching.com

Social Media @johncorbellini

Ingra Sparkman

4

~ Wisdom ~

The Spirit of wisdom ignites knowledge's path, guiding hearts and minds to profound understanding. It empowers individuals to unravel complexities, embrace truth, and dissolve doubts. In its presence, ignorance fades, clarity prevails.

Letting Go of Your Old Stories

by Ingra Sparkman

Even though my passion is storytelling, I can't recall the exact time or even the specifics necessary to make the following particular tale more captivating, but what I CAN tell you with all certainty is that what happened over time, changed the entire trajectory of my life.

As a biographer, I've had the audacious spiritual benefit of hearing thousands upon thousands of stories in my lifetime.

I've even had the heart-wrenching privilege of being seated at the bedside of men in their final hours of life, hired to pen their most precious details in the hope that by sharing their words with me, between labored breaths, their legacies will live forever.

My life's work is based on the belief that it will.

But I didn't always write other people's stories. For many years as a young adult, I just relayed mine.

Over and over and over again.

My anecdotes of anger, my songs of suffrage, my poetry of past pains... they followed me everywhere I went. They were so much a part of me that I was very much afraid to let them go. Those stories were my whole identity. Those stories justified my insecurities, my aggression and, most importantly, my excuses.

I told them ad nauseum, to anyone who would listen.

And then one day, and I don't recall which day it was, I stopped talking and just started listening instead. As much as talking gave me the power to hold on to the past, listening freed me for my future. Breaking the chains of your past is one of the hardest challenges you will ever face, but when you get there, what's waiting for you is nothing short of magic. Now I get to live in the future and share the magic, and for that I am eternally grateful.

Over the years, I've heard incredible stories; people have shared some of the truly most horrific experiences a human can have, and yet there in front of me, sharing their words, would be a survivor. And it slowly occurred to me — and not just on one particular day or memorable moment — that as spirit beings having human experiences, we do indeed have the remarkable ability to survive.

And to thrive.

With every story shared with me, I grew more and more fascinated with the knowledge that we are remarkable beings, and, along the way, I learned the true way to happiness, genuine happiness, is through forgiveness and letting it go. Your story of the past, your anger, your grudges, your fears, your doubts, your indiscretions and insecurities, your paradigms… just let them go.

If you can't let it go, you won't be able to grow.

What purpose does it serve you to hold on to anything other than love and light?

Accept what is, let go of what was, believe in what will be. Lao Tzu gives us this wisdom: "When I let go of what I am, I become what I might be. When I let go of what I have, I receive what I need."

Ancient wisdom from books we've carried down for millennia. Stories you could hear tomorrow that might very well change your life, in the same way mine changed too.

I could have carried the massive weight of the books I had

written from my own past on my back until I was truly broken, but it was in the listening that I was freed.

Learn from yesterday, live for today, and hope for tomorrow.

Leave who you were, love who you are, look forward to who you will become.

I can't say it was one story, one moment in time that I can pinpoint as my own tipping point, but I can tell you that, over time, I began to understand that the most beautiful thing about writing a biography is that just like comic books, just like the best fictional book ever written, there is always a hero.

Some days you are the hero, and some day you're just scanning the book praying you'll get to the last page unscathed without a surprise ending, or at the very least a decent last sentence, because nothing sucks worse than a good book with a terrible ending.

You are writing your story every day too. We all are.

One of the best quotes I've read recently goes something like, "Make sure you put into perspective your current state of mind when you're going about your day and accidentally start allowing your mind to control the narrative. Try saying out loud: 'The story I am telling myself right now is...' because understanding that just because you think it, doesn't make it true, is life-altering knowledge."

The same can be said for the stories of your past. What do we tell ourselves about our past stories that keep us anchored in where we are right now?

Seshat, the ancient Egyptian goddess of writing and the ruler of books, soulfully understood the power of words. Words are true magic. After all, we call it 'spelling' for that very reason. Words can cast spells, they can alter your future, they can change the narrative of your past, they can bring you life and, oh yes, words can take you down. The stories we tell others are powerful, the stories we tell ourselves are almighty. Be most conscientious about the words you tell yourself. Those words, that storyline running through your head day in and day out… that's your lifeline. Take care of it and take charge of it.

It's amazing the power, the energy words carry, the vibration of each sound within the letters. T A Barron offers in his book, "The Wisdom of Merlin", that there are seven simple but powerful words that answer cosmic questions. They are gratitude, courage, knowledge, belief, wonder, generosity, and love.

What are the most powerful words in your story right now?

Choose your words well. Wake up to the narrative that's repeating in your head. How much power does the story you're replaying in your head right now have over you?

See how listening to someone else for a change can help clear your head?

When was the last time you sat with someone with the sole intention of just listening to them, offering nothing else but your time and attention?

When was the last time you replayed that story?

I cringe sometimes when I think about the amount of time I lost replaying the stories of my past. There is a part of me that truly believes that, if I hadn't started listening more to others and writing down their words of wisdom, I would have driven myself crazy. I would have burned pathways through my brain to create an unhappy ending to every situation I was experiencing in the present.

It's a very daunting revelation, learning there is always someone out there who has or has had it much worse than you but, at the same time, it's so freaking powerful, and half the beauty is you don't know who you're going to learn from — or when you'll learn it — until you engage. I still say that "Hello" is the most powerful word on this planet.

What about talking to a complete stranger? There is this incredible study by Gillian Sandstrom that offers the idea that not only does talking to strangers make you happier, it makes you smarter too.

Over the years I've learned a few interesting similarities about the human condition, and I feel like I can share these with you with confidence.

Consider these as being just the tip of the iceberg of incredible advice you can get from others when you're just willing to ask the questions and truly listen.

Everyone has a story.

One thing I've learned is that most people I've spoken to agree they would NOT want to go back in time if it meant going back to the beginning of junior high school to start their life over. Countless people I've interviewed over the years offer that they wish they could travel more. Bob Marley once said, "If traveling was free, you'd never see me again." Marley's quote resonates with me daily.

Most often the people I heard stories from, who had previously retired, said retirement was so boring they'd decided it was better to go back to work than to just do nothing at home.

I have entire notebooks filled with the wisdom of others. But my favorite stories are the ones I write about my future. I am so happy and grateful now that... Write it down! Bring your story to life.

There is another quote I love which reads, "The thing you are most afraid to write? Write that."

When was the last time you sat down and wrote for the sheer joy of it, scribing your biggest dreams or inspirations because you understand the power of words?

Words made manifest.

The Bible says, "Write the vision and make it plain upon tables, that he may run that readeth it. For the vision is yet for an appointed time, but at the end it shall speak, and not lie: though it tarry, wait for it; because it will surely come."

We've known for as long as we could create it, that the written word had dominion; that the pen truly is mightier than the sword; that if we ask, we shall receive.

What are the most powerful things you've ever read? The most powerful words you've ever heard? The revelations that were relayed to you that moved you to tears or brought you the greatest joy?

What stories have compelled you enough to share them?

Pen and paper in hand, I sat down abruptly at my desk with the intention of writing down the whole damn thing, every last word, every gory detail. I was turning 50 years old in six months, and I still hadn't even started typing the next great American novel. My plan wasn't to leave anything out, even though I hadn't started yet. I swore to sit my rear down and not to leave that spot until I had used every drop of ink in that pen. I'd spent hours that day, off and on, scheming in my head the working title and trying to recall the horrors I would share. Not, at this point, with the intent to expose every person who had ever hurt me as a child, but mostly so I could get the pressure of writing "the book" off my chest once and for all. Time was ticking and if not now, when? Never… as it turned out.

Because here is the most beautiful part of my own story. The book I'll never write because I don't need to. After 50 years of fighting with it, struggling with how much truth I could or would tell, I looked back down at this blank piece of paper and realized I had nothing left to say, much less write. I had witnessed and written so much about the beauty of other people who had defeated their demons, sat with so many heroes who had overcome so much incredible adversity that I hardly even cared anymore to consider what my past was like, much less try to memorialize it with the written word.

There was no anger left inside of me and I smiled, understanding at that moment, I had inadvertently forgiven everyone who had ever hurt me. I was truly at peace with myself.

I had completely outgrown those first few chapters of my life.

I was totally freed from the past.

Everything, every moment, from that day forward became the future narrative I was choosing to create, and I owed a great part of that to everyone I had ever sat with and asked, "What's your story?"

That's the power of stories; you become a part of them the very moment the words reach you.

Surround yourself with good ones.

Write the good ones.

Share the good ones.

In that way, you too are positively embodying and projecting the true power of stories, words, and yes, even of the Goddess Seshat herself.

Inhale Love Exhale Peace

by Ingra Sparkman

Deep breath.

In for four.

Hold for four.

Out for four.

Relax for four.

Deep breath in...

In this breath I bring the power of source
knowing we are one with all.

I hold in my heart the knowing
that I am peace and love.

We are all love.

I exhale releasing all negative energy
within me. I forgive. I am forgiven.

I sit with source. We are one.

I inhale gratitude.

Thankful for all that source has given to us.

From the breath to the water,
from the light through the darkness I offer thanks.

I hold in my heart the knowing
that love is for each of us. I am divine love.

I exhale sending with this breath
this love to those who need it most.
To those who need it most. I send love.

I sit with love. I am love.
I inhale love. I exhale peace.

In this breath I cleanse my body.
Sending healing light through me
from breath into every part
of my human form.

I hold that light. I am light.

We are all light.

And we are all right.

Exhaling the light of source,
sending it through me
into the universe.

We are one.

Inhale Love.

Exhale Peace.

About

Ingra Sparkman

Ingra Sparkman known in her South Texas community as Ingra Lee, is the cohost for the Jp and Ingra Lee Morning Show on KIXS 108 in Victoria. She brings her positive vibes to the airwaves every morning in the hopes of inspiring thousands of people with her opening line, rain or shine " Good Morning Sunshine!" and she means it.

As a DJ, a writer, and a podcaster for her latest project, 'The Story I Needed to Hear' on Spotify and Apple Music, Ingra had dedicated her life to helping those who have triumph over trauma share their stories in the hopes of bringing peace, healing and understanding to everyone. She believes it's through storytelling that we heal. And we all have a story worth telling.

When she isn't on air or in her studio writing, you can find Ingra running around the ranch with her husband of 30 years trying to keep up with never enough grandkids and way too many damn dogs.

thestoryineededtohear.com

Dr. W. Garrett Goggans

5

~ Valor ~

His resolute spirit ignites the flames of courage in warriors' hearts, propelling them to face daunting challenges with unwavering determination. In the heat of battle. A beacon of inspiration, he champions noble causes, guiding champions to achieve remarkable feats against all odds.

Breaking the Chains of Guilt

by Dr. W. Garrett Goggans

Guilt. It is often described as a relentless shadow, constantly lurking in the corners of our minds, ready to pounce when we least expect it. It possesses an uncanny ability to emerge uninvited, yet forceful, causing us to doubt ourselves and question our worthiness. For me, guilt was an incessant barrage of self-criticism, whispering in my ear that I wasn't deserving of the success I so desperately sought. Like a cruel puppeteer, guilt would pull at the strings of my confidence, dragging me down from the heights I had worked so hard to reach. My relationship with guilt was complex and profound, and through that journey, I learned a crucial lesson.

At the age of 16, I made a decision that would alter the course of my life: I ran away from home. While others may have seen it as an act of rebellion or teenage defiance, for me, it was a desperate attempt to break free from the constraints of a constrictive religious upbringing. I craved independence and yearned to pursue my own desires, particularly when it came to dating. I also held other ambitions and aspirations that I felt were being stifled within the confines of my previous life.

Running away offered a taste of freedom, but it also came with its own set of challenges. I dropped out of high school and faced the uncertainty of finding shelter and employment. It was a tumultuous period in my life, marked by moments of hardship and resilience. I worked multiple jobs to sustain myself and eventually secured a small apartment. While I appeared to be living a life of independence and adventure, my emotional and psychological growth lagged behind.

Eventually, I was afforded the opportunity to go back to high school and ended my educational career achieving my doctorate. However, the years between were filled with a rollercoaster of experiences. I faced numerous setbacks, including failed marriages, lost jobs, and shattered dreams. From the outside, it may have seemed like I had achieved considerable success, but internally, I saw myself as a failure. No matter how many times I picked myself up and reached new heights, I would inevitably find myself back at square one, plagued by self-doubt.

It was during a period of profound despair that I attended a transformative training event. A speaker's words resonated deeply within me, challenging me to take ownership of my successes and failures. They emphasized that external circumstances and other people were not the primary factors influencing my life's trajectory; instead, it was my own mindset, beliefs, and actions that shaped my reality. These words struck a chord within me and propelled me into a journey of self-discovery.

The initial stages of my journey focused on personal development, seeking to understand myself better and unlock my true potential. However, it was during this exploration that I stumbled upon a pivotal realization: I had been carrying around the weight of guilt for the greater part of my adult life. It had become a constant companion, holding me back and preventing me from fully embracing my journey of self-discovery.

Seeking guidance and healing, I had the opportunity to work with an individual whose wisdom and spiritual insight transcended conventional boundaries. Although he did not identify as a shaman, our time together was spiritually transformative, delving into the depths of my emotions and experiences. It was during these sessions that I became aware of the immense impact guilt had on my life.

Through our work together, I began to understand that guilt was not an external force imposed upon me, but something I had internalized and clung to. It had become entangled within my sense of self, masquerading as a part of my identity. The process of unraveling this connection was both challenging and liberating.

One particular session stands out vividly in my memory. It was a moment of profound confrontation with my guilt — a battle for inner peace. In a vision-like experience, I found myself locked in an intense struggle with guilt. It was as if an ominous creature had taken residence within me, its grip tightening with every attempt I made to force it out. I fought with every ounce of strength, determined to expel the guilt once and for all.

The battle was taxing, stretching on for what felt like an eternity. The creature resisted my efforts, refusing to let go. It seemed as if the struggle would never end, and I grew exhausted, questioning whether I had the strength to prevail. But in a final surge of determination, something shifted. The creature dissipated, and I emerged from the vision with a sense of release and healing.

In the days and weeks that followed, I processed the profound experience, slowly unraveling its significance. It became clear to me that the fight had not been a battle against guilt, but rather a struggle to let it go. Guilt, like many negative emotions, does not attach itself to us; we attach ourselves to it. The guilt had been trying to leave my being, seeking its own liberation, but I had held onto it tightly, fearing what might happen if I were to let it go.

This revelation marked a turning point in my journey. I began to realize that guilt no longer served a purpose in my life. I had carried it for far too long, allowing it to define my self-worth and limit my potential. It was time to break free from the chains of guilt and embrace self-forgiveness and compassion.

With newfound clarity, I reevaluated my past actions and choices. I recognized that running away from home was not an act of rebellion, but rather a courageous pursuit of personal growth and authenticity. It was an expression of my desire to break free from societal norms and carve my own path. While the journey was filled with challenges and setbacks, it ultimately led me to discover my own voice, beliefs, and truth.

In my quest for healing, I also found solace in connecting with others who had experienced similar struggles with guilt. Sharing our stories and vulnerabilities created a sense of empathy and understanding, reminding us that we are not alone in our journeys. It was through these connections that I realized the universality of guilt and the transformative power of compassion and support.

As I continued on my path of self-discovery and healing, I discovered the importance of integrating the lessons learned from guilt into my present and future. I recognized that guilt could serve as a valuable teacher, guiding me towards greater self-awareness and growth. By acknowledging the lessons and insights gained from past experiences, I could shape a more empowered and authentic present.

Moreover, I began to recognize the impact of releasing guilt not only on my own well-being but also on my relationships and interactions with others. When burdened by guilt, it becomes challenging to fully show up in relationships and offer genuine connection and love. By freeing myself from guilt, I could foster healthier relationships based on authenticity, vulnerability, and compassion.

Today, as I reflect on that transformative chapter of my life, I do so with a deep sense of acceptance and gratitude. I have made peace with the guilt that once consumed me, understanding that I am shaped by both the joys and the hardships I have experienced. My path may have been unconventional, but it has molded me into a resilient, compassionate individual.

By sharing my story, I aim not to justify my actions or seek validation, but rather to shed light on the complexity of human emotions and the pursuit of personal growth. Each of us is bound to make choices that others may not understand or agree with. It is in navigating those choices, learning from our past, and embracing our own truths that we truly find ourselves.

As I carry the memories of my rebellious teenage years, I do so with a mix of gratitude and reflection. I have learned that it is okay to challenge societal norms, to question the status quo, and to forge our own destinies. My journey has taught me the importance of self-discovery, self-acceptance, and, above all, the power of embracing our own truths, even if they lead us down unconventional paths.

The relentless games of guilt have shadowed much of my life. It has challenged my self-worth, clouded my judgment, and stifled my growth. However, through a process of self-discovery, healing, and self-acceptance, I have learned to release the weight of guilt and embrace forgiveness. This transformative journey has shaped me into a stronger, more compassionate individual who understands the complexities of human emotions and the power of personal growth. By honoring our own truths and carving our unique paths, we can navigate the challenges of life and find true authenticity.

Guilt can be a persistent force that holds us back and prevents us from fully embracing our true potential. However, through self-discovery, healing, and the power of forgiveness, we can release the weight of guilt and embark on a transformative journey of personal growth. It is through embracing our own truths and navigating the complexities of life that we find authenticity and fulfillment. May we all have the courage to let go of guilt and embrace self-acceptance and compassion.

Prayer of Liberation

by Dr. W. Garrett Goggans

Prayer From Self

As I navigate through this journey of life, I often find myself feeling lost and uncertain of who I am meant to be. I pray that you guide me on the path towards discovering my true self.

Help me to let go of the expectations and opinions of others that cloud my judgment and prevent me from embracing my authentic self. Give me the courage to explore my passions and talents, and to pursue the things that truly bring me joy.

Open my eyes to the beauty that lies within me and help me to recognize and appreciate the unique qualities that make me who I am. Show me how to use these gifts to make a positive impact on the world around me.

I trust that with your guidance and grace, I will find the true me that you created me to be. Thank you for always being by my side and for loving me unconditionally.

Prayer From Source

As you navigate through this journey of life, I understand that sometimes you may feel lost and uncertain of who you are meant to be. I am here to assure you that I will guide you on the path towards discovering your true self.

Allow yourself to let go of the expectations and opinions of others that cloud your judgment and prevent you from embracing your authentic self. I encourage you to find the courage within yourself to explore your passions and talents, and to pursue the things that truly bring you joy and fulfillment.

Open your eyes to the beauty that lies within you and recognize and appreciate the unique qualities that make you who you are. I will show you how to use these gifts to make a positive impact on the world around you.

Trust in my guidance and grace, and you will find the true essence of who you were created to be. I am always by your side, loving you unconditionally and supporting you in every step of your journey.

About

Dr. W. Garrett Goggans

Dr. W. Garrett Goggans is an accomplished International Best-Selling Author, Speaker, and Mindset Coach. He is renowned for his exceptional coaching style, which he refers to as mindset engineering. His passion for helping others achieve success stems from his own life experiences. He realized that our thoughts are the single most contributing factor to achieving success.

Having been a runaway high school dropout, Dr. Goggans knows firsthand the feeling of going against the flow while attempting to achieve goals and obtain success. But through the application of proven mindset principles, he emerged victorious. He has made it his mission in life to help others see that with the proper mindset, they can propel themselves to success in ways they never thought possible.

Dr. Goggans' unique approach to coaching revolves around positivity, encouragement, and an overwhelming sense of faith. He has helped countless individuals look past their current situations and find success in any endeavor. Through his works, he has offered motivation and guidance to many, inspiring them to pursue their dreams and live their best lives.

www.garrettgoggans.com

Facebook, Instagram @drgarrettgoggans

YouTube @garrettgoggans

Hilary O. Betson

~ Empowerment ~

With unwavering conviction, this divine muse instills within us the unwavering belief that we possess the capacity to shape our destiny and transcend any obstacle that stands in our way. 'Rise, for you are the architect of your own triumph, and the master of your own narrative.'

The Forge of Empowerment

Red flags burning away in the embers
of the fire of transformation.

by Hilary O. Betson

Picture it. Summer of 2017. Total solar eclipse and major planetary congruence. Apparently, this occurred on August 21, 2017, but I have no recollection of the date. This major celestial event was witnessed by me — and, tangentially, with new friends — as a sunrise from a big window in a mental health ward at a hospital in Santa Fe, New Mexico. As we wrote, basking in the experience, our poems bloomed in the desert sunrise, flowing around the darkness of the full eclipse.

How did I get here? I felt tingly and out of it, floating in and out of awareness, but experiencing joy and hope in this disturbing circumstance. I was still in there somewhere. Divine Love was still with me.

I now know, this phasing awareness was dissociation, as well as probably a spiritual awakening of sorts, through the fires of damnation, at any rate. Burn it up. Burn up a career, a life, an identity. You're crazy.

You know your name, but you are so terrified of your life, of your husband, you simply aren't there anymore. You've been airlifted out by your own brain. As you flail about in an existence you've only seen in old movies involving Jack Nicholson that couldn't possibly persist in our modern world, you seek anything safe. This place, this sudden, farcical life is not safe.

Your latest defense to these cold walls of this stigmatized prison is to marry yourself. Then no one else can marry you. No one else can take control, like he did, of your fractured heart and sundered mind.

You analyze the pros and cons. You use your insight and knowledge as the forge of your own empowerment.

Is this legal? I'm a lawyer, I do divorce; I should know. If marriage is no longer defined as between a man and a woman, why couldn't I just marry myself? The utmost protection. I could never fall into that trap again. He shows up, sits across from you during visiting hours. You tell him. You've painted your face with your makeup to celebrate. It's beautiful and wild and guttural. You look insane. You ARE insane.

It's your wedding day and you've dressed in a set of mental hospital gowns, cobbled together, that look and feel like a heavy blanket dress. My "God/essence", the fabric was so thick and safe. So cottony. With integrity.

You feel the dress around you.

You have no idea what color it was or when this occurred. You pop in and out of the physical world, of your conscious mind, of your hippocampal ability to create memory.

You know he came. You know you conveyed your new marital status, and you truly embodied the Loon of the Loony Bin in that moment, only confirming and validating a conclusion he salivated for: she's crazy, she left you because she's crazy. For what? Why, brain? To protect yourself, at least the shreds of self not already immolated on the pyre.

Your mind pulling out all the stops. The shock and awe of splintering; the greatest act of self-love possible; the love that can only be expressed by shattering pain and fear into an ever-changing merry-go-round of new realities. A mirrored fun house of perception. A parade of characters, thoughts, ideas, and new

76

people to be. Dissociation. Because deep down, your amygdala loves you enough — even if no one else does — to protect you.

But, you know, deep down you are still there. You feel the empowerment of joy, of hope, of demystifying this experience.

Suddenly, you are determined.

Hurt People Help People.

You know this is your core.

You realize you are there to shatter the glass houses, the sheer prisons of antiquated paradigms that can only be … smashed. The splintering is thunderous and stunning. The beliefs, rules, expectations, and servile roles are liberated into glittering shards in the burning light of clarity.

Suddenly you are present. You are powerful.

I will not let another woman go through financial and personal debasement.

Building Glass Houses

I think we are all a bit afraid of shining light on certain shadows of our past and on who we've become. I sit here, today, just a Montana girl. A simple house, a business I love, a life in which I feel not only content, but empowered.

My chapter began in a house. A mansion, if you will. A mansion that is the dwelling of my subconscious. Exploring this house is exploring my personal architecture.

It is the house that law built. It is my glass house and shelters my story of intergenerational trauma, shattering a pattern that is thousands of years in the making.

The house is around 6,000 square feet and resides on half an acre in the capital city but what is truly a small town in Montana. It begins with a childhood initiated by a split family and a restructured home on different sides of the country. A man who fled corporate law and its rat wheel on Wall Street for a simpler life in Montana. A woman from the East Coast working for Congress. They created a home.

It housed a constellation of generations of bullshit relationship conditioning through years of war, servitude of the divine feminine, two little girls, and eventually the glass house that law built. My emotional world.

Where I live. I have a body that attacks itself and a mind that copes by taking flight. My mother's latchkey childhood in DC (following an unheard-of divorce in the Sicilian community in Brooklyn) is easier to understand and digest than my father's upbringing as the son of a G-Man. I suppose the juxtaposition is somewhat telling: the cultural family of the tertiary reaches of the mob, and the feds who brought it all down. The culture of abuse in families of European immigrants coming to the US at the time of World War 2. Service and servitude. In households. By women. By children. Who should be seen and not heard. Children who ultimately raised themselves because their parents became vacant or explosive, or both.

Then those people raise their own children, like my parents did. Generation X, geriatric millennials, and the shining aspirations of the Zennials. This is a story not just of my quirky beginning but of the impact of thousands of years of patriarchy running the show. Trauma? Try endemic existential drama.

So, hurt people hurt people and little kids learn to cope. The "Body Keeps the Score", right? Yes, and it certainly turns on itself, if we've learned anything about autoimmunity in the last 50 years. Since my grandmother died in a wheelchair at 65, married to her ever-devoted, quiet, and angry FBI-man husband.

What I don't think we all realize is that the mind also holds all the secrets. In its recesses. In its crawl spaces. The mind keeps the fears safe and in lockdown. It vaults the memories away into little boxes we don't have the keys to, embedded in the synapses of our trauma-bonding psyche.

Until it reaches its breaking point. Compassion is often born of experience.

I had a bad first marriage. I repeatedly gave in and gave up my legal and financial sovereignty to move states for my ex-husband's job. I was an attorney, well-educated, and successful. Moving from Montana, I failed the California Bar, over and over. I sacrificed my legal sovereignty and financial power while my ex-husband gaslit the pyre for my ruin.

In 15 years of family law, I've stewarded hundreds of women through their de-coupling, co-parenting, and loss. I use insight, knowledge, and compassion to empower.

Narratives vary, but there is an endemic undercurrent of intergenerational, cultural women's legal disempowerment, emboldened by the legal system itself. Essentially, we give our power away to shore up partners or provide for our children because "they" tell us to. Who "they" are depends on your narrative.

My personal narrative was losing my mind, my sense of identity, and my livelihood.

In the last five years, I have overcome impossible odds, rebuilding my mind, my nervous system, my own sense of identity and power. I'm back and stronger than ever. I've always used education and knowledge to empower myself through painful circumstances and I've done that again. I voraciously study and train in professional knowledge, skill-building, and personal and spiritual growth. I am here to use my professional and personal experience to empower others.

I am here to be present when you can't be.

My shame, guilt, disgust, and fear have been burned away by the fire of clarity and purpose. I step from the charred remnants of my destruction, immolated and yet reborn, and into my Renaissance. I have my own house that law built because I married another lawyer. However, our house brims with love and opportunities for understanding. We are determined to change the narrative, to smash our fragile patterns, to purpose through our pain.

I've chosen my own personal, legal, and financial sovereignty over outmoded roles and rules this time. I've rebuilt my agency. I challenge my conditioning, people-pleasing, and limiting beliefs. I focus on abundance, evolving, thinking outside the box, and holistic healing. I bring empowering insight and compassion to the table for myself and my clients.

I am not asking anyone to join me in an easy conversation. It is a mired path studded with sharp stones. It requires us to show up, be present, get vulnerable, and confront shadows. Stepping into your legal sovereignty means recognizing your worth and planning in advance to quell potential legal storms.

Now I have my own business, bringing my own personal gift of empowerment through insightful knowledge to help my clients heal through transition.

I practice family law with heart. I practice compassion, presence, and grace. I practice holding space. I am a wholehearted lawyer, mediator, and coach, because stepping forward with your whole heart is power. It is stepping into your sovereignty. It is stepping into Divine Love, purpose, and truth.

I will do the hard work with you. I will tell my story. I will hold your hands and walk with you. Come with me. It's time to smash all our glass houses. I've got you.

Prayer to the Goddess of Empowerment

by Hilary O. Betson

Goddess of Empowerment, ethereal embodiment of Strength gained through Insight, Knowledge, and Compassion.

Please be with me. Sit with me in my pain and grief. Grant me the presence of mind to slow down, to quell the storm of my racing thoughts, to feel the sovereignty emboldened by my own knowledge and experience.

Bless me with grace in this flow of change and infuse me with Divine Love.

Help me hear your reassuring words and feel your presence. "I am with you. I am here. I will hold your hand and walk with you."

Help me navigate this murky path of complexity and indecision.

Bring me clarity in your forge of empowerment. Rebuild me to be sovereign, powerful, insightful, mindful, and compassionate toward myself and others.

Let me bring my whole heart forward in all stages of my life. Let its fullness overflow with Divine Love, purpose, and truth. May I be reborn of the ashes of my pyre. Re-form my elements, crafting the foundations and scaffolding of expansive beliefs, courage, and abundant heart.

Empower me in your image, fill me with your grace, bless me with your insight. Guide me on my path, sure of step. Empower me to compassionately love myself and those who cross my path. In Grace in all and Grace within.

About

Hilary O. Betson

Hilary O. Betson is an attorney, mediator, and holistic coach. She survived legal, financial, psychological and potentially professional ruin due to divorce. She has come back stronger, smarter, and even more compassionate than before and is soaking up professional training and personal development opportunities like dry grass in a Montana fire season. Already heavily educated with B.A.'s in Psychology and Print Journalism and Sociology, her J.D. and a Master's in Public Administration,

Hilary has also completed over 100 hours of mediation and Collaborative law training and is a Certified Holistic Divorce Coach. She is a change-maker, a community builder, and a life-long advocate. She is the founder of Compassionate Family Law™ and is always thinking outside the courtroom to change the legal system for the better. Her mission is to change the family law paradigm worldwide to whole-hearted legal advocacy, coaching, and planning to keep families out of court no matter what their stage of life.

Hillary spends her time channeling tremendous love into her legal business, Whole Heart Matters, LLC, growing in mindfulness, and exploring spirituality. She is currently delving into a life coaching program and writes, draws, and cultivates joy in her free time. She also hones her skills in energy healing, Reiki, mindful movement, and meditation through her other passion project, Mountain Magic Intuitive Healing, LLC. Find Hilary at **www.wholeheartlegal.com.**

Robin Tapp

~ Trust ~

The goddess of trust is the divine personification of ease and joy in the world. She radiates a serene aura, embodying the confidence that All Is Truly Well. She thrives in times of change and upheaval, helping those who seek her wisdom to feel seen, cared for, and worthy of all good things.

With the Darkness Comes the Dawn

by Robin Tapp

From the day Robin was born, some people saw her as different. Before the nurse had even brought her in for her mother to hold for the first time, she was described as "not perfect". This nurse, thinking she was being kind by preparing Mom for possible disappointment, set the stage for a unique life. Robin was born with a large birthmark on her face; a mark that couldn't be hidden, a mark that would become a focal point for others. Some people pitied Robin for this imperfection. Some, especially other children, could be mean and cruel about it.

To compound the situation, her father, being a career Air Force man, moved them around the country every couple of years. Just as she was beginning to be accepted somewhere, just when those around her saw something beyond the "little girl with the unfortunate birthmark", they would move to another town, another state, another school, and Robin would have to start all over again. But Robin soon realized that others' opinions didn't need to define her, and she decided to retreat into her own world.

She became what others would call shy, but what they didn't know was that Robin had a deep inner life. School was the only constant, and that's where she found solace. Learning became her connection and her joy. Reading provided a great escape. The characters in a book didn't judge her. Her teachers, for the most part, were kind and gave her a quality of attention that allowed her to ignore (or at least minimize) the teasing or meanness that came from the other children. The feedback she received from teachers and from her proud mother became a great source of joy for her.

Robin became very good at directing her attention. When others were unkind, she could retreat into a book, or into a daydream or memory that soothed her. On occasion, when the situation was really bad, she'd cry or get upset in the moment, but had a way of quickly putting the situation out of her memory by focusing on things that would make her feel better. While not perfect, most of her early years seemed almost magical. Things would just "happen" for her, even when she wasn't exactly cooperating.

Robin was a procrastinator when it came to things that she didn't enjoy doing. During her senior year, when she was applying for an ROTC scholarship in order to attend college, her guidance counselor had to continually badger her for her paperwork. She finally returned it to him but, unbeknown to her, it was a day late. Years later, she ran into this man, and he shared that he had had to "call in a favor" with his buddy, the postmaster of the local post office, to backdate the packet in order for it to even be accepted.

Robin just naturally trusted that everything would simply work out for her. She didn't worry when she hadn't won that scholarship. And when it came time to pay the tuition for her first semester, she and her mom scraped together the money and she left for school. It never even crossed her mind to worry about what they would do for the second semester, or for the rest of the four years. She simply knew it would work itself out. Months later, she was notified that she'd been awarded her own four-year scholarship from ROTC, and that it would be retroactive. She was happy, but she also thought to herself, "Of course! Of course I did." Her unconditional trust that things would somehow work out allowed no room for doubt.

This seemingly magical time lasted into her first several years of adulthood. She moved to Colorado, found her career and life path, met a man, and married.

A few years later, Robin flew back to her hometown in Pennsylvania for a visit. She spent the days talking and laughing, telling stories, playing cards, and drinking beer with her family — just enjoying each other's company.

At the end of the visit, Mom drove Robin to the airport, getting there in plenty of time to sit in the small terminal just talking about stuff. Then the announcement came. "Boarding flight 463 to Denver..." They continued talking; Robin didn't want it to end.

"Boarding all seats to Denver, Colorado. Last call."

"Honey, it's time to go. You don't want to miss your flight." As Robin reluctantly stood up, picked up her bags, and started walking toward the gangway, a strong urge suddenly came over her. She decided she wasn't leaving without a hug. Robin always trusted her feelings, so she dropped her bags, whirled around and grabbed her mom in the best imitation of a bear hug that she could muster. Mom stiffened. Then, just as quickly, she completely relaxed and put her arms around her daughter.

"Love you, Mom."

"I love you too, honey, now go on before you miss your flight." Robin let her go, picked up her bags and threw a "See you soon" over her shoulder as she floated toward the airplane.

Three weeks later, Robin was attending a party at a friend's house when the phone rang. Her friend said, "Your father-in-law's on the phone. He says there's been an emergency and it's urgent that you call home."

Confused and worried, she dialed the familiar number. "Hey Todd, it's Robin. Is Mom there? Can I talk to her?"

"Are you sitting down? You need to sit down." She looked around to find a chair as her friends surrounded her. "I'm afraid there's been a terrible accident. Your mom was killed this morning." Robin's knees buckled and, if it weren't for her friends catching her, she would have hit the floor.

In the weeks and months that followed, Robin began to feel as if nothing made sense anymore. All the coping skills she'd used as a child just didn't work. Nothing could make her forget the circumstances. Nothing she did could soothe her grief.

Her mom had been her rudder, her feel-good focal point. Her husband's family tried to take the emotional place where her mother had been but of course they couldn't live up to the image Robin had of her mother.

Mom had been "home" for Robin. Whenever they had changed cities, Mom was the constant — Robin's main source of love and acceptance. Without her mom, nothing made sense. Doubt began to creep in.

She lost her sense of trust in the world, her trust in life itself. She began to reexamine everything. She started to realize that without knowing it, she'd been using her mom as her guidance system. She'd always just "gone with the flow" of what Mom and other adults had told her to focus on, but she'd never really taken the time to think about what she wanted, what she truly desired for her life.

Did she even want an Air Force career, moving all the time as she'd had to do in childhood, or did she want to settle down somewhere? This allowed her to consider even bigger questions. "What is truly important to me?" As the questions came, for the first time in her life, she felt lost.

She began realizing that her Air Force career wasn't fulfilling to her. It was at the beginning of the war in Iraq and, when she realized the satellites she helped to manage were directing the bombs that were being dropped, she felt sick. She concluded that she didn't want to be part of the war machine anymore. She knew that rather than hurting people, no matter how indirectly, she wanted to help them. On the advice of a friend, she used her mom's insurance money and enrolled in massage school.

As she transitioned from Air Force officer with an engineering degree to massage therapist, she caught plenty of flak from those around her.

"How can you throw away your career and your degree like that?"

"You're being so stupid. What about your military pension? Just suck it up, it's only another 15 years and you'll be set!"

The comments only increased her determination to trust her new focus.

As Robin transitioned in her professional life, her marriage began to fall apart. Her husband admitted to cheating on her with a co-worker. Robin was shocked by his infidelity. She felt hurt and betrayed. Once again it seemed she'd been handed an unfair situation, that someone else was causing pain in her life.

Instead of wallowing in the discomfort, Robin felt that all of this was happening for a reason. She moved from despair through anger, even allowing occasional thoughts of revenge, eventually accepting that what was happening was needed. It became evident, week after week, that this relationship no longer served who she was becoming. These events are what allowed her to step into the woman she was always meant to be. And Robin trusted she would get there. The next steps were for her to file for divorce and begin investing in herself.

This led Robin to search for a broader view of life, a more spiritual view. She attracted different teachers in this arena, noticing the vast variety of beliefs. She became enamored with the idea that each of us has the right — and responsibility — to define life for ourselves. At a spiritual book group, her friends introduced her to the concept of the Law of Attraction. At first, she scoffed at the notion that somehow, she had caused any of this to happen. But, over time, she allowed her skepticism to soften into curiosity. She watched for opportunities to test this "law". One soon presented itself.

During their divorce hearings, her soon-to-be-ex was awarded possession of their home. And worse, Robin had just a little over a month to move out. Rather than being angry with the judge or worrying about how she was going to find a rental, she decided to trust the process and test the theory. Again, she trusted everything would work out as intended. She started thinking, imagining, and talking about how exciting it would be to have her own place for the very first time in her life. She'd never before lived completely alone, and the prospect was very freeing. Once she'd made the decision, she noticed that helpful information came to her from a variety of sources. So many people were eager to cooperate.

"Make a list of your needs and wants. Then prioritize them and begin to focus on them."

"Have you checked the ads in the 'Thrifty Nickel'?"

"Drive around in the areas you're willing to live and look for 'For Rent' signs."

"I think there's a nice apartment building near me that allows pets."

She followed every piece of advice and slowly the life she'd imagined began to piece itself together.

Robin had attracted all these helpful steps just by focusing on her new life. It took just over two weeks to find the perfect place — a small house with a fenced yard at exactly the price she'd written on her list. When she went to view it for the first time, she discovered the property managers were the same people who were managing the building where she had her therapy office — they'd already worked with her for several years and they liked and trusted her! They told her exactly what she needed to do to become their tenant and two days later she'd secured her new residence.

As the new version of herself unfolded, people and things that no longer matched seemed to just fall away and those more in alignment appeared. She had a new path. By focusing on the end goal of becoming a higher version of herself, her intuition kicked in. Timing became exquisite. She would continually rendezvous with exactly who or what she needed at exactly the right time.

Robin discovered that having trust in her emotions and focusing on the optimistic perspective will guide her through life's difficulties. When we follow the path that feels good, or at least better, good will always come. We can trust that the path is unfolding perfectly, that any apparent blockage is just guidance toward a new direction. Any unraveling is simply allowing a new life to be woven. And no matter how dark the skies may get; we can trust that the sun is always there waiting to shine again.

Prayer for Trust

by Robin Tapp

Things are always working out for you.
Worry and doubt only steal the sweetness of Life.
Focus on the desired outcome,
listen for Guidance and trust enough
to take the first step.

Life is easier when you stop the struggle.
Slow down uncomfortable thoughts
by doing something
that feels better now, in this moment.

Pet your dog.
Enjoy a cup of tea.
Take a walk.
Dance.

Do you trust that the Universe is on your side?
Trust the process.
Trust your instincts.
Trust your emotions.
Trust your ability to see the guideposts
that are always there.

The roughest of waters will always smooth out, eventually.

About

Robin Tapp

After earning her bachelor's degree in aerospace engineering from Penn State University, Robin became an officer in the US Air Force, working as a Satellite Vehicle Engineer for the Global Positioning System satellite program. Following the tragic accidental death of her mother, Robin changed the focus of her life and career to include helping others on a more one-on-one basis. For over 30 years as a hands-on practitioner of the healing arts,

Robin has combined her passion for scientific principles, her understanding of our inherent ability to self-heal, and her well-honed sensitivity to the natural rhythms of the body to assist her clients in creating space for the unfoldment of the natural well-being that is the birthright of each of us. She understands that total health and vitality are the basis of our being and that it is illness that is the anomaly.

Robin Tapp is a Craniosacral Therapist and Wellness Consultant who loves hiking and camping and simply being in Nature. She lives in Colorado Springs with her husband Douglas.

linktr.ee/robinstapp

Instagram, Twitter & TikTok @RobinTapp2

Caroline Biesalski

~ Reflection ~

Behold the Goddess of Reflection. Through her sacred mirror, she illuminates the path to self-awareness, empowering all who seek to embrace their true essence and unlock the secrets of their own reflection.

Through Reflection To Freedom

by Caroline Biesalski

I wake up from a deep, dreamless sleep, slowly opening my eyes. The room I am in is dark and cool. Where am I? Water drips down on my head from the ceiling. I rub my head, my skull humming. I feel moss and earth under my naked feet. The surroundings are unfamiliar to me. Seems I've never been here before. An invisible noose tightens around my neck. "Hello?" I yell out scared. "Is anybody out there?" No answer. Immediately, I feel alone. "Hera, breathe," I repeat to myself as I feel an oncoming panic attack. "Relax! What's the last thing you remember?" I think for a moment. Oh yes, the party!

When I received the invitation to Morpheus' birthday party, at first my breath caught in my throat. He was my best friend Maira's boyfriend, but I had never been invited to his house before. I come from a poor family, whereas Morpheus' family is one of the richest in town. I felt uncomfortable. What should I wear? How should I behave appropriately without my background betraying me?

As long as they were in a committed relationship, I envied their great happiness in love and their wealth. Morpheus' birthday was celebrated with quite a stir. His parents had even placed an ad in the newspaper so the whole town would know that their heir, who was worth millions, was now entering the serious side of life.

Maira picked me up from my house. She helped pick out an outfit and did my makeup. We set off to have the best party of our lives — or so we thought. It turned out so completely different to what we had imagined…

We drive up the long driveway to the estate of Morpheus' family and are already welcomed with appetizers by the servants. We find our other friends in the park-like garden, which includes a river pool. The terrace leading to the garden offers a breathtaking view of the city, and the garden itself is protected from views by cypress trees. In the midst of the party, I run into Morpheus. We begin talking and I compliment him on his home.

Back in the underground hole, pitch dark, far away from any civilization, I feel as if I have been buried alive, left alone in this eternal darkness to face my sins. Water continues to drip from above. One drop, another one.

A small light comes on in the far corner of the room, and I dimly see a small trap door on the floor. I pull the handle and investigate a black hole. I can just make out a ladder, leading down. Carefully and step by step, I climb down. At the end, I gather all my courage and... jump!

I land softly on straw. I don't rest but continue to feel my way through the room. On the other side, drops of water fall from above onto my head again. This time they are warmer and softer. I move on and feel a door handle. "When were you innocent?" asks a whispering voice. I shudder and think.

I enter the third room. It reveals a movie theater with a big screen, a couple of chairs and a projector in the back. As soon as I take a seat, light falls onto the screen and the countdown starts to play.

Morpheus suggests having a drink. Talking at the bar, he invites me to his house for the next day. I want to remain civil, but I can't resist his beautiful words and caresses. So I spend a breathtaking night with my best friend's boyfriend without ever sleeping at all.

I feel uncomfortable on my chair in the underground cinema; water flows from the ceiling like a shower. In vain I try to get to a dry corner of the room. There is no such place. I resist the water and begin to hate it with my whole being. "Get me out of here!" I scream. Finally, I find the door, well-hidden and painted in the same gray color as the wall itself. I try to open it. "What happens after you've betrayed your best friend?" the soft voice whispers. After that night, in the morning, when the sunlight fills the room, I realize what I have done. To myself, to my best friend, and to my own boyfriend. At that moment, I swear to God and to myself that I will never be happy again. Never again will a smile appear on my face. I lose all and condemn myself to a cave of 28 years of darkness.

What happened during all this time? I rummaged in my memory. I was living my life according to the intention I had set.

A very short period after my affair with Morpheus, a new student arrived at my school from a foreign country. He revealed that his parents had been shot in a riot and so his life was at risk too. I decided to save his life by marrying him. What I didn't know was that I had given up my own in return. I had ceased to live my truth.

As I walk through the corridors to the next room, I suddenly become aware of all the other people walking in front of me, behind me and beside me. For so many years, I had excluded every person out of my perception because I didn't want to feel pain again. At that moment it clicked, and I stood still, clenching my fist. I was determined to get my life back. Here and NOW.

"Forgive yourself," a small voice murmurs and, for the first time, I'm not sure anymore if the voice is outside my head or inside. "Let go. Let go of the past. It's over. The past is just a thought you keep on thinking." I fall to my knees and ask for forgiveness. As I open my eyes, I recognize the water drops from above.

At that moment, I understand that this is the right path. At the end of the tunnel, I perceive a door with a mirror. I'm afraid of looking in the mirror and seeing the person I had denied for so many years. I knock and the door swings open.

I enter a golden hall of mirrors and see myself a thousand times in a thousand mirrors. Immediately, I get angry at the person I see. "Why did you do all that?" I yell at the mirror. The mirror yells back in an ugly grimace. I search the room for a tool to destroy it. I find a huge hammer on a table, exactly as if someone, who knew what I had been up to, had placed it there. I hurl the hammer repeatedly and persistently against the innocent mirror, which cracks but I can still see my face. Exhausted, I sink to the floor, crying. I realize I cannot change what's reflected, by destroying the mirror. I have to deal with the cause.

I stare into the biggest mirror in the room and tears run down my cheeks. For the first time, I recognize my beauty. My inner beauty has now become visible on the outside, following a path I am courageously beginning. I look into my eyes and say, "I love you, Hera!" Drops of water fall from the ceiling and merge with my tears in a very magical yet strange way that I have never experienced before. Gratitude floods my heart, and I am overwhelmed by the intensity of the feeling. Intuitively, I put my hands on my heart. As I stand in front of another door, I know the curse is broken. My restless journey in the darkness is finally over. I'm ready to enter the light.

As the door opens, I see a green pasture with the most beautiful flowers I have ever seen, in a multitude of colors. I move forward and bend down to smell the scent of the flowers. I inhale deeply and absorb it completely. Then I recognize a little pond and I walk over. I am so happy and grateful, that I forget myself and I fuse with this holy moment. I watch the surface of the pond and suddenly, it strikes me like a thunderclap: in the reflection of the water, I see myself for the first time in my life as the most beautiful person on earth. "Where have you been all these years?" I ask her. A serene, familiar voice answers, "I was always there for you. You just weren't aware of it. I watered the seeds of awareness which were planted before birth. And it worked. You made it, room by room by room, until you reached this very moment of peace and freedom. It's alright now. You are saved! It is done. Now that you have everything you ever needed and wanted, we are complete."

I stretch my arms and give a hug to the whole world before I continue my path toward the sunset and my new life!

HERA:
Heals, Envy, Revenge, & Anger

by Caroline Biesalski

A goddess has no such attributes.

Nothing is done to me.

All I have done; I've done to myself.

Today is the day to stop these feelings.

I turn envy into gratitude
for everything I have, had, and will have,
anger into serenity
and revenge into generosity.

Everything's perfect.

All is well.

You are strong.

You are healed!

You are free!

About
Caroline Biesalski

Caroline Biesalski, a numbers enthusiast, and structured worker discovered her passion for accounting during a commercial education after A-level. She pursued economics studies in Germany and France, specializing in finances, and earned a master's degree. Throughout her career, she gained experience in various institutions and companies, even starting a successful business with six employees.

While building her professional life, Caroline also focused on creating a loving home and raising her two remarkable sons, Nelson and Jakob. In 2021, a simple question—"What do you really, really want?"—ignited a transformative journey for her. She compiled a shopping list of dreams and immediately began fulfilling them.

With the flexibility of her self-created work situation, Caroline traveled for four months in 2022, expanding her horizons. Inspired by her own journey, she became a successful coach, guiding others to achieve their deepest desires by sharing the steps she had taken.

Caroline's ventures extended beyond coaching, as she ventured into screenplay editing for Hollywood and embarked on her second book project. In 2023, she set her sights on California, eager to establish new companies and undertake thrilling projects.

Caroline Biesalski exemplifies ambition, resilience, and a relentless pursuit of personal growth. Her story inspires others to follow their passions, overcome challenges, and create a life filled with purpose and fulfillment.

Caroline is happy to connect with you. She speaks three languages fluently: German, French and English. She's open for new projects and helps you to turn your dreams into reality by high-class elite programs. Join her journey! It's the story of courage and freedom.

www.reflection8.com

Debbie Laney

9

~ Mercy ~

The Goddess of Mercy, with boundless compassion, embraces all beings in her loving arms, showering the world with eternal grace and guiding humanity towards compassion and kindness.

There's No Place like Home!

by Debbie Laney

In the words of Dorothy of the Wizard of Oz, "There's no place like home." From the very beginning, my home and life were filled with challenges. Home is supposed to be happy and filled with love. When I was a little girl, our home was anything but happy or filled with love. In fact, it was full of struggles, strife, and stress. All of which could've defined me and set me up for failure. Thankfully, I learned early on how to make my circumstances work for me. As I grew into young adulthood, I focused on building a home that could withstand the stormy winds of life.

The struggles which created my foundation shaped me into the person I am today. At the root of my struggles were my father figures. It all started when my father, battling alcoholism, attempted to suffocate me with a pillow when I was just one year old. The pattern repeated with my second father, who was also an alcoholic and subjected me to sexual abuse. The third father figure in my life had his own set of issues, including alcoholism and he had four children of his own and had another child with my mother. So, to say that I've had my fair share of father figure problems would be an understatement to say the least.

When I turned fifteen, my mother sent me to live with my grandparents for the summer, hoping to pressure my father into fulfilling his obligation of paying back child support that he never paid which was only $50.00 a month for each child. Unfortunately, it backfired. My grandparents, believing that my mother had abandoned us, called the police. As a result, my brother and I were placed in a detention home for three months until a foster home could be found. We stayed there for 9 months. These were experiences that no child should ever have to endure. My upbringing is proof positive that there should be a license to parent required before people can have children. In my mind, if someone chooses to have children, they must seriously consider how they can provide the love, support, guidance, and education necessary for a child to thrive in this world. They need to be ready, willing, and able to create a loving home for their children.

None of the men who played a role in my life should have been allowed to have children or be a part of my life. I grew up in a household where I was treated as a mere servant, responsible for cooking, cleaning, babysitting my younger sister, and whatever else they demanded of me. There were no family visits, no shared experiences such as going out for dinner or taking trips. Laughter and playfulness were nonexistent in my home. I grew up feeling unloved, unwanted, and unappreciated. Family should be a source of strength, a support system that helps each child navigate through difficult times and share the joys of life. Family should provide unconditional love, guidance, and security. In my opinion, family should prepare you for life. Such a life begins with the home the child is raised in.

Instead, I learned to be a servant rather than a cherished child in my family. I believed that serving others was a universal expectation, a way to demonstrate my love for my mother. However, as I grew older, I realized that serving others did not necessarily equate to being loved in return. Nevertheless, the act of serving taught me that the more I did for people, the more they seemed to like me. Service has become one of my love languages, and if someone plans on becoming a parent, they should carefully consider this aspect. As I entered adulthood, acts of service became one of my core values.

I see parenthood as an opportunity to demonstrate

unconditional love, teaching valuable life skills, and taking pride in one's child. Parents should instill hope and provide their children with the belief that they can achieve anything they desire. A child growing up without love or feeling unloved is an injustice on multiple levels. Additionally, parents should not wait until their child is 35 years old before expressing their love. "I love you." The impact of those three little words on a child is truly remarkable.

If it weren't for God, I would never have survived any of the hardships I faced. God has always been there for me, listening, giving me strength, and providing guidance. For me, His unconditional love is like no other, filling the void left by the absent father figures in my life. Knowing that God is always with me and within me has brought me the peace and comfort I needed to face the rest of my life. It is like having a full-time bodyguard, always present and protecting me. As Matthew 28:20 states, "I am with you always, even to the end of the age."

In the early eighties, I ventured into the mortgage industry with a clear purpose: to help people achieve their dreams of homeownership. I wanted to make a positive impact on people's lives and provide them with the support and guidance they needed during the complex process of obtaining a mortgage. I believed that the direction one's life would go began with their home life, which was dramatically impacted by the home they would be raised in. The doors of life are often opened by the mortgage we obtain. The problem is that obtaining a mortgage is often a very difficult acquisition for young couples who either have or will bring children into the fold of life.

Through hard work and determination, I excelled in the mortgage industry. I established strong relationships with clients, earning their trust and respect. I made it a point to educate them about the intricacies of mortgages, ensuring they understood their options and could make informed decisions. My commitment to service went beyond the transaction itself—I genuinely cared about their well-being and long-term financial success.

Over the years, I witnessed the joy and relief on the faces of countless families as they received the keys to their new homes. The satisfaction I derived from helping them achieve their dreams was immeasurable. It fueled my passion and motivated me to continue making a difference in the lives of others.

As my career progressed, I also became involved in the community and the military, volunteering my time and expertise to assisting families and individuals in securing affordable housing. I collaborated with nonprofit organizations, and other professionals in the industry to create initiatives that provided access to homeownership for those who faced financial obstacles.

Through these efforts, I saw firsthand the transformative power of a stable home. Families were able to establish roots, children had a safe and nurturing environment to grow up in, and communities thrived. Witnessing the positive ripple effects of my work reinforced my belief in the importance of service and the impact it can have on individuals and society as a whole.

Outside of my professional life, I also made it a priority to build meaningful connections with loved ones and family of friends. To create a nurturing and loving environment. Having experienced the absences of these elements in my upbringing, I was determined to break the cycle and provide love, support and security to all those I came in contact with. I made it a point to be present, to actively listen, and to foster open and honest communication. I built a H.O.M.E. I honored God. Opened my heart to serve. Made connections to home and community. Embraced my experiences as my purpose.

Reflecting on my journey, I realized that my difficult upbringing had shaped me in profound ways. It instilled in me a deep sense of empathy, resilience, and a relentless pursuit of creating a better life for myself and others. While I would never wish my experiences on anyone, I had learned to find strength in adversity and turn my pain into purpose.

My story is not just one of personal triumph, but also a testament to the transformative power of love, service, and the indomitable human spirit. Through acts of kindness and genuine care for others, we can create a world where every individual has the opportunity to thrive and be surrounded by the love and support, they deserve. And with each person we uplift, we contribute to a ripple effect of positivity that can change lives, communities, and even the world.

Throughout my journey, I have found solace, guidance, and strength in the words of the Bible. The scriptures have been a constant source of inspiration and a reminder of God's unwavering love and presence in my life. Here are a few Bible verses that have resonated deeply with me along the way as I created my H.O.M.E.

1.   Psalm 34:18 - "The Lord is near to the brokenhearted and saves the crushed in spirit." In my darkest moments, when I felt broken and lost, I found comfort in knowing that God was always near, ready to heal and restore my spirit.

2.   Jeremiah 29:11 - "For I know the plans I have for you," declares the Lord, "plans to prosper you and not to harm you, plans to give you hope and a future." This verse reminded me that even amidst the challenges and uncertainties, God had a purpose for my life and a future filled with hope and abundance.

3.   Philippians 4:13 - "I can do all things through Christ who strengthens me." Whenever self-doubt or obstacles threatened

to derail my journey, this verse served as a reminder that with God's strength and guidance, I could overcome any adversity and achieve great things.

4.   Matthew 7:7 - "Ask, and it will be given to you; seek, and you will find; knock, and it will be opened to you." This verse taught me the importance of seeking God's guidance and relying on His providence. It encouraged me to approach every challenge with a spirit of prayer and trust that God would provide the answers and open doors along the way.

5.   2 Corinthians 9:8 - "And God is able to bless you abundantly, so that in all things at all times, having all that you need, you will abound in every good work." This verse reminded me that God's blessings are boundless and that He would provide everything I needed to fulfill His calling in my life. It inspired me to be generous in serving others, knowing that God's abundance would always be present.

As I reflect on my journey, I can see how God's hand has guided me, protected me, and brought incredible individuals into my life to support and uplift me. Through faith, prayer, and a deep belief in His promises, I have found the strength to persevere and make a positive impact in the lives of others. I continue to hold onto these verses, allowing them to guide me as I navigate the challenges and joys that lie ahead. With God as my guide, I am confident that my purpose will be fulfilled, and my life will continue to be a testament to His unfailing love and grace. Be intentional about creating your personal H.O.M.E. as it will transform your heart and mind into a home you can be proud of. Honor God first. Open your heart and hands to serve. Make connections to your family and your community. Embrace your experiences as the things that will mold and shape who you ultimately become. There's no place like H.O.M.E.

Prayer for Mercy

by Debbie Laney

Dear Heavenly Father, bless me indeed and enlarge my territory. Help me to depend on You for everything that I want, desire, and need. Grant me the wisdom and courage to pursue my dreams and aspirations, always aligning them with Your will.

Lord, I humbly ask that Your hand be upon me, guiding me on the path that leads to abundance, strength, love, and light. May Your presence go before me, paving the way for success and fulfillment in every endeavor.

I surrender my plans and ambitions to You, knowing that You hold the ultimate authority over my life. Teach me to trust in Your divine provision and to seek Your guidance in every decision I make.

Father, grant me a spirit of contentment and gratitude, that I may appreciate the blessings You have already bestowed upon me. Help me to recognize and seize the opportunities that come my way, knowing that they are gifts from Your loving hand.

As I rely on You for my every need, may Your grace and mercy be evident in my life. Mold me into a vessel of Your love and use me to impact the lives of others positively.

In the name of Jesus, I pray, believing that with You, all things are possible.

Amen

Debbie Laney

Debbie Laney is a seasoned professional in the mortgage industry, known for her expertise and unwavering dedication to her clients. With over 30 years of experience, she has established herself as a respected figure in her community and has also earned a strong reputation among military personnel.

Specializing in purchases and refinancing loans, Debbie guides her clients through the intricacies of the lending process with confidence and expertise. She understands the unique needs and challenges of her clients and provides personalized solutions tailored to their specific circumstances.

Outside of her professional accomplishments, Debbie embraces a vibrant and fulfilling life. She thrives on adventure and finds joy in activities such as skiing, hiking, biking, and golfing. These pursuits allow her to connect with nature, stay active, and find balance in her busy schedule. Additionally, Debbie's passion for entertaining shines through as she hosts memorable gatherings for friends and showcases her culinary skills by exploring new recipes.

Travel is another significant aspect of Debbie's life, with a particular love for exploring European countries. Immersing herself in diverse cultures, savoring local cuisines, and exploring the rich history and arts of different regions enriches her perspective and fuels her curiosity.

In all her endeavors, Debbie is guided by unwavering principles of integrity, honesty, and fairness. She believes in treating each client as a valued member of her community, forging relationships that extend beyond the scope of business transactions. Building connections that last a lifetime is at the core of her philosophy.

Debbie's passion for helping others extends beyond her professional pursuits. She is a compassionate advocate for children in need and actively supports organizations such as Compassion, One Child Matters, Children's International, and Mission of Mercy. Currently, she provides support to 21 children, ensuring they have access to food, water, and basic supplies for survival. Her ultimate goal is to support 5,000 children, enabling them to live the life they were born to achieve.

With her commitment to exceptional service, continuous learning, and genuine care for her clients and the well-being of children, Debbie Laney stands out as a mortgage professional with a deep sense of purpose and a desire to make a positive impact. When you choose Debbie, you not only receive expert guidance in your financial endeavors but also contribute to a meaningful cause that brings hope and opportunities to children in need.

mindsetboutique369@gmail.com

Matthew Gibbons

10

~ Perseverance ~

Through the depths of adversity, he stands as a relentless force, inspiring souls to push beyond limits, endure hardships, and rise above tribulations. With steadfast determination, he fuels the flame of resilience, empowering individuals to persist until triumph is achieved, reminding the world that true strength lies in never surrendering.

life is an Inside Game

by Matthew Gibbons

"The world as we have created it is a process of our thinking. It cannot be changed without changing our thinking." ~ Albert Einstein

I was born on November 14th, 1968. My mom was born November 15th, 1945, and my father was born December 15th,1944. My parents are very loving; they worked really hard to provide for our family. I'm the oldest of three other siblings, which, as I got older, came with more responsibilities to help out while my parents were working. My childhood was good; my parents worked; we went to school; we played in the neighborhood with all the other kids; and we were very close with my aunts, uncles and cousins — we did stuff with them all the time. At the age of 8 years-old, my parents purchased another house and we moved to a different neighborhood. At this time in my life, it was a little scary leaving the environment I was comfortable in, leaving the friends I had made, and moving to an area that I was unfamiliar with and where I didn't know anybody. I felt like I was abandoning them, and that I was being abandoned.

All my young life, I was bigger and heavier than most of the other kids. That came with a lot of criticism, teasing and being made fun of — as you can imagine — so I had to learn how to stick up for myself really quickly. This really affected my self-confidence. Fortunately for me, my grandma lived with us for quite a while as I was growing up. She was one of my biggest fans and a huge influence in my life, especially in the way she taught me how to think, use my mind and talk to myself. She always told me I could be, do or have anything I wanted.

115

One of the things I learned from my grandma was how to think and do things differently. When I was 12 years old, I had my very first newspaper route. One of the things I did very differently was put everybody's newspaper on their porch, not just throwing it anywhere in their yard or on their driveway. Very quickly, I became my customers' favorite newspaper boy. As a young entrepreneur, I thrived. I was blessed with extra tips and gifts. I believe the reason that happened is because of the level at which I served my customers.

My teenage years were filled with ups and downs. I played sports, I was the lead in the school musical, and my name was in the local newspaper all the time. One day after one of my baseball games, my mom's sister was waiting at our house to inform her and my grandma that their brother, my uncle, had died. I loved him and I felt like he abandoned us. I believe he committed suicide. During this time my mom worked a lot. My father was a truck driver and not home very often, so this left me and my siblings to ourselves until Mom got home. For most of the events in my teenage years — football games, baseball games and concerts — my mom was always there and did so much. Because of my father's profession, he often wasn't able to make it to my games or my concerts. For a long time I resented that, because I felt I didn't have the encouragement or the support from my dad so that I could get better and go farther with sports. My dad is an amazing human being and I know he did the best he could, but I missed that extra push only a dad could provide.

All my life I learned to hustle, work hard, always striving to have more because what I had wasn't good enough. You know, to "keep up with the Joneses" so to speak. In fact, I heard that most of my young life. Learning to stay focused and work hard served me well. In my mid 20s I got married to a wonderful woman; I think we made a great team. It seemed like we always got what we wanted. We worked hard; we took life head on. Before we officially got married, we decided to have a baby and that amazing little boy was 6 months old when we got married. That little guy changed my whole world, I don't know if I'd ever been happier in my life.

During this time, I started a business that my sister ran for me, while I worked my day job. After a couple weeks of that, I decided to quit my job and jump into my new business 100%. My wife was not a huge fan of that move because she liked security, which I respect. There was something inside of me not satisfied with working for somebody else. This turned out to be an amazing experience for me. Within six months of starting this business, I was making $50,000 a month with very little overhead. That continued for quite some time. In my mind, life was good! But just because I began making more money than I had ever made before, it didn't solve the challenges my wife and I were having. However, somehow, we manage to work through it and stick together.

Two years after our first son was born, we had another baby boy. This was a different experience for me because we were continuing to go through some ups and downs and then, all of a sudden, I found out she's pregnant. Initially I was a little scared and unhappy about this; in fact, I resented it because of our relationship struggles. She and I continued to work through our challenges while being parents of two amazing little boys. Things turned the corner for the better; we started accomplishing more of our goals and eventually building a new home. I was excited about this home; I had wanted this home for a while.

We finally moved into our home after it was built. The boys were getting bigger, they were so much fun. We were very busy with work, the kids playing sports, playing instruments, getting involved with martial arts and all the other events that happen with kids, raising a family and running a business. Once again, life was good.

One year after living in our new home, I came home from work only to meet my wife at the door telling me she wanted to divorce. I was shocked to say the least because from my perception our life was good and getting better.

Over the next few weeks, I attempted to get us to do anything to work this out because I wanted to avoid a divorce, no matter what. I realized quickly that it takes more than one person to be invested in a relationship. I did everything I could to put up a good front, making it look like I had it all together, that everything was going to be fine, that I was good. The truth of the matter is this was the beginning of a very long battle. Depression crept up on me ever so subtly; it was like this slow, steady energy that just kept grabbing hold of me, influencing my thoughts, determining how I was looking at things, controlling the way I was feeling. Looking back now I was literally in a fight for my life.

This one event changed everything — you know, the things we take for granted: waking up in the morning; listening to your little kids playing, fighting, screaming, having fun and simply growing up or taking them to school; being there when they got home; sitting down with them and having dinner; helping them do their homework; tucking them in for bed… Just being there and experiencing your kids growing up. I missed out on most of that because I didn't live with them every single day. Unknowingly this began to take a toll on me, and I quickly became very unhappy. I kept wondering why somebody was doing this to me. Why was God punishing me? What in the world had I done that would cause somebody else to cause me this much pain?

My thriving business that I loved started to struggle. I was in such a bad way that I didn't even care about it and very quickly I was losing my business. I felt helpless. I knew the inevitable was going to happen and I was going to lose this business. While this was unfolding, I was approached by a couple of gentlemen who wanted me to start another trucking company and work with them. So, with my brother, my father and a family friend, we started another trucking business.

I like facing new challenges because it drives me and lets me do what I'm really good at, which is to create and make things happen — at least that's what I thought at the time. We were fortunate to hit the ground running with this company because we obtained a whole line of business right out of the gate that we didn't have to go look for. This gave the new company a great start. However, this time it was different because it wasn't just me. Now I had to work with my brother, my father, some family friends and go through all the different dynamics that this brings.

Consciously, I thought this was going to change everything for me. It didn't, however, because deep inside, my world had been turned upside down, I was angry, upset, and unhappy. It didn't matter what I did, nothing worked out. It was a constant battle of robbing Peter to pay Paul, arguing and fighting with my dad and brother over how to run the company, and what was the best things to do. This created so much turmoil. The one thing I had going for me is what my grandma had taught me: to think positive and hope for the best.

I was getting tired of the daily grind and arguing with my brother what seemed like daily about the operations of this business. So I decided to move on with all the optimism and positive thinking I could muster. Meanwhile, I was falling farther and farther behind on my financial responsibilities. I couldn't pay my Child Support. I couldn't pay the mortgage on my duplex. I literally couldn't pay for anything, and you can imagine what was coming. First, my truck got repossessed, then my mortgage went into default, and I lost my Duplex. Meanwhile my Child Support was racking up and I couldn't figure out anything to do to stop this complete collapse I was experiencing. I did everything I could think of. I never imagined in a million years I would be in this position.

One of the things that matters to me the most are my two boys. On some level, my relationship with them got strained because I only got to be with them every other weekend and whenever I went to their games or events. I resented not seeing them grow up every single day, so much so that it began to consume part of me on the inside while I was doing my best to make everybody else think that I had it all together and everything was going well.

I finally hit what I thought was rock bottom, at the age of 40, and I had to move back home with my parents. I am very thankful for them and what they did for me. As you could imagine, this wasn't very much fun. I'm 40 years old, divorced, I've lost everything, I'm barely making enough money to somewhat survive, and I live with my parents. What a résumé, huh?

Life was moving by really fast. I was getting older, and it seemed like I wasn't making any progress towards achieving any of my goals. I began to think why am I even here? Nothing I do makes a difference, I'm alone, my boys are taken care of, nobody needs me and all I seem to do is cause more problems.

One quiet afternoon I found myself sitting on the edge of my bed feeling overwhelmed, depressed, and useless. Sitting beside me I had my gun. All these thoughts kept running through my head… I'm not good enough, I don't make a difference, nobody cares about me, everybody would be better off if I wasn't here because then I would no longer be a burden… The constant wave of thoughts kept rolling through my mind, then those thoughts evolved into I should just kill myself; how should I do that to make sure it is successful? Do I shoot myself in the side of the head? Do I stick the gun in my mouth? Do I shoot myself in the heart? I sat there contemplating how to go about this and mustering up the courage to do it.

Suddenly, something came over me and brought my two boys to my awareness. It was like this incredible pattern interrupted my suicidal thinking. I began to see my boys in my mind; it was like watching a video of what their life would be like if I were to abandon them. The movie seemed so real and what I saw was a horror movie with my boys being the stars. The energy that came over me reminded me that all those suicidal thoughts were just bullshit and how in the world could you abandon your two precious boys? This stopped me in my tracks. This truly is the only reason I didn't follow through.

I knew right then and there, something had to change. I had to change. I had to change the way I was looking at life and how I was thinking, because living and not abandoning my two boys mattered more to me than anything else. Over the next few days, I reflected on what was happening. I remember my grandma talking to me about the power thoughts have. I replayed over in my mind the thoughts I was thinking and how those suicidal thoughts were leading me to act on taking my life. This was an incredible awareness for me and a wake-up call.

I embarked on a journey to heal. One of the first things I learned is that nothing just happens to me. Experiences happen for me, and I had a choice: do I want to be a victim of circumstance, or do I want to embrace the power that I have and know that I created these experiences so that I could grow and make different choices so that I could experience something else? I remembered that I had the power to choose what I thought about, and when I did that, those thoughts moved me to take the actions needed to achieve my goals and experience life on my terms. I understand this is an ongoing process and will be like that for the rest of my life. It's the one thing we all have in common. We have a powerful mind, and we are the captain of that ship, and our thoughts determine the direction it's going to take us.

LIFE IS AN INSIDE GAME! REMEMBER...

Every condition, every experience of my life is the result of my mental attitude.

I can do only what I think I can do.

I can be only what I think I can be.

I can have only what I think I can have.

What I do, what I am, what I have, all depend upon what I think.

I can never express anything that I do not have in my mind first.

The secret of all power, all success, all riches is in first thinking powerful thoughts, successful thoughts, thoughts of wealth, thoughts of plenty.

In order to have it, I must build it in my own mind first.

Concentrate and think about things that you want, not on things which you do not have.

Think from having it. Think from being it.

Think from doing it.

Think from appreciating it! WHAT YOU MAKE IMPORTANT MUST COME INTO FORM!

Prayer of Perseverance

by Matthew Gibbons

I am filled with gratitude and awe
for the blessings surrounding me.

With unwavering optimism,
I seek your guidance and strength.

Grant me the courage to face challenges
and the perseverance to overcome them.

May I find resilience in adversity,
knowing you are always by my side.

With a grateful heart, I embrace life's journey,
filled with gratitude, courage, and unwavering faith.

About

Matthew Gibbons

Matthew is a manifesting mentor with a passion for helping people unlock their full potential and live their best lives. With over a decade of experience in the field of personal development, Matthew has helped hundreds of clients align one's thoughts, feelings, and actions with their desired outcomes so that they can thrive. He is a certified NLP and Theta practitioner. In his free time, he enjoys playing golf, traveling and being with family and friends.

"My purpose is to make a difference in our world by harnessing the power of our minds. I believe that our thoughts have a profound impact on our lives and the world around us. By cultivating a thriving mindset and focusing our energy on creating a thriving lifestyle, we can transform our lives and the lives of those around us. Through my words and actions, I strive to inspire others to tap into their own inner power and use their minds to make a difference in our world."

mrmattgibbons.com

Doe Renée

11

~ Grief ~

With her divine presence, she transforms grief into the seeds of growth, empowering us to rise above our pain and embrace a future filled with strength, purpose, and an unwavering spirit.

The Gravity of Grief

by Doe Renée

I jolted up in bed. I had just woken up from a jarring dream.

I turned to my right to see that Clint was still lying next to me, and he was OK.

The dream was just exposing my greatest fear.

"He would never do that to himself. He has told me that he would never do that," I thought, as I reassured myself shakily.

A couple years later, in the women's restroom of a marina in Puerto Vallarta, my friend hands me concealer as she lovingly puts her hand on my back. I breathe through tears while trying to hold the rest of them back. We both look at my reflection together, as I take the concealer pad to my black eye.

In a moment that transcended time, the eyes of my future self-found my reflection in the mirror, and she seemed to say telepathically, "What are you doing? Why are you pretending nothing happened last night? When will you stop allowing this?"

September 16th, 2019:

With my 6-month-old son, Leo, in my arms, I show up at my parents' house and ask to move back in. I tell them, "I've finally found the courage."

September 5th, 2020:

Our family finds out from a local inpatient facility that Clint came in for help due to suicidal ideation but left before being admitted.

After hours of not hearing back from him, and being worried for his mental wellness, he calls me back the next morning.

September 6th, 2020:

We talk about how he was driving all night and didn't sleep. At the end of the call, he is silent for many moments and then says, "I love you." At that moment, I know his decision has been made. I know there is nothing I can do but pray.

Later that day, I see I missed a call from Clint when I was away from my phone. I try to call back. No answer.

Late that night, I receive a call from the Denver Police Department. Under the blue horse statue at Denver International Airport, Clinton Craig Cooper's spirit had left his body. I realize the dream I had years ago, of seeing him take a gun to his head, has become a living nightmare.

Present Day:

The moment I found out Clint had died, I screamed out loudly, and literally fell to the floor. My sister rushed over to me.

Torrential waterfalls of tears flooded down my face. Memories of everything flashed through my consciousness.

The good times. The nights out when we owned the dance floor for hours and hours. All the people he helped on the side of the road when their car had broken down. Seeing him speak at the front of the room in personal development courses, and declaring freedom from the traumas he has faced.

The scary times. The moments I felt terrified for my life. The times I lied for him. The many car rides where I was so scared we would crash due to his road rage.

The beautiful times. When we made the choice to try for a baby.

The first time we held Leo together. The times he confided in me in his depression, even when we had separated. The times we apologized after a horrible fight and came back to love. How we would say the Hawaiian phrase "Ho'oponopono". The sound of his laughter when he did stand-up comedy. The last phone call I had with him earlier that day.

I thought of the sound of his voice I would never hear again.

Survivor's guilt and asking "What if" questions, is something I experience often whenever I replay that day. What if I hadn't missed his last phone call? What if I hadn't separated from him? Could I have done more to help him heal his depression? What if I had listened more, and didn't tell him to "just smile through it"?

I also experienced a twisted sense of relief. Relief that his suffering and pain were over. Relief that I didn't have to endure the challenges of co-parenting with someone who had such a large ebb and flow of emotions.

It was also at this time I discovered what I call the "Circular Model of Emotions".

In other parts of the world, workplaces often grant months or even a year to an employee after experiencing a traumatic death in the family. In the US, it's often barely a day or two. Thankfully, I was able to take two weeks off from my role as a charter school STEM teacher. Then, after returning from Clint's Celebration of Life, I got back to school. It was still my first few weeks at a new school when Clint died.

After returning to teach, there was a time when I was lightly sobbing during my lunch break, as the grief suddenly hit me uncontrollably. I breathed and tried to compose myself while wiping my tears with a blob of tissues. Then an 8th-grade student walked in with a 3D-printed octopus in his hand. He was coming in to share his success, as he had become my right-hand man in our 3D printing project. As he got closer, he could see I was crying.

"I'm sorry to interrupt, should I leave?"

I took a moment to blow my nose and wiped my wet eyelashes. Thankfully, I'd had a lifetime of experience of being pretty open about my emotions and experiences. "No, it's OK, I'm actually glad you're here. I have accepted that sometimes I just need to allow the tough emotions to fully flow and then the next moment, it's easier to move forward. Then, hours, days or weeks later, I might be back there again. It's the circle of life."

He then thanked me for being such a real teacher and proceeded to share his 3D printing win with me. I taught there for two years, and I am proud to say, many more students thanked me for being a "real" teacher, and many also confided in me in their own times of inner turmoil. I listened and didn't try to change them, and just by listening, it provided a natural space of transformation.

It wasn't until I began truly listening that I realized, for much of my life — including my marriage to Clint — I didn't truly listen.

When I was a student, I was the positive one who always saw the bright side. This was often a huge contribution to my friends and family. Unfortunately, this also meant I was toxically positive. I jumped straight to being happy without honoring the grief someone was experiencing. While I did listen, I was listening to respond and fix, not truly just to listen. I did that in my marriage with Clint and in my friendships with others who died by suicide or overdose. My survivor's guilt wondered if I had listened better, would the outcome still have been the same? Because of Clint's emotions throughout our time together, I often labeled anger and sadness as "negative" emotions that had "negative" consequences. While he was alive, I was anxious whenever he was angry or sad. My coping mechanism would be to pretend it wasn't happening.

After his death, I finally began to honor the fact that I'd felt so unsafe for years. I began to allow dormant anger to rise up within me about how he died and about how I'd allowed myself to be a target for his rage when he was alive. I realize all that rage represented his unprocessed emotions that had come from a lifetime of trauma before we met. And yet, it was taken out on me. With the help of my mentors, family, and friends, I used modalities like dance and the conscious allowing of emotions to transmute this anger. There are moments I still feel it today. I allow it to rise, in safe ways. I affirm, "Thank you for showing up. Thank you for showing me what I need to witness and let go of."

Now I realize I can honor grief as a gift, and that all "negative" emotions come up for a reason, as a part of the Circular Model of Emotions. I find the next deeper level to truly listen to myself and others, and hold infinite gratitude for my family and my life as my medicine.

My husband today, Garrett, has naturally become "Daddy" for Leo, our son. He has been there to witness our grieving and healing process. Leo was a year and a half when Clint died, so it's only in more recent years that Leo has been able to understand the facts and acknowledge his feelings about it all. He is aware that he has his first father, "Daddy Clint", as his guardian angel in heaven.

When Leo was 3, we were sitting on the couch, looking at memory reels of him and Clint. In my favorite photo of them together, they are both beaming and laughing.

Leo excitedly exclaimed, "Daddy Clint! He didn't die anymore!

We could FaceTime him! Aww, I can see his face!" The pure innocence of his words crushed me. He was still understanding the finality of death. I reply softly, "Well, his body did die, so we can't FaceTime him... His spirit is always with us, and we can always talk to him in our hearts, in dreams and in meditation."

I witnessed his realization as a few tears fell down his face. My heart ached to see him mourning.

"It's OK to feel sad. Are you sad that he died?" He nodded yes and came in for a hug and to put his head to my heart. "Me too." I suddenly became breathless as I allowed tears to flow. I was surprised by the waterfall of emotion. Unexpectedly, Leo was now actually the one holding me at that moment. As I sobbed, I experienced infinite bittersweet gratitude for Leo. A gift of love that Clint had created with me. Leo looked up at me to check in, then leant back in for another hug.

At that point I was aware the tables had been turned and my 3-year-old son was now holding space for ME as we grieved together. He took a deep breath, grabbed a toy, and began to play with his sister, Zelda. He allowed the grief, and being a true model for me, felt it fully and then naturally moved forward. Leo became my teacher.

While I was initially comforting him, I softened, and allowed dormant grief to rise within me. I let myself be held by my son, rather than always being the one to help or fix another. Leo taught me to sit with my grief, breathe into it and give it a place to live. This was a breakthrough moment in my mourning process.

These grief sessions with Leo come naturally as I consciously share positive memories of his first dad, and often last a few minutes at a time. As he builds his spiritual gifts, he will more deeply understand the truth that Clint's spirit lives on. I know and trust that his spirit lives on, as I have had many sacred connections with him after his physical death, in experiences via dream time and meditative communications. Even knowing this, I still feel the deep sadness of his physical loss and still feel guilt that I could have done more.

These affirmations help me mend survivor's guilt whenever it arises.

"I forgive you for doing the best you could."

"Grief can show up as anger too. I let it arise in safe ways."

"I forgive you for the times you wanted to run from your anger or grief. You were just doing what you could to survive."

"Thank you for showing up. I love you. You have a place… you can go now. I know I may see you again."

Grief has appeared in so many ways for me. Sometimes it was a joyful grief when I would come across old photos of good times. Sometimes it was an angry grief, realizing all the milestones of Leo's growth that weren't witnessed, or remembering a time I felt so scared for my life.

I allowed myself to express some grief and anger, one warm, autumn day, outside during my movement practice. I was physically kicking the air and crying at the same time. I was remembering times I wanted to fight back, and abusive times when I just wanted him to be gone. Then feeling guilt for ever wishing that, and somehow feeling I was the ultimate cause of his suicide. I got down on my knees and began to cry out. I lay down on my yoga mat and felt my inner guidance say, "Let it out. And look around… for signs."

Suddenly, I felt like I was being hugged. I felt the sensation of being embraced, despite there being no one physically there.

The next moment, a red cardinal flew close by me, landed on a tree and looked right at me. As I locked eyes with the cardinal, tears welled up in my eyes. I felt my heart burst open energetically.

All at once, I was overtaken with a waterfall of visions and feelings. I sobbed deeply and allowed my tears to be absorbed into the earth. The red bird was chirping loudly and flapping its wings, acting as a messenger for these words from Clint that I sensed.

"I am so sorry, Meral. I wish all the time it wasn't this way. I can still feel regret even here in Astral City. And there is something greater that is growing now, which will aid the collective, from our spiritual friendship which spans across space and time. Your love wasn't enough to save me. No one's love was enough. Especially not my own self-love. Not while I was in my body. Please help Leo understand the truth of my struggles and help him know the best of who I was. Also, be honest with him about my struggles when he is ready. Leo is our gift I was able to help you create before I left. He is the best of both of us. Ho'oponopono."

Later that day, I wrote a letter to Clint and telepathically mailed it.

"Ho'oponopono. I am so sorry for all the times I tried to fix and change you or just wanted you to smile through your pain. I am grateful for our spiritual friendship where we can honor the hurt anytime we feel it, even when we thought it was healed. Leo is teaching me to feel it deeply and then let it go, over and over. YOU ARE OK. I AM OK. LEO IS OK. WE ARE ALL OK. I will remind myself of this often. Always and forever. It's OK not to feel OK. Because, in the end, we will always be OK, and our spirit always lives on."

Writing this chapter as the Oracle of Grief has been a breakthrough in my empowered healing process. I am stepping up as a leader for honoring grief as parents and as a community. I invite you to join me as we co-create unprecedented vulnerability and courage as a collective.

Prayer To Surrender

by Meral Doe Renée

I allow myself to surrender to this brutiful grief.

It's okay for me to feel.

It's safe to cry.

I am allowed to feel weak.

Mindful and heartfelt grief is a superpower.

We are meant to experience darkness and lightness.

I integrate duality into wholeness.

I embody the circular model of honoring emotions.

Everything I feel is welcome and safe to be here.

My grief is equal to my Joy and they are welcome to rise together.

My loved ones are forever connected to me, across space and time.

Grief is my powerful force of transmutation, emanating into eternity.

All loved ones who have passed physically… are still with me. They continue their mission in spirit.

Even if I feel far away from a loved one who has passed, I trust in my knowing: Energy never dies. It only transforms.

About
Doe Renée

Doe Renée is the author who expands time. She is a mom and a visionary leader for Peace on Earth and the Cosmos. She is a publisher and authorship coach with Author Catalyst Academy (ACA) and is also the Director at the Pueblo Heritage Museum. ACA provides author wellness support, hosts co-creation flow sessions, creativity retreats and more!

She stands by this truth: We are completely shifting the paradigm of humanity such that a peaceful and regenerative society is emerging.

She is the author of several books including the Cosmic Sagas and the Sacred Feminine: A Collection of Insights from the Higher Self.

Connect with her at **linktr.ee/doerenee** or @doerenee on social media, especially if you're ready to start your authorship journey.

Lisa Regan

12

~ Faith ~

The Goddess of Faith illuminates the human experience, unveiling the limitless potential that lies dormant within each individual. She champions the cultivation of belief and trust, fostering an unbreakable bond between mortals and the sacred essence that permeates all existence

A Love Letter To My Daughter

by Lisa Regan

You can have, do, and be whatever you want! I hold firmly to this belief, and it fills my heart with faith.

What happens, though, when life seems to kick you in the gut over and over again? And you don't understand why you're attracting another narcissistic control freak into your life? What happens when your internal navigation system, your true North Star, meets with pain and trauma? Faith seems to fail you every step of the way, and your reality is the opposite of your hopes and dreams.

It is my sincerest intention that you open your magnificent heart and allow yourself to connect to your true North Star so you can have the freedom to be and do whatever it is you really want – not someone else's vision for you. In this inner space, you can give yourself permission to awaken to the truth of who you are, why you're here, and what you came to do. Your North Star guides you through faith. Just as it has for me.

 Faith reveals itself in reflection.

To heal my emotional trauma, I needed tools. And this piece of wisdom from Steve Jobs, which was given at a commencement address in 2005, has impacted my life significantly: "You can't connect the dots looking forward; you can only connect the dots looking backwards."

In Proverbs 4:7 it is written, "And in all your getting, get understanding." Understanding my choices has given my healing journey shape and form. My heart's desire has been to understand myself deeply and profoundly, to embody faith with all my senses, and to know there is hope for me.

Thank you for indulging my preaching nature. It's a piece of me and it's how I have healed.

I am a strong-willed, determined person. I was the child who threw temper tantrums in the grocery store. I was the child who would hit my head on the floor to get what I wanted. It's these attributes in my journey of healing that have brought experiences of great joy and great sorrow.

My faith was first tested when my parents divorced. I was 4 years old and couldn't comprehend how I was not to blame for my dad leaving. Prior to my him leaving, my life had been filled with joy, fun, and lots of play.

Now I understand how my parents' divorce molded and shaped one of my core beliefs of being unworthy to receive what I really wanted: a healthy, happy me.

I sought relationships with men who, on the surface, appeared to be strong, powerful, and caring. Instead, I attracted narcissistic men, who loved using me so they could look better. The first serious relationship I had was in high school. This guy represented a knight in shining armor who would save and protect me. Throughout our time together, I dismissed my gut instinct to get out of this relationship. I didn't trust my faith. So, I accepted his decisions for my life as my own. This pattern continued until my sophomore year in college. With enough pressure from within my internal being, I made the decision to end that relationship. I felt relieved and free to be me. But wait, this personality type doesn't go away that easily. Interestingly, he followed me to the city I'd relocated to, and attempted to resume the romantic relationship under the guise of friendship.

His true motives were revealed when I agreed to join him on a road trip to see his family.

Gratefully, I trusted my heart and cut all ties to him. Now, I am able to understand why I put my trust and faith in someone else. I had lost faith in my North Star. Free from a controlling relationship, I gave myself permission to explore my beliefs and what spirituality actually meant to me as a 20-year-old. I moved away from Catholic beliefs, away from any religious beliefs. Being open to my North Star, my heart, I moved into an alliance with my soul.

During my initial spiritual awakening, I met a man 20 years my senior at a Unity Church in my hometown. I was so open and naive during my spiritual awakening that I didn't see the human in front of me. What I saw was another spiritual being with very similar beliefs about God and the universe. I said yes to this experience.

It turned out that my decision to join my life with this man was one of my hardest – yet greatest – lessons of faith. This test of faith connected me to my core, to the center of who I am.

This test was born out of my desire to defy the conventional principles and opinions of family and friends. The rebellious side of my nature was flourishing. Feeling restored in my heart (my true North), I was confident this guy was my soulmate. I felt alive again, enjoying life in a way that felt unrestrained, where I was free to express all emotional aspects of myself. I thought I was free to be me - not the me others expected or wanted me to be. I felt unstoppable, powerful, and in charge of my life.

For a short period of time, that was how I chose to exist.

At the two-year mark of my relationship, I became pregnant for the second time (my first pregnancy ended in a miscarriage).

After my daughter's birth, I convinced myself and held on tightly to my belief that we would be a happy family. However, the reality was my partner became more physically distant and emotionally demanding. I remember comments like, "You wanted this baby, you live with the consequences", "Don't depend on me to help you" and "You still need to have sex with me when I say so". I accepted the responsibility. In public, he took credit and boasted to anyone within earshot, including my family, what a great dad he was. He painted a picture that he was the brains behind our financial and philanthropic success. I didn't dispute or disagree with his boastfulness, publicly or privately. My grandpa would cringe anytime we visited as a family (my husband, daughter, and me). He would tell me privately that my husband was a jackass, and that I was raised to know better than to let someone put me down. Sadly, depression and disharmony spread through my body and spirit. And the hope I held that a baby would bring us happiness was misguided and misplaced.

As each day passed, my fantasy of a happy family was met with the stark reality of unhappiness, pleasing my partner, and buffering the sharp emotional blows of "You are not enough" towards myself and my daughter.

The darkness of this relationship and all my past traumas of betrayal, shame, and unworthiness overtook my being. During this period of my life, I also became aware of my first sexual trauma at the hand of my dad. I'd buried this trauma so deeply it could only surface after the birth of my daughter for me to consciously acknowledge and admit it.

Ultimately, I lost access to my North Star, my heart. I felt like my life force was leaving me. I used all my spiritual practices: prayer, meditation, affirmations, naturopathic treatment, massage treatment, healing circles, energy shrouds of protection, hugging trees, and calming herbs. Everything I tried provided only temporary relief. Then, much like any medication, the effects wore off. I was still facing myself in the mirror. I survived by leaving my body. I felt like a zombie, and this was my way of protecting myself from emotions I couldn't bear to feel.

Every decision I made through the marriage and dissolution of that marriage centered around what I could do that was in my daughter's best interest. I took all my will and determination and focused that energy on raising her.

When I made the decision to leave my husband, quivering and shaking, the unexpected happened. He announced to my daughter, just as she and I were leaving for school, that I was moving out. He then followed that with a question to her: "Who do you want to live with? Your mom or me?" I was shocked and hurt. After all the marriage counseling, a person would think that his power move wouldn't have come as a surprise; yet it did. My intention was to work out a parenting agreement so my daughter would have us both in her life.

Because my physical and emotional safety was in jeopardy, I moved in temporarily with my mom and stepdad. I continued therapy sessions to help heal, and I was advised to move back in with my partner for six months and say no to him, especially when it came to sex. I followed my therapist's advice and moved back in with my partner and daughter. The 6-month experiment lasted two weeks. Following my therapist's instructions helped me understand my partner's dominant, narcissistic, and psychopathic behavior. Fortunately, I trusted my heart and left that house for good. I made a note to myself: listen to what others have to say but put your trust and faith in your own guidance system.

Thankfully and gratefully, my family gave me a soft place to land, direction to a divorce attorney, and funds to rent a place of my own.

During the two-year separation, I saw my daughter every other weekend maybe, and occasionally one day during the week. I hired a guardian ad litem as a protective measure for her.

With the pending decision from the guardian ad litem, my daughter mounted a fierce defense to protect her own self-interests. During the first summer of the separation, we were swimming at a local hot spring, and she flatly told me, "I would rather die than live with you." I felt her statement, and I absolutely knew she was not joking. Being as strong-willed as I am, I could see myself in my daughter's eyes.

This pain pierced my heart. It was the greatest pain I experienced as her mom.

 Faith reveals itself in reflection.

Just before Christmas, the guardian ad litem ruled that I should be the primary parent. Yet again, my daughter informed me that if I forced her to live with me, I would never see her again. In my heart, I knew she meant every word she said.

My daughter continued her path with her father, and I remained the custodial parent for the remainder of her minor years. Even the judge, during another custodial hearing two years after the initial separation, ruled in favor of her wishes to remain under her father's primary care. She was 12 years old then.

Another test of faith.

When my daughter was 15 or 16 years old, she accused my now husband of sexual assault just after our engagement in 2007. My daughter had met my husband only once! We were at her 8th-grade track meet, and they were not left alone, not even once. She made her accusation to another woman who was a foster type of parent. This unfamiliar woman accused me of letting my daughter be raped by my now husband. In my heart and rational mind, I knew my daughter was lying, and I knew she was testing me. Thankfully, my daughter had the courage to admit she lied, and she apologized for her actions. I held tightly to my faith to see me through.

The reality of the physical, emotional, and spiritual alienation from my daughter took hold of my heart. Faith tested me. I questioned myself almost daily: Do I hold steady and believe that somehow, someday, my daughter and I could reunite and really love each other? I kept hearing in the soft silence of my heart: "Trust your North Star; I am your guidance system."

Throughout the 12 years of alienation from my daughter, I felt as if I were being denied by fate, God, and the universe to be mom, one who is grounded, confident, steadfast, authentic, and fearless. Like a lioness who nurtures, protects, and hunts to feed her cubs, I wanted to embody these attributes for myself and for my daughter.

Faith's reward. The present healing transformation for my daughter and me is one in which we have a divine sisterhood. We are business partners, and we hold mutual honor, respect, and love for our individual light and dark.

Acceptance, harvesting the good, and forgiveness practices have helped heal my emotional pain and move me from victim and survivor of emotional and sexual abuse to a confident woman who loves herself; and has gained victory over the conditions, and circumstances that life dishes up.

My North Star, my heart, connected back to me through faith. Faith found me and waited for me ever so patiently, ever so gently.

Welcome home, dear one.

I love you always. I love you eternally. I am your ye

Prayer for Inner Peace

by Lisa Regan

In the presence of the Goddess of Faith,

Love radiates ceaselessly, permeating the vast tapestry of Creation.

Boundaries dissolve as sacred Doves, we soar, embodying empowerment and spreading the seeds of peace.

Your Love knows no limits, coursing through every nook and cranny of existence, uniting all in its embrace.

I ask the Goddess to intertwine with our essence, dispelling self-doubt and nurturing unwavering trust.

With deep reverence, we yield to your infinite wisdom and graceful guidance, trusting your navigation through life's twists.

May blessings cascade upon us, filling our hearts with unshakable faith.

So be it, may it be so, as we manifest this sacred covenant.

About

Lisa Regan

LiteHouse Lady, Lisa Regan, is a radical transformative spiritual teacher. Her passion is for every person, especially women, to harness the power of their divine greatness claiming their worthiness to co-create a cooperative, compassionate, global community.

With the awareness of life being a journey, not a destination, she has fostered a deep desire for learning. Tempering the learning with FUN creates inspiration for her, so family amusement park and waterpark vacations are an annual event including unBirthday Birthday parties. Lisa has found tremendous joy with gardening and loving quiet time with her plants and trees.

With two post-secondary degrees, a Bachelor of Science in Business Finance from the University of Montana and an associates of science Registered Nurse from Montana Tech, Lisa continued to immerse herself in personal development programs. She has studied with motivational great Les Brown in the Power Voice program, the great Bob Proctor and Darren Hardy.

Locally Lisa received certification in Soul Purpose Hand Mapping© from Sara Gasch, Certified ThetaHealing® Master, Registered Holy Fire® III Karuna Reiki® Master Practitioner and Certified Advanced Hand Analyst. She loves this modality as it awakens clients through their handprints to their Divine selves, shifting their paradigm of beliefs and negative karma into one of empowerment and purpose.

Driven to expand into coaching and personal development from the life insurance industry, Lisa and her business partner/daughter Caitlin Graves started LiteHouse Enterprises to educate people about holistic wealth. Combined with being ambassador coaches with Napoleon Hill Institute, Lisa is a beacon of lite for people to realize their unlimited potential.

litehouseladies.com

lisa@litehouseladies.com

YouTube @litehouseladies

Facebook & Instagram @LisaRegan8

Chris "Maverick" Miller

~ Will ~

Will Power is the fiery essence that transforms dreams into realities, for it knows no bounds, recognizes no obstacles, and forges paths where none exist. In its presence, failure cowers, doubt dissipates, and greatness awakens.

Honoring the Darkness

By Chris "Maverick" Miller

"I think I can, I think I can, I think I can."

Those powerful words have had more of an impact on me than any other. Simple, yet effective. Taken from a children's book titled "The Little Engine that Could." My first memory is that of my dad reading to me this remarkable story about resilience and WILL. Throughout time, this recurring theme to be strong during difficult times has manifested in my life in an assortment of ways.

In Kindergarten, I was diagnosed with A.D.H.D. As a result, I received Special Education services and was teased profusely for one reason or another. The difficulty I experienced with focusing made learning quite a challenge which led me to have low self-esteem. I started believing that I was inadequate and so the programming had begun.

When I was 11 years of age, I joined the Boy Scouts of America. My first camping trip began just as any camping trip would. What soon followed would change the course of my life. One night, the person I was tenting with proceeded to masturbate in front of me. I was thoroughly confused. I wasn't yet a teenager and honestly didn't even know what masturbation was. He threatened to beat me to a bloody pulp if I said anything. I remember thinking, "what the fuck is this person doing?" This was only the beginning of a long, torrid path to inappropriate sexual deviations.

After a while, I checked out emotionally. Staring out into space and visualizing that I was in a fantasy world rather than the nightmare my life had shifted into became an everyday activity. Although I'm certain this almost catatonic existence I created as my coping mechanism concerned my parents, the sad part is no one asked me what was going on. I felt so isolated, like no one genuinely cared, my parents in particular. It seemed that my parents and everyone else were too busy to notice the traumas I was enduring. Looking back on it, this was one of the most challenging aspects of the abuse period. I began stuttering and was unable to speak up for myself or tell my truth. I had no one to turn to and things truly seemed hopeless.

The sexual abuse continued on until mid-junior year. At its peak, I was raped. To cope with the nightmare reality that I was too ashamed to talk about, I turned to drugs. Smoking reefer and drinking became a common occurrence. By the time high school graduation came, I had been smoking cigarettes regularly and was on multiple medications, anything to repress the emotions I was afraid to express. It wasn't until after graduation that things began to shift. I could feel a change brewing in the air, and my WILL to keep pushing, regardless of how hopeless things seemed, was growing stronger.

One afternoon, the abuser decided to pay me a visit. The moment I saw him walking up the driveway, I called the police and ran to my room. It was at this moment that my WILL to be brave and end my cycle of trauma finally showed up. I told my truth and took back my power! I felt like a Superhero. Of course, it was scary, but for the first time, I felt bigger than myself and the pain that I had been sitting with for so long.

While I thought life was going to be so much better after confronting my abuser, I ended up just wallowing with the effects of my traumas. I was living a redundant and rather mundane existence, shuffling around from job-to-job and experimenting with a whole host of drugs, not really knowing or caring whether I lived or died. Realizing there was no future for me if I continued on this path, I began looking for a way out. I was longing for purpose, to belong to something, even if that meant doing something really difficult.

I knew something had to change. I contacted a childhood friend who had recently joined the U.S. Army and about a week later, I signed my life away. When I enlisted, it all happened so fast, I didn't pay attention to any of the details. All I knew was that I wasn't going to be living in that horror show any longer! Enlisting into the Military and not knowing what each new day would bring was scary. In fact, being away from familiarity scared me to death! Although, the alternative of staying in that shit-town and continuing the dead-end monotony loop seemed like certain death, so, despite the fear, I dug deep and took a leap of FAITH. I look back on it now and know without a shadow of a doubt that I made the right decision. Sometimes in life, the best decisions are the ones that pull us out of our comfort zone.

I never fully adapted to Military life. The A.D.H.D. programming made it impossible to fully step into the leadership role that is expected of Soldiers. I was constantly getting screamed at, sometimes on a daily basis, because my performance was not to standard. Verbal abuse was my new norm. I had gone from one nightmare to another. Running away from my hometown had been the right decision at that time, but I had traded one poison for another. I had a desk job that required me to multitask, which at that point I was incapable of doing. My boss was a bit of a perfectionist and he loved to scream when given the opportunity to, and working with me, the opportunity was always there.

In between the daily screaming sessions, I had corrective vision surgery. A common side effect showed up with my postoperative care, I fell in love with Percocets and Klonopin and the sensations of feeling absolutely NOTHING! Once again, I had descended into an emotionless robot fumbling around with no known purpose, no rhyme or reason as to why I was residing on this planet. On the inside though, there was a hideous beast of anger, rage, and immense hurt that had been growing inside of me since early childhood.

A few months into my addiction, I reached my breaking point. I overdosed on a combination of Percocets, Klonopin, and alcohol, ending up in a drug rehabilitation center soon after. From a stress point of view, cigarettes became my new best friend. Contrary to popular belief, cigarettes SAVED my life and were truly what kept me sane!

While at rehab, I developed bronchitis. It hurt to cough and even breath, but I kept smoking despite knowing how bad it was. I was so angry and disappointed in the way my life had turned out that I couldn't muster up enough desire or willpower to stop smoking or at least cut down. Ironically, I have learned since that time that getting sick to that degree is something that stems from having so much anger built up that I could no longer speak. My throat chakra was completely blocked due to repressing my truth for my entire life. My body showed me, in the form of illness, the necessity to change.

One of the assignments while in Rehab was to write our story, explaining what had led us to drugs. Though initially resistant, once I began writing about my life trauma, I went full in. Like one of the messages conveyed in the "Friday the 13th" films; I came to realize that if we do not face our childhood traumas and the things, we detest about ourselves, they will continue to haunt us. Similar to that of horror villain Jason Voorhees, those unhealed wounds will reanimate repeatedly throughout our life and seem like they are quite literally trying to kill us. That is, until we face them head on and deal with them.

The truth of the matter was that I had not processed what had taken place in my childhood. All the bullying and abuse had taken its toll on my entire being and left me timid, tattered and torn. The voices in my head began taunting me, causing me to question whether or not I was really a man. For a period of time, these voices made me question my sexuality, despite having been in a few relationships with women. They asked, "Why didn't you tell anyone? Why did you let it go on for so long?" Writing my story helped me to reconcile those questions and restored my voice. The more authentic we show up, whether that be through writing or speaking our truth, our mind and body honor that and the results in our life change because WRITING IS VOICE.

Paradoxically, while I began speaking my truth for myself, in other areas I was banned from doing so. Upon returning to the Military after my time in rehab, the abuse continued. I was not allowed to stand up for myself in that environment. Like it or not, authenticity and the Army are not mutually exclusive. Being faced with mostly men who had difficulty expressing themselves in a meaningful way and then adding in PTSD was a recipe for a toxic work environment.

Flash forward a few years later and following being Honorably discharged from the Army, I was sitting in an IHOP at about 3 in the morning after a night of drinking with a friend and his one night stand. I mentioned I was longing to have a girlfriend, but what this young lady said gave me something to think about. She suggested not pursuing a relationship at all, and instead to work on me, to get to know myself better, not just the light, but the dark too. This is where my life began to change for the better.

Thus began my journey of riding solo, looking inward for comfort, assessing myself, and learning my habits. My WILL to straighten myself up and start attracting better things into my life was growing stronger. My indomitable WILL was gnawing at me to seek out a better life that on some level I knew was already here, I just hadn't aligned with it YET. I always had the WILL to get myself out of toxic situations, but this time I wasn't escaping them, I was changing and healing them.

After a much-needed chaotic period of floating around and living in some interesting and character developing living situations, I signed for my own apartment. Things really started coming together now. I began working for Uber and making more money than ever before. However, with the good we can most certainly expect the perceived "bad" and so in comes the duality. Throughout most of 2018, I fell into a deep and dark depression. As much as I wanted to change, my mind very much did not and so I allowed myself to give in to the darkness.

I watched the movie "The Secret," and my eyes were opened to the power of law of attraction. The message was clear, and it could not have come at a more perfect moment in my life. That documentary helped me to see that everything that had happened in my life was due to what I was thinking and feeling. I started taking responsibility for everything that had happened; the good, the bad, and the ugly. I started owning the things that I did, where I was in life, and started looking at the man in the mirror. Things made more sense than ever before, and now, I became more deliberate with my thoughts. I started writing lists of gratitude and affirmations and living with more deliberate intention.

On September 16th, 2021, I attracted an Uber rider who told me things that I loved but simultaneously intimidated me with her words. Things like, I am worth better than this job and that I am fully capable of having more of what life has to offer. I recognized that this was the Universe knocking on my front door with a loud and thunderous sign or in other words, this is what my WILL had been calling forth. Exactly a month later, on

October 16th, I got another ride with the same woman, and we exchanged phone numbers and soon after she started giving me personal development assignments. As it turns out, she is a Coach who works for Proctor Gallagher Institute (PGI) which is the biggest personal development company in the world. About 2 months later and 3 years to the day of watching The Secret for the second time, on December 30th, 2021, I invested in myself and enrolled in one of the PGI programs.

On a similar bandwidth to winning the golden ticket from the chocolate bar in "Charlie and the Chocolate Factory," this truly was the golden ticket. All the manifestations and affirmations that I had been writing out, were suddenly coming to life. It was not "luck" though. These things came to be out of persistence and perseverance. My WILL is the emotional force that kept me moving forward regardless of how impossible the obstacles of life seemed. Everything that had happened, both by happenstance and the decisions I had consciously made, created the space I am in today. This is truly why I am grateful for absolutely everything because ALL of it is necessary! Simply put, if merely one of the events didn't happen in the exact way in which they did, I would not have been given the opportunity to create the Warrior that I see today.

Times of crises breed miraculous advances. The Chinese define the word crisis as meaning both danger and opportunity. In other words, we always get a choice in how we perceive the reality in which we are presented. Now that I am the Warrior that I only dreamed I would become as a child, things are different. As difficult as it was throughout much of it, I look back and like Steve Jobs once said…

"You cannot connect the dots looking forward; you can only connect them looking backwards."

Things don't quite make sense when you are going through the storms of life, but when you hang in there long enough, you begin to see how the dots line up.

A profound quote from Robert Collier's book, "The Secret of the Ages," sums up my story.

"It is the difficult things in life that develop our mental and moral muscle that build up courage and stamina."

My ability to look at myself and own all my mistakes, where I am in life, childhood traumas, my flaws and insecurities, all of it (many of them that I am still working through), is something that takes time, patience, and FAITH. Now when I look in the mirror, I am proud of the man that stares back at me because I know that whatever happened had a purpose. It happened so that I could share my truth with the world and help them find their inner WILL and strength.

Investing in myself helped me grow and TRUST THE PROCESS... I think I can. I believe I can. I know I can... and so can YOU!

Water

by Chris "Maverick" Miller

Dearest Omnipotent Forces from above, below and within: We come together at this point in time, space and from this current perception of Our reality to proclaim that no matter what happens during Our time spent in this Human form and this paradoxical experience that is life, that ALL truly is well. With each breath taken, we are becoming more in harmony with God's laws. We embrace this MARVELous duality reality as it comes with wide open arms, a perceptive mind, and a LOVING hEart.

We recognize that there will be chaos, but from that opportunity, the inevitable order will follow. We TRUST in our understanding of time and that everything unfolds perfectly. We are guided by Our FAITH and that serves as Our foundation that makes absolutely ANYTHING possible! We openly LOVE all energy because we KNOW that everything has its divine purpose.

With each storm that life can be at times, We know that the Sun WILL rise again. With each friendship that dissolves, new members of our SOUL Tribe will emerge. With each intimate relationship that may end, We KNOW that our perfect partner will manifest at precisely the right moment.

So, as We step forward into this New World, We utter these Heavenly words . . . Everywhere We Go We Are Loved, Guided, Protected and Touched by God's Divine Grace.

About

Chris "Maverick" Miller

Chris Miller is a resilient and empathic individual who has discovered a way to embrace positivity in any situation. Born and raised in the city of White Plains, New York, he spent his formative years in the idyllic town of Woodbury, Connecticut, nestled in the heart of New England.

Upon graduating high school, Chris made a life-changing decision by enlisting in the U.S. Army, where he served for an impressive 11 ½ years in the Human Resources field. His time in the military instilled in him a strong sense of discipline, dedication, and a profound understanding of the value of teamwork.

Driving for Uber is what gave birth to his awakening and recognizing that all humans are doing the best that they can. It also shook him quite literally in recognizing that coaching is the job he is best suited for. Amidst the global awakening that has captivated humanity, Chris emerges as a steadfast Warrior, offering guidance and support to those in need. A devoted father to a 12-year-old Starseed, Benjamin Jacob, he draws inspiration from his child's unwavering Spirit and strives to actively contribute to the unfolding of a beautiful future.

Continuously seeking personal growth and the opportunity to make a positive impact, Chris is currently studying to become a coach with the prestigious Napoleon Hill Institute. Simultaneously, he is engrossed in the creation of his autobiography, scheduled for release later this year. Through his memoir, he aims to share his inspiring journey and lessons learned, touching the hearts of readers far and wide.

In addition to his writing endeavors, Chris is preparing to organize transformative retreats centered around medicine journeys and other guided escapes. These sanctuaries will serve as peaceful havens for those seeking solace in a fast-paced world. Through these immersive experiences, he intends to facilitate profound healing, self-discovery, and spiritual growth.

Chris Miller's unwavering resilience, boundless compassion, and commitment to personal and collective growth make him a beacon of light in a world yearning for guidance and transformation.

Facebook @Chris Maverick

Instagram @fiercespiritualwarrior369

TikTok @chrismaverick369

wideopeneyez247@yahoo.com

Harlow Richmond O'Brien

14

~ Love and Light ~

The Spirit of Love and Light, a radiant beacon of compassion and illumination, embraces the world with her ethereal grace, uniting hearts and guiding souls to embrace the transformative power of pure love.

From Darkness To Love and Light

by Harlow Richmond O'Brien

I listened quietly while the woman across from me spoke. "You must have lived a charmed life," she said. This was her reasoning for me being positive, lighthearted, and loving. Charmed? Not so much. Blessed? Without a doubt.

I have come to understand there are blessings in everything. Some come with exuberant joy, love, and connection, while others present with painful tears and anxieties. However, all come with an opportunity to grow.

Let me take you back to a moment in time where my "charmed life" became so dark I couldn't find my way out. Love, as I defined it to that point in my life, seemed to be just a word, a privilege meant for others, and something I could no longer grasp.

I was 36 and thought I had it all: a wonderful marriage to a man I absolutely adored and two incredible children. I had a beautiful home full of beautiful things, and an incredibly successful career in the high-tech industry — one I could have never imagined, being "just a girl from Indiana" with no college degree. I had an abundance of friends and was deeply rooted in my church community.

Then, in a blink, it all came tumbling down. My marriage was destroyed through infidelity. I had always believed that if there was infidelity in my marriage, good riddance, full stop, move on, and I wouldn't skip a beat. After all, I had already overcome a number of traumas — including an emotionally and physically abusive relationship — all by the age of 19. I was so strong and

163

on top of my game that this was just one more thing. Countless people go through divorce. Just a bump in the road of life, right? I could not have been more wrong.

I tried with everything within me to save my marriage. However, it ultimately failed and I spiraled to depths of grief I had no idea existed. Divorce, a word that previously had no energy or meaning for me, was now defining who I was. As if that were not enough, other challenges started to stack very quickly. The company I worked for was acquired and I was let go. I was months from losing my home and many of my "friendships" quickly melted away along with my marriage. I lost virtually every relationship I thought I could count on. So many of them simply couldn't understand my grief. Comments like "His loss", "There are plenty of other guys out there", and "You will find another job" were meant to be helpful, but in reality they left me feeling unheard, misunderstood, and completely disconnected.

For the first time in my life, I had severe anxiety and had lost so much weight that at five-foot three, I had shrunk to a mere 93 pounds. I was so frail and, after passing out multiple times one morning, was rushed to the ER with an irregular heartbeat. The doctors were very clear that if I didn't start eating, hydrating and taking care of myself, I could die. I was so despondent that my faith, the one thing I had relied on in challenging times, was hanging by a string. I was angry at God for allowing all of this to happen to me and for all the crippling questions that were now looping constantly in my head.

How did I end up here? How am I going to make ends meet? How am I going to raise two children on my own? How do I just get through today, let alone tomorrow? Why am I not good enough? Will I ever be able to find joy or even smile again?

Through my profound grief and a stint with the divorce cocktail (antidepressants, antianxiety pills and powerful sleeping pills), I was a shell of my former self and aimlessly wandered like this for several years. At my lowest moment, I had completely lost the will to live. It was from that place of darkness, despair, and complete exhaustion of living lifeless that I made a choice to do something different.

Choice. That was a word that triggered so much anger in me. I heard it all the time: "Happiness is a choice". Every time I heard that, I would think to myself and sometimes say out loudly, "Don't tell me all I have to do is 'choose happiness'." It enraged me! I wanted to know HOW to choose happiness. What was missing in me that I couldn't simply choose to be happy?

Discovering the "how" of choosing happiness started with a decision to accept being uncomfortable and to embrace a new way of thinking. It was a painstaking process of rejecting my newfound emotional home of sadness, where I had become "comfortable". I felt justified in my pain and grief. This allowed me to avoid truly looking inside and doing the work required to rebuild the beautiful life I loved. I never asked for any of this, and I truly felt it was unfair that I was the one who had to change and do the work to fix it. But there was no way around it. It was either live the rest of my life hurt and angry or do something different.

But what was that different? What was the first step? I had a close friend who had been through the same pain of infidelity in his marriage, which had also led to divorce. It brought him to his knees just like it had me. That said, I was in awe of how he seemed to rise above it all and live a truly epic life. What was his secret? The answer was, he looked inward, got uncomfortable, and did the work. He plunged headfirst into learning and healing to create Life 2.0. He recommended I go to a personal growth seminar called "Date with Destiny". Again, I thought, great for him, but that is just not me. And what if it doesn't work? What if I spend my last $5,000 on this seminar and I end up right where I am today?

The bigger question, and the one that motivated me to take action was, what would happen and what would my life look like if I did nothing? That answer wasn't something I could live with for one more day. So, with all the self-doubt and every excuse in the book as to why I shouldn't go, I signed up for an intensive week of self-exploration, mindfulness, and learning a new way. Before leaving, that man gave me a word of advice. He said, "Forget everything you think you know and be willing and open, just for this one week, and see what happens." Right then, I made the choice and promised him, my parents, my children and, most importantly, myself that I would go all in and do the work, hoping for a better future.

That week proved to be a turning point for me. I learned that my pain wasn't special. Everyone there also had pain just as profound as mine, some even more. I learned concepts like "Life is always happening FOR me and not TO me". It sounded nice, but seriously, how was something that broke me happening for me? I now smile as I look back at my former way of thinking. I had to choose to see the love and light in every situation. Every yin has a yang. Without a doubt, life is truly ALWAYS happening for each one of us. In every single challenge or adversity, I can now point to a gift or lesson that came from it. Being not only open to seeing it but actively looking for the gifts made all the difference for me. While no one likes it when life throws us a curveball, I now know there will always be something good and I will be better for it. Does it mean it's easy? No.

Learning about where I put my focus, what meaning I give to things, and what action I was willing to take was the difference between living a truly epic life or accepting one of suffering. That week was incredibly difficult. I was emotionally and mentally filleted. I had to traverse through many emotions of anger and sadness and, at times, wanted to give up. However, I could feel things changing. I could see light on the other side for the first time in a very long time, and I could feel my soul start to stir and wake up. This told me I had to get even more comfortable being uncomfortable because that is where true healing, growth, and expansion happens. In truth, it is where life begins.

I was on a path now, and one I would choose to stay on — a path that would require committing time to myself for learning and growth and, at times, would necessitate me prioritizing family money to continue my journey of healing. As much as I wanted to skip to the end, my journey was just beginning.

Once I was home and outside the bubble of the seminar, I found myself starting to slip back into old thought patterns and white-knuckling my newfound "happiness". When I felt this, I made the choice to reach out for help and it came in the form of a life coach. On one of my first calls, she asked me, "Harlow, what are you grateful for?" Thinking for a second, I responded that I was grateful for my children, my parents, and for my health. She asked me what else, knowing those answers were low-hanging fruit. I truly couldn't come up with anything. She immediately told me the call was over and that when I could find something else to be grateful for, we could continue. Wait. What? Did she just end the call with me? Her ending the call so abruptly shocked me.

So, I made the choice to dig deeper and find what it is I am grateful for. It was through this exercise that my eyes were opened further. I am grateful for the sun that beautifully rises for me every single morning and for the way it kisses my cheeks on warm summer days. I am grateful for my legs that effortlessly take me anywhere I want to go and hold me up as I dance with delight whenever I choose. I am grateful for the sound of music and how it tickles my heart with every note. She was right; it is all around me, but I had to be willing to find and see it. I had to choose to see the love and light in every part of my world. This started a daily practice of gratitude which filled me up and became a place I return to whenever the outer world is too overwhelming. I have found love and happiness truly lives in a grateful mind and heart.

Much like finding gratitude, I also realized love was always around me, even in my darkest days. It was in a smile from a stranger. It was in the laughter of my children, in my mother and father who selflessly stepped up for my children when their father left. It was my driveway mysteriously being shoveled for me after a snowstorm. It was everywhere. But because it was not showing up the way I wanted it to, I had been blind to it, and that kept me locked away in a prison of sadness, loneliness, and self-loathing. Now, I choose to find the love and light in my world, as well as create those moments both for myself and for anyone I encounter. It can be as simple as making eye contact and giving that stranger a warm smile. It is sending that "Thinking about you" text or baking cookies for no reason and sharing them with everyone. It is touching the hand of the person you are talking with or giving a heartfelt hug to anyone who needs it. It is doing random acts of kindness — just because.

However, I had to extend that kindness to myself, which included forgiveness. I had always believed forgiveness was saying: "it" is OK. Through my faith in God, I have now come to understand that true forgiveness is also a choice. It is deciding to release all feelings of resentment or vengeance toward another. The act of forgiveness is not only a loving gift to the person who hurt us, it cleanses our own hearts and minds from the toxicity festering inside. In forgiving myself, I had to release past versions of myself and give them grace. By holding onto the resentment of what I had become during this dark time, I stayed imprisoned where I was. I had to release to soar. This didn't come overnight, but rather with an abundance of choices and extending myself the love and light I found and gave to everyone else. I had to forgive myself for not knowing a better way and for all the precious time wasted in my head, feeding thoughts and emotions that kept me from experiencing and creating love and light.

"Watch your thoughts, they become your words; watch your words, they become your actions; watch your actions, they become your habits; watch your habits, they become your character; watch your character, it becomes your destiny." — Lao Tzu

This quote is one I often reflect on. I made a choice to step away from the darkness, the shell of myself. I wanted to be light and unburdened from the heaviness I had felt for so long. That meant embodying love and light in my thoughts, words, and actions. I had to choose to see love and light in the world around me. I had to choose to give love and light to myself just as I did to others. As I continued to work with love and light every day, the world became a more beautiful place, and I with it. Love and light are how I healed myself and how I am able to offer healing to others. In a world that tends to focus on the negative, be love and light. And in moments of doubt or darkness ask yourself, "What would love do?"

I AM love

by Harlow Richmond O'Brien

Love is all I am.
Love is all I want.
Love is all I need.
Love is what I was made for.
I AM Love.
And Love is me.

May I reflect love to myself
and to everyone I encounter.

May I be an impeccable listener,
deeply feel others where they are,
and become the embodiment
of selfless giving and love.

May I see the beauty
and love in all people and creation.

May I give unconditionally
with an open heart and treat others
as I would like to be treated.

God, please grant me the courage
to BE the love
in this world I seek.

About

Harlow Richmond O'Brien

Born in the heart of the Midwest, Harlow is an avid adventure seeker and lover of the outdoors. Whether it be fire walking, skydiving, whitewater rafting, snowboarding or surfing she fully embraces the idea of LIVING A GREAT STORY. She is most at peace when fully immersed in nature whether that be at the ocean, a hike in the woods, quietly sitting in the jungle by a rolling river or marveling at the majestic beauty of a sunrise or sunset. Harlow also loves to travel and considers herself a life-long student at the University of the Universe. She is now retired, however enjoyed a long and successful career in the online tech industry. While she is a proud mother of two beautiful children, married to her best friend, ride or die partner in adventure and love of her life, she is most known for her kind, loving heart, listening ear, and huge magical hugs.

linktr.ee/harlowobrien

Nicole Cosentino

15

~ Pride ~

The Goddess of Pride, in her resplendent glory, unveils the radiant truth of one's inherent worth, guiding souls to embrace self-acceptance and bask in the magnificent tapestry of their unique being.

The Journey Within: Unveiling True Worth and Self-Acceptance

by Nicole Cosentino

For years, I felt like something inside me was holding me back. I didn't have the awareness or courage to question myself. I only knew how to look at my external results. I've always been a big dreamer, achieving anything I put my mind to. But this time, I felt off and disconnected from my own desires. I felt stuck but comfortable. I'd been feeling unsatisfied without really knowing it. How did I get to this place where only things on the surface mattered? I began to look back at my life, collecting mental puzzle pieces to understand how I'd got here.

Both my parents were immigrants, and my brother and I were living the American Dream in San Francisco, CA. My parents met in Panama, where my dad was stationed in the Canal for the US Army. My mother was only 21 when she came to the US with my dad. Mom didn't have many options: she was alone with no immediate family; didn't speak English; didn't know how to drive; and couldn't work. My father was strong and in control of everything, especially the finances. They fought a lot and there was no real partnership in their marriage. I grew up with mixed feelings about money because the fights were about its scarcity, even though we lived a very abundant lifestyle compared to our family in Latin America.

My father held all the cards. He made the money and all the decisions. He had come from nothing and had achieved the American Dream. He never let the discrimination he felt hold him back. His image was always on point, and you would catch him in the mornings with a clean-shaven face and his hair always brushed. He aligned his value with his job, possessions, and achievements. He always had nice cars to represent his symbol of success. That material success was a sign that he belonged in America, that he had made it. Money and possessions determined his worth on a superficial level that bled deep into my veins.

My mom relied on my dad because she wasn't independent. She tried to leave my dad once and we had to go to a women's shelter. That was so scary because we weren't accepted there by the other families. One of the boys randomly hit my brother with a bat not long after playing with him. A few days into our stay, our room was vandalized, and all my mother's jewelry was stolen. We were forced to return home. Mom had to go back to her toxic marriage for our safety. My parents' marriage became a façade and they finally divorced when I was 14 years old.

I made a promise to myself I would never depend on anyone, especially financially. I didn't want anyone controlling me like my father did my mother. I wanted to have options in my life, and I kept that promise to myself by working from the age of 14. I got my driver's license the day I turned 16 and I moved out on my own at the age of 21. It gave me pride to be self-reliant as I achieved each one of my goals.

I grabbed my father's playbook and learned to align myself with fancy brands so that I could feel like I was a part of something bigger than myself. I bought my first Mercedes Benz at 21 to look and feel like my dad. I remember he was happier about that purchase than when I graduated from college! I felt a sense of pride obtaining something I desired so much, and which caused my dad to feel proud of me. My father was from Argentina and worked for everything he wanted. Having anything nice, symbolized success and worthiness. I started associating myself with luxury brands so I could be an extension of what that brand meant to the world.

I bought knockoff brand bags to complete the look I was selling. In my mind, no one would question whether it was real or not. My image became part of the brand I was projecting. I ran with the mantra "you have to fake it to make it", which served me well when I worked in the world of sales. People want to buy what you are selling if you are projecting success. My pride helped me believe I was successful, important, and valuable because of what I possessed, where I worked, and what I had accomplished. But never for who I was.

When my parents remarried, I realized that marriage was something I wanted, so long as it was with the right person. I married my best friend, and we created a partnership on every level imaginable. The negative parts of my parents' marriage served as a "what not to do" and all the good parts served as the best "how-to". In marriage, we operate as a team and we find ways to lift each other and, most of all, grow together so we don't grow apart.

Years later, I entered the chapter of motherhood. I knew my life would change on so many levels, but I wasn't prepared for what that meant. I instantly pulled what it meant to be a mother from my mom, who believed in sacrificing herself for others. It's how her culture defined love. She found value by being selfless and sharing our secondhand clothing with the family she'd left behind. The house was always clean, home-cooked meals were always ready, and everything was extremely organized. I found her always sacrificing her own happiness so everyone around her would have more opportunities. Without realizing it, I had immediately embodied my mother's playbook and found pride in my family and home.

I ended up leaving my corporate job and became an

entrepreneur. I thought the only way to have a career and be a mom was if I created my own path. I instantly loved being a mom and took my role very seriously. I read, went to classes, and connected with other experienced moms. I learned all about play dates and child development. I kept my little one busy.

For my business side, I used my passion for fashion to offer working women stylish business attire. Ironically, you would find me mostly wearing gym clothes because that went hand in hand with having a newborn. Gone were the days when I could just go to happy hour after work on a moment's notice! My reality consisted of playdates, feedings, and nap time. On some weekends, I would set up racks to sell my clothes at local markets. I loved working on the weekend because, for a few hours, I was Nicole and not a wife, mom, or stepmom. It was liberating to connect with other women and keep that side of me alive while keeping my "boss" image present. I even started a digital agency to help other women with their businesses. I couldn't let go of the person I was, and it was this productive nature that fed my pride, making me feel valuable.

The pandemic nudged me to release the identity I'd created due to my father. I closed the online fashion boutique and got rid of my luxury car. I stripped myself of the things I felt most defined me. I knew I had to learn to love myself, but I didn't know how to do that. I did the best I could but always had these feelings of not being enough. I kept trying to go forward but always found a way to take two steps back. It was hard to feel worthy no matter how hard I tried. Whenever I did work for my clients, I felt as though I was on top of the world. Then there were days when I felt like a loser and that I didn't add any value anywhere. There was a constant battle in my mind of who I was.

As time went on, I began feeling more aligned with my new role in life, and I thought I was happy. That was… until I lost my 19-

year-old stepdaughter. After her death, I jumped back onto the hamster wheel. Pride took over, as my attention was permanently fixed on external things. It was a form of distracting myself from my grief. Despite such a traumatic loss, I had to continue living for myself and our family. I kept saying yes to everything, as though I had this need to please everyone around me, and not once did I ever stop to ask myself whether I really wanted to do it. I continued to make sure my appearance and my attitude with everyone remained perfect. I did everything for everyone and, when it was time to do something for myself, I had no energy left. I was running on mindless productivity. It became my distraction to avoid really looking at myself and all my emotions.

I was everywhere but nowhere, at the same time. I was comfortable but I didn't have any desires. All I could do was to be of service to everyone around me. I had no purpose unless I was helping someone in some way, shape, or form, hoping they would define my value. In my mind, I wasn't worthy of saying no or charging people for my services. People would take and I would continue to give. I was slowly dying inside, and no one knew it, not even me. I tried focusing on understanding myself more and changing my life, but I always found an excuse to put myself last on the to-do list.

I kept adding to that to-do list to feel worthy. I didn't want to let anyone down. But in the process, I let myself down every day. I would try to stand up for myself and even practiced what to say, but whenever it was time to say something, the words never came out. I just didn't have the courage to stand up for myself. I wanted people to like me and, if I said no, I believed it would change the way they saw me. If they didn't like me or see me as important, my pride would get hurt and I would begin the spiral of not liking myself. It would make me look inwards in disappointment. So, I made everyone love me, no matter the cost because that disappointment was something I never wanted to face.

I began feeling angry, but I didn't know who I was angry at. I was angry I couldn't speak my truth. I was angry I couldn't say no and not feel bad. I was angry I couldn't make decisions boldly. I couldn't believe I had turned into someone I didn't recognize. I had always been very assertive and spoke my mind. This behavior overtook me, and I was frustrated with everyone but mostly with myself. I began doubting my talents and wanting to give up all my hidden desires. If someone mentioned the word loser, I would get so upset. I felt that was me; I was an imposter. I was no one important, no matter how much I thought I was.

I'd been using the external forces to define my worth my entire adult life: the job, the car, the image, the associations, the experiences, and all the things. As a marketer myself, life is designed to make you feel like you need all the external things to feel good, worthy, important, and to give you a sense of belonging. I was a part of that without ever being aware of it. I needed all the things to fill the void inside. Any time I remotely felt out of alignment, within seconds I would do something to satisfy the need to feel whole — whether it was a post to get that instant social media love, or a few clicks on Amazon to instantly make me falsely whole again. I distracted my emptiness by feeding my pride with excess.

Things began to change as I settled into being a mother. Being a mother made me realize what love really looked like instead of what I had adopted it to be. I loved my daughter for who she was: a beautiful, sweet, intelligent girl. I love her for her bravery and confidence. I love her for her, not her good grades or because she is pretty or any other shallow reason. She is stronger than I, and her strength inspires me to love myself the same way.

Alongside seeing what true love really was, I began digging

178

deeper into myself. I invested my time in personal growth and learning about myself. My patterns of pride and sacrifice became very apparent to me. Aligning my self-worth with external gratification had created a constant pressure to maintain a certain image or level of success with myself. I never realized how exhausting and unfulfilling this was in the long run. There was a deep feeling that I was never good enough despite contrary belief —- and now I know why.

I had to change the way I valued myself, change my pride. I fed my pride through every form of external gratification; sacrificing myself for others and being who they wanted me to be. For my dad, I was financially successful with a collection of possessions we admired. For my mom, I was the "giving daughter" she wanted me to be. Once I realized those characters weren't me, I began to look at who I was at my core. I was intelligent, strong, determined, and loving. More than that, I was also as successful as my father and as giving as my mother.

I came to realize that my past self, who used pride to succeed, was never a "bad" version of myself. That version allowed me to move out at 21; graduate with three degrees; start multiple businesses; and create the beautiful life I have today. Those traits allowed me to be an amazing mom, wife, and daughter. That mental programming allowed me to survive and thrive in my life. But what was important, was being aware of when that mental programming no longer served me. Like I said, it had gotten me to this point in my life and I am so grateful it did. I don't need to survive anymore; I am already successful, and I am already loved. I have everything I need within myself.

I choose to move forward from a place of presence and love, instead of chasing external validation from people and money. If I were always chasing my future, I would never live in the present. And I love the present. This choice to love myself for who I am is where I put my pride.

I am proud of myself for being me.

Self-Acceptance

by Nicole Cosentino

Dear Higher Power,

I come before you today with a humble heart and a sincere desire to embrace the power of pride in my life. I have come to understand that pride, when grounded in authenticity and self-acceptance, can be a guiding force for personal growth and fulfillment.

Grant me the wisdom to recognize the difference between unhealthy pride and the kind that nourishes my soul. Help me release the need for external validation and instead find solace in celebrating my unique qualities and personal achievements.

May I always remember that true pride comes from within, rooted in self-love and acceptance. Guide me to embrace my worth and live authentically, free from the constraints of societal expectations.

As I navigate my journey, grant me the strength to overcome obstacles, the courage to follow my passions, and the resilience to stay connected to my core values.

I am grateful for the lessons learned and the transformation pride has brought to my life. May it continue to be a source of inspiration and motivation as I strive for greatness and find my rightful place in the world.

With humility and gratitude, I offer this prayer.

Amen

About

Nicole Cosentino

Nicole Cosentino is an innovative branding and digital strategist fluent in English, Spanish and Portuguese. With nearly two decades of experience in Marketing & Advertising, she has made significant contributions to organizations such as Spanish Broadcasting Systems, the W Hotel, and Seminole Hard Rock Hotel & Casino, spanning major cities like San Francisco, Los Angeles, Dallas, and Miami.

After leaving her corporate career, Nicole established Downtown Chic, an online fashion boutique catering to professional women. Through her curated collection, she inspired women to embrace confidence by dressing for success in the workplace for almost 5 years. Her expertise in branding and e-commerce led her to support fellow entrepreneurs with their business strategies full time.

Driven by her passion for marketing, Nicole launched Chance Digital Agency, which has evolved to offer a comprehensive suite of services tailored to meet the evolving needs of businesses in the digital realm. Nicole Cosentino offers a holistic approach, providing strategic consulting, insightful eBooks, and exceptional voiceover services to empower individuals and businesses in their digital endeavors.

In addition to her professional pursuits, Nicole actively contributes to her community. She volunteers at Dress for Success Miami, empowering women to achieve economic independence and self-sufficiency through career development & image services. Nicole also volunteers as an Assistant Director for the Miss Miami Scholarship Program under the Miss America

Organization, where she promotes personal and professional development for young women. She also serves as a board member volunteer for The Rosales Sisters' Scholarship Program, raising awareness and funds for immigrant and first-generation students in California.

Nicole's educational journey reflects her adaptability to the ever-changing business landscape. She holds an Associate of Arts degree in Merchandise Marketing from the Fashion Institute of Design & Merchandising, a testament to her early foundation in the dynamic field of marketing. Building upon this foundation, she pursued a Bachelor of Science in Business Marketing and a Master's in Business Administration from Woodbury University, continuously equipping herself with a comprehensive skill set that evolves alongside the rapidly transforming professional landscape.

www.NicoleCosentino.com

Instagram @nikki_cosentino

Facebook @nicole.cosentino.1

LinkedIn @nicolecosentinomba

Brendaliz Cintrón

16

~ Redemption ~

The Goddess of redemption, with her unwavering grace and divine power, offers strength and courage to all who seek her, guiding them towards their liberation from fears, limitations and difficult situations by illuminaing their path to ultimate redemption.

The Swing of My Dreams

by Brendaliz Cintrón

I was born in Ponce, in the beautiful island of Puerto Rico. I grew up in the barrio, a low-income environment where a lot of families were just surviving. In my culture people are friendly and happy but also content with just having enough to get by. Most of the people in my neighborhood were just following each other's footsteps, having the same things others were having. There were many times in my childhood when I lacked basic needs. Sometimes I didn't have proper shoes to wear, and only ate one meal a day. Even though I was a little girl and was surrounded with an environment of lack and need, I was a dreamer. There was a big tree in front of my house with a swing for the neighborhood kids to play on. I called it the "swing of my dreams", and I made it a game to swing and dream of my future life. Every time I would go up on the swing, I would see a flash of my future life in my mind. I dreamed of a life of abundance where I had all the things I wanted. I dreamed of a life where I was traveling the world and contributing to other people in need. I dreamed of having a life of freedom and stability but overall having happiness and lots of love!

The next part of my life was very difficult. I arrived in the USA at the age of 15, speaking no English. I'd left behind part of my family, friends and my beautiful island but I kept my dreams in my heart. I knew that in order to fulfill my dreams I was going to have to work hard. I was determined to excel in school to get into a good college so that I could get a good job which would lead to a good life. In keeping my promise to the little girl in the swing, I did just that.

However, at 16 I fell crazy in love and got pregnant. While most people would look down at my situation or think I messed up, my pregnancy only pushed me harder. My desire to improve my life magnified and that tiny person growing inside of me ignited it even more! My son Frankie became my reason why, my obsession and my purpose. I had to provide for him and give him the best of me so that he could have the things and the life I didn't have growing up. As a single mom, I worked day and night and at times, I had to hold down three jobs, while going to school, to be able to provide for my son. It took me seven years to finish my bachelor's degree and proudly graduate as a registered nurse.

I dedicated my life to raising my son and providing him with a safe and loving upbringing. I was focused on him and my nursing career. I quickly progressed up the ladder, becoming a charge nurse and later a nurse manager. During all of this, I didn't realize just how much time I was dedicating to work. I had been working over 50-60 hours per week and under a lot of stress. I was exhausted and burnt out. This was the life I had worked so hard for. I remember thinking to myself, "I've made it. I have a good job, savings in the bank, and I can provide for my son." I didn't realize what I had become: a SLAVE to my job. I had no life! I thought I was trading time for money but, in reality, I was trading my life for money.

The day came when my son left for college. I had been focused on him for 18 years and suddenly, he was gone. I was alone and I became depressed. All those years of my life working so much and taking care of everyone except me. This is when things got real. It was the first time I was able to look at my life, reflect and think of myself. I had abandoned myself for so long, and now I was overweight, weighing over 200 pounds.

I remember feeling defeated and confused. How did I do everything right and yet not feel happy? In reality, all those things

I'd accomplished were external, but I was empty inside. I had no goals, no destination and to make matters worse, I didn't even know who I was. This wasn't the dream that little girl on the swing had. Her dreams were of freedom, abundance, and happiness. It seemed I had forgotten about her along the way.

One day, the unexpected happened. I was walking down the street and fell backwards. I became unconscious and sustained a big head laceration. When I opened my eyes everything around me was swirling around non-stop in circles. Closing my eyes only made it 100 times worse. I felt like I was going to die! There was no way to get away from it other than to submit to the uncontrollable and debilitating feeling that took over my entire body. I lost total control of everything in my life. The doctors told me they didn't know exactly what was wrong with me, but they diagnosed it as vertigo.

The vertigo went on for months and had taken control of my body and my entire will. I couldn't take care of myself, work, drive or even walk as I was unable to keep my balance. For over 30 days, I was in bed with everything around me spinning in circles. I was surrounded by a lot of people but at the same time, felt so alone. I felt so worthless, everyday lying in my bed, not being productive. Every time I wanted to move, I was hit with both the spinning and the hopelessness that followed.

I became depressed, feeling as though everything I had worked for had been for nothing. I had hit rock bottom. How was I ever going to do anything in my life when the world just kept spinning? Day after day would pass and the voice in my head kept reminding me that I was born to do something big and instead I was wasting my life.

The inner voice allowed me to see what little confidence I had. It showed me all my insecurities, my fear of not being good enough for others, my fear of failing and not accomplishing my dreams. But my deepest fear was to not achieve that little girl's dreams, her true purpose and happiness.

One morning I was in bed, immobilized by the awful sight of the walls moving around in circles and the feeling of my guts spewing out. My vision was fixated on a dot in the middle of the ceiling lamp. Staring at that dot made the room slow down a bit, so I would often stare at it for hours and even days. It was in the middle of focusing on that light when suddenly a thought flashed in my mind, and I heard that same voice yell at me. "Aren't you tired of this? Get up! It is time to rise! It's time to REDEEM yourself. It's time to claim your life back!" The voice was right. It was time to do something about my situation and start fighting to get my life back.

As I focused on the dot in the middle of the ceiling lamp, I began to draw on whatever energy I had to start moving. That moment was the first time in a long time that I'd felt ready to make my first move. The voice gave me hope. I realized that the voice was my higher self who was talking to me and guiding me all along showing me the way. I decided I was going to do whatever was needed to redeem myself from my paralyzing circumstances and take back control of my life.

The next morning, I woke up determined. I felt something was illuminated in my mind. Taking my first steps intimidated me more than anything. I could hardly get myself out of bed as my body had weakened over time. However, I pushed myself to go to the bathroom, holding onto the walls to prevent myself from falling. Every step I took required so much strength and courage, as the spinning would intensify. It would have been easier to stay in bed. I had cold sweats and felt nauseous in my stomach. It felt impossible to get to the bathroom, but I was determined to make it, so I did.

When I got to the sink, I didn't want to look at myself in the mirror.

I was ashamed. But the voice in my head told me, "It's time to look at yourself and start accepting the face looking back at you." As I looked in the mirror, I was shocked to see my face looking so different. I looked older, sick, and tired. I cried intensely for a long time until I could cry no more, just standing there, looking at myself.

I became a victim of my vertigo. It was easier than moving. Everyone around me validated my illness, gave me their pity and love. Being in bed allowed me to validate the feeling of being a failure to myself. I was putting blame everywhere except on me. The weight I gained, the lack of motivation, I was able to blame it all on my vertigo and no one judged me about it either, because I was sick. I allowed myself to stay in the comfort of my illness.

I felt uncomfortable looking in that mirror. I saw a person that I was not. I felt the worst I had ever felt. Looking back at myself was a worse feeling than the vertigo because, for the first time, I acknowledged that I had abandoned myself and needed to put myself first. The voice was right; it was time to move. Only I could help myself. As I looked in the mirror, I thought of the little girl on the swing. I thought of my swing of dreams, and decided I was going to achieve them. I wasn't going to be just happy; I was going to be successful, and I was going to have it all.

From that day forward, I started looking at myself in the mirror every morning and saying "I Am" affirmations. I was telling myself, "I am strong, I am powerful, I am in control, I am beautiful, I am guided!" As I repeated these, tears would run down my cheeks because I was feeling the opposite. The war within my mind was relentless. Some days were harder than others. I continued walking slowly to the bathroom every day and made slow but steady progress. This became my morning routine. I also started visualizing in my mind clear pictures of the amazing life of the little girl on the swing. I kept repeating over and over to myself, "Every day I am getting better and better." I started believing it, and it started to come true. I started changing from the inside out.

This one action rippled into bigger ones. Walks to the bathroom turned into walks to the kitchen. I began eating healthily and studying my body. I became a vegetarian and started losing weight. I was feeling healthier and stronger day by day.

This was all part of a bigger lesson: learning how to put myself first so I could be a better mother, a better sister, and a better friend. I started doing less of what weighed me down and more of the things I loved. I made Fridays my "self-care days"! I started getting massages and going out to lunch with myself. I started meditating and the voice within kept guiding me. I continued looking at myself in the mirror every morning and I was seeing a reflection that I loved and was proud of. As I spent more time on me, the vertigo became, in part, a thing of the past. I bought myself a journal and started writing down my feelings, my goals, and my dreams!

But progress isn't linear and it sure wasn't for me. As I worked on my recovery the vertigo episodes continued on and off for years. Sometimes the vertigo would come back unexpectedly after years of not having it. There were difficult days where I would go back to bed feeling sick and helpless. I understood that sometimes I had to let myself rest and recover. I learned to give myself grace. While resting, I would think of the little girl on the swing, and she would remind me of what I really wanted, which was my freedom. Therefore, the next day, I would force myself to get up for her and go through the recovery process all over again.

Going through this experience, I learned that there are no accidents in life. Everything I've experienced since the moment I was born, including all those difficult times in my childhood; all those difficult challenges I had while raising my son; all the difficult moments when I wanted to quit, and the moment I thought I was going to die, all those moments were preparing me to become the woman I needed to be, the woman that I am today.

Today my vertigo episodes are almost non-existent and, whenever they come, they only last minutes. I am a redeemed woman! I am no longer a victim of my circumstances but instead the leader of my life. I love who I am, and I know my worth! I have an amazing life full of joy. I am healthy and take care of myself. I have peace and serenity within. I am in a constant connection to God who lives within me. I have a beautiful relationship with those around me but most importantly with myself.

I move forward in my life with purpose, love, and contribution. I created a foundation called "Heart of Gold Foundation" that helps poor kids with basic needs around the world. I live a life in commitment to helping others around the world find their purpose, and unleash their inner power, so they too can redeem themselves and create the lives they truly love!

I redeemed myself from a life with no purpose or direction. I pushed past my inner struggle and against all odds and created the best version of me. I learned to listen and follow the guidance of my voice within. The voice within is my guardian angel that protects me and guides me every day. I now have control of my health, my life, my decisions but most importantly I have control of my thoughts. My life now is meaningful, and I am forever grateful that my greatest pain turned into my biggest blessing. I released and redeemed all previous versions of me that I created to survive. And with that choice of redemption, I achieved and created every dream I promised I would to that little girl on the swing of my dreams.

Prayer for Redemption

by Brendaliz Cintrón

Oh, Divine Goddess of Redemption

I stand before you today with an open heart full of gratitude and joy.

I was stuck in patterns of limitation, doubt, fear, and loss.

I have learned that I have the power to let go of the past, find the strength to move forward and create a new path.

I am not perfect, and I have made mistakes. I have hurt myself and others, but the pain revealed the way.

From this moment forward I know my worth. I forgive myself and others and the fears are truly gone.

Oh, Divine Goddess of Redemption

Thank you for being my inner voice.

I can feel your everlasting presence and your love, which is the most precious gift of all. Your voice of redemption guides me all the way.

Thank you for the reminder that I am not alone, that I am always guided, protected, and loved.

Oh, Divine Goddess of Redemption

You have guided me through the darkest hours of my life and helped me to find my way back to the light.

You have given me the opportunity to start over. I will not take it for granted. I will live my life to the fullest and create a ripple effect of love in the world so that others can create the life they truly love.

Thank you for your guidance, your strength, and your hope.

Thank you for the courage to try again and never give up.

In your divine name this prayer I send, knowing that no matter which challenge I face, you will always illuminate the way.

Amen

About

Brendaliz Cintrón

Brendaliz Cintrón was born in the beautiful island of Puerto Rico. She graduated with honors from George Mason University with a Bachelor's in Science Degree. She quickly climbed the corporate ladder and became a nurse manager working for different health organizations.

During her 16 years working as a nurse, she discovered that her true purpose and passion was to lead others on a self-development journey to become their best version of themselves and to live lives of abundance, growth and contribution.

She personally went on that journey, worked and trained with the best mentors and leaders in the Self Development Industry to develop her skills and potential to become the powerful Latina leader that she is today.

Today, she is a transformational Global Coach, Speaker and Trainer who is on a mission to awaken people from all over the world to understand who they truly are, the power of their mind and how to use their power within to create the life and business they truly love. In 2015 she founded "Dare to Conquer Institute" to take her mission globally.

Brendaliz has been a philanthropist from an early age. She has always been involved with the community and has been leading missions to different countries to bring relief and help to families in need. In 2014 she founded Canastas de Amor, a movement of Love providing food baskets to families in need in the DC metropolitan area. This movement continues to grow and is now serving families in Latin American countries including El

Salvador, Guatemala, Honduras, and Puerto Rico. Since its founding, the Canastas de Amor team has assisted more than 1200 families in need.

These efforts motivated Brendaliz to found the "Heart of Gold foundation" a nonprofit organization to continue the work and expand the reach to those in need around the world.

Brendaliz's has been recognized and received different awards for her leadership and philanthropic work including, among others: Personality of the Year; Woman of the Year Leadership Award; Top 100 Latina Leaders in Washington DC; and 2020 Woman of the Year Humanitarian Award

Brendaliz joined forces with the Napoleon Hill Institute as a Master Coach, and she is at the forefront of the Latino market expansion. She currently works with the Institute to carry out Napoleon Hill's legacy and is helping people master his principles of success. She has decided to dedicate the rest of her life to sharing and teaching his material to everyone around the world.

www.BrendalizCintron.com

Instagram & Facebook @ brendalizCintronofficial

TikTok, LinkedIn, & YouTube @ brendalizCintron

Foundation: www.heartofgoldglobal.org

Michelle Osborne

17

~ Infinity ~

She embodies the unwavering power of self-belief, where strength, resilience, blessings, and faith converge, propelling one forward with unwavering hope and the realization that they are truly chosen.

The Chosen One

by Michelle Osborne

April 10, 2013, was one of the scariest days of my life but also one of the most freeing days of my life… I just didn't see it.

A few months earlier, I had gone off to work, as on any other normal day, with a husband of 17 years, a 13-year-old son, a 10-year-old daughter, and two mini goldendoodle dogs in my home. I was driving to a job where I wasn't happy or fulfilled; however, I had taken this job — at a reduced pay — to support my husband, who wanted to be an entrepreneur and have his own business at this time, which I supported. What I didn't realize I'd ever hear, when I returned home that day, were words coming from someone who supposedly loved his family.

As I walked up the stairs to the fourth bedroom in the house, which was now his office, I could feel this tension in the air and a silence that seemed strange but familiar. When I walked in, he was sitting at the desk with his back to me and his head slumped. I stood in the doorway, wondering, as I did many days, what had he actually done today, and whether he'd done anything to support his family in bringing in any income. Our debt had been increasing drastically in support of his endeavors. As I said "Hi", he turned around in the office chair, and I will never forget the look on his face. With a blank stare, hands clasped and resting on his lap, he calmly looked at me and said, "I don't want to be married anymore." With a slight pause he continued, "I want to be able to do what I want when I want with whom I want!" Now, how do you respond to such a statement after being married for 17 years, together for 20, and the only life I'd known since I was 25?

I'm sure, as many of you know, marriages don't fall apart overnight. It takes many years to come to a place where you feel like you cannot go on, you can no longer seek counseling or even fake it. Many try their best for the children's sake; some stay for the money and stability; and some are just too scared to take that leap or are afraid of what others might think or say. So I simply responded and said, "Um, OK, if that's what you really want." My brain automatically switched into fight-or-flight mode, and started processing all the things I would have to do next. It wasn't the first time I had to survive and figure things out, but I was damn sure it would be the last.

As many of us are taught growing up, relationships are about compromise, about sacrifice, and not always about getting what you want. However, sometimes we compromise who we are for the sake of others. We completely lose our authenticity, and who we really are — or think we are! At that moment, I realized I had done exactly that: I had spent my entire life trying to please everyone else, and never pleasing myself at my core. At that moment, I knew I was free.

> ~ Love does not hurt, love does not abandon, love does not criticize, and love does not judge. Love is independent, love is co-creation at its finest, love is respect, love is being authentic and true to yourself without jeopardizing anyone else's feelings. Love is freeing, and in that moment, I decided to love me. ~

April 10, 2013, the house went on the market. There was no turning back now, the damage had been done and the decision in my mind was made. The house sold in one week and we had to be out in six weeks. This was where bravery and desperation took over and the work began. I had packed up 4500 ft.² of house with two teenagers, two dogs, and a full-time job. Every night consisted of packing one or two boxes, feeding the children, doing homework, sports, and the dogs — never pouring into my own cup. I didn't recognize the strength I had. I was physically weak. I was unhappy. I would cry to myself to sleep every night alone, and I was scared. I knew I had conviction; I knew I had a better life ahead of me, and this was my opportunity to make an amazing life for me and my kids.

Deep down inside of me, I knew what I had in me and what I was capable of, and each and every one of us has the capacity for more, a true calling that is knocking inside of you pulling your heart every day, and I finally realized I didn't have to sacrifice what I wanted for the sake of everyone else. I was finally able to see what others saw in me, and what I could see in my children, who I was for my children, and that was my "why". My children were my life, and I wanted to show them that love always avails, and that persistence and willpower come from within.

I'm not sure when we were taught that living a life unhappy and unfulfilled is the way God intended us to live. I knew this wasn't the example I wanted to set for my children, nor would I ever want them to live this type of life for themselves, so I must lead by example, and this is what my mantra was every day to get me through.

But my belief system asked, "Who can you rely on, Michelle?" You can only rely on yourself, and this is the story I told myself. It is not a story that serves you to think that you can do this journey of life alone without community, without family, without love, without help. We need to recognize that where we've been, who we are, and who we are becoming can all be different. It's OK to change, to grow, and it's OK to create the version of you that you want to be. My father wanted me to stay in the house and said he would help, but it was too late. It sold and I had to be out in the next four weeks.

I put on a brave face every day I got up. I got the kids ready for school, made them their breakfast and their lunches. I would go to work and pretend like everything was fine. I put on a brave face and told myself I wouldn't settle for anything other than a step forward every single day. This is where you find out who you really are and what you're made of. Do you crumble in the face of adversity, or do you thrive? This is where you meet your Maker. This is where you see what inner strength is, and that just because this is your story today doesn't mean this is going to be your story tomorrow. You get to write your story; you get to decide who's in it and who isn't. It's your life and you create it. This was the biggest blessing for me.

There is a seed that is planted in every adversity we face that is greater than the obstacle we have in front of us, and this is the mentality I carried with me every day, coupled with the faith of who I am, how I was raised, what I deserved, and what my children deserved. This was going to carry me across the finish line and into the promised land at 43 years young!

May 24, 2013, was the Victoria Day holiday in Canada which meant I was off work and doing my normal driving around neighborhoods, looking for houses to live in with little to no money. I only had a couple of weeks and we had to be out of the house, and I still hadn't found anything affordable. When the marital home sold, I found out we were in even more debt than I knew, and I had to pay the bank to leave my home! I was fully prepared and imagined I would be living in a basement apartment with my two children, and I figured this would make me stronger, which is something I have subsequently learned is not the case!

We do not have to suffer to be stronger; we can actually build our strength through our awareness — our awareness of all the abundance and prosperity available to us in the smallest things that surround us every day. We can build our strength in a positive way — not just from a negative experience — and this is the richest, most fulfilling way to build strength: through recognizing the blessing of adversity that has been given to us all.

As I was driving down the street that day my brother called me on the cell phone, asking if I wanted to go for lunch. I said jokingly, "Sure, I'm just driving around this neighborhood one more time, looking for a house to live in." He said, "OK, I'll see you soon" and, as I turned the corner, I decided to turn right and go down a street I had already been down because it just felt right. When I turned that corner, I noticed this house with hedges all along the front of the house, all up the side of the house, and I could see there was this man who looked like he had just put some sort of sign in the ground, in front of the hedges, and walked away.

I thought maybe it was an advertisement for a garage sale or painting services or something and, as I got closer, I noticed it was a For Sale sign, so I immediately pulled into the driveway. There was a hose lying across the driveway that he had just used, a pair of old running shoes, but no sign of him. The garage door was wide open. I noticed it was an older home and an older neighborhood — a back split with gray brick, white garage door, white front door, and this red, wooden deck on the front of the house. I was by myself but was desperate. I got out of my car and walked up the driveway. I looked into the garage but couldn't see him. I looked up the side of the house and still didn't see him. I walked up this red deck, which was about three or four steps, and I went to the front door. The old screen door was closed but the front door behind it was open. I knocked, no answer, I rang the bell and finally this older gentleman came to the door. I smiled and said, "Hi, I was just driving around the neighborhood and I noticed that you just put out a For Sale sign on your house." He said, "Yes, I just put it out there, but it's actually not on the market yet. My girlfriend is a real estate agent, and it goes on the market tomorrow." My immediate response was, "Well, you need to go take the sign down because I'm buying this house!"

I told him the situation I was in: being a single mom going through a divorce, and I needed a place to live with my children and two dogs. He looked at me, dismayed, and said, "OK, do you want to look at the house first?" and I said, "Sure" and stepped inside. I asked him how much he wanted for the house, and he told me. I said, "OK, I'm gonna give you what you are asking." He said he had lived there for 30 years with his wife and three daughters, and his wife had passed away 10 years earlier with breast cancer. He walked me through every room in this house, and I could feel the love in the walls. I envisioned my bedroom, my son's bedroom, my daughter's bedroom, and then we went down a few steps and there was a family room. We then went back out into this beautiful backyard, backing onto a ravine, and there were three huge apple trees in the backyard. "These were just little plantings when we moved in here," he commented. There was just a feeling of such love and good memories in this house, and I thought this was so perfect for me and my children. This was a sign from God that everything was going to be OK.

It may not be easy but it's going to be OK, and so I told him I would come right back with a check for $5,000 for him. I asked him to take the For Sale sign off the property, which he did while I went to the bank. The house was ours an hour later, now all I had to do was get financing and close on the property. This was another lesson in taking action: not knowing the how but doing it anyway. When you feel that nudge, listen and act. This is your chance!

I remember the feeling of excitement telling my kids I had found a house for us to live in. So I took them to the house, and told them we had to go to this person's house to pick up a barbecue that I was purchasing, and I needed both of their help to lift it. I had also told the kind man whom I'd bought the house from about this plan, which he graciously agreed to.

When we got to the front door, I told the kids, "OK, let's go in. We have to go to the backyard to get the barbecue." However, I intentionally walked them the long way through the house, and said things like, "Oh, this is a cute house", "This is a nice neighborhood", etc. Then we went into the backyard, and I could see their eyes widen. They were shocked at the size of it all and by the three huge apple trees! It was the best part of the entire house. This expensive backyard, backing onto a ravine with trees and forest, set in nature, a place of serenity, a place I could envision them hanging out with their friends and me; feeling comfortable and having fun; having our family over… The feelings of happiness and joy slowly started creeping back in. No one could take those feelings away from me, because I was their mother and I only wanted what was best for them.

Finally, my son asked me where the barbecue was, and I replied, "Well, to tell you the truth, there is no barbecue. This is our new house. This is our new home. This is where we're going to start our new life. What do you think?" The look of shock on their faces was a look I wasn't prepared for. I could tell it was mixed emotions, realizing that this meant finality. We were now just a family of three, living in a new home, that was very different from the home we had just come from.

Overall, when I think back, it gave them some feeling of stability. We had a home, and something I have always tried to do for my kids is to let them know I love them; I will always be here for them; and that we are stronger than we know. In these moments, when you have a strong enough desire or dream you want to achieve, when you find your true character, you dig deep and then find what you're made of.

Ten years later, we have spent many nights living, loving, laughing, crying, fighting, growing, break-ups, make-ups, accidents, flipped cars, Christmases, birthdays, Hallowe'en graduations, basketball games, and soon-to-be weddings.

I believe we choose our parents when we are born. I know my kids chose me, and I know they have taught me more than I have ever taught them, and for that I am forever grateful and honored to be their mother. I may not have known the how, but I did it anyway. I knew why, and I simply put my two feet on the ground every morning and took one step forward every day in the direction of where I wanted my life to go, and who I wanted to be.

~ Strength comes from within, strength finds you, resilience finds you, blessings find you and faith keeps you moving. Faith keeps you hopeful, faith stands you up when you don't have the strength to stand any longer. Love yourself, be proud of yourself, and know that you are the chosen one.

Infinity

by Michelle Osborne

With an adoring heart, I kneel before you,
Seeking your boundless wisdom, passion, and truth.

In this sacred sanctuary, where eternity collides, Ignite my soul
with the fire of your eternal strides.

Grant me the unyielding strength to face life's storm,
To rise above the challenges that try to deform.

Infuse my being with a passion that's untamed,
So I may triumph, with resilience unashamed.

Goddess of Infinity, your beauty burns like a flame,
A burn that kindles souls to make a triumphant exclaim.

Bathe me in your fiery, passionate embrace,
And let me embody your ardent, fierce grace.

With every step, shall my presence ignite,
A force that sparks courage, shining ever bright.

May its profound meaning fill every moment I encounter,
Forever guided by divine wisdom, love, and fervor.

As I emerge, may passion flow,
Conquering challenges that may sow,

Goddess of Infinity, I offer devotion,
A flame that burns with fierce emotion.

Blessed unto thee, forevermore,
With gratitude, my heart will soar,

I carry your ardor, love's decree,
With a passionate heart, forever free.

In her name, I embrace the magnificence presented by the
Goddess of Infinity.

Knowing that within its boundless embrace,
An eternal journey, forever evolving in grace.

Lies the essence of my life's purpose and meaning,
In unity with the infinite, I find purpose and belonging,

About

Michelle Osborne

In the realm of technological marvels, where digital landscapes intertwine with human ingenuity, there exists a luminous soul who has spent over two decades crafting her destiny amidst lines of code and networks of innovation. Michelle Osborne is a visionary seeker who has embarked on an extraordinary journey, fueled by a deep-rooted passion for personal development.

From the earliest days of her career, Michelle recognized the power of technology to shape our world, and she wholeheartedly embraced its endless possibilities. With each new challenge she encountered, personally and professionally, her skills flourished, and her expertise grew like a majestic oak. Yet, as her professional achievements multiplied, an unwavering stirring within her heart whispered of a greater purpose, a calling that transcended the confines of technical proficiency.

Guided by an inner compass, Michelle embarked on a profound inner exploration, delving into the realms of personal growth and self-discovery. She immersed herself in the timeless teachings of wisdom traditions, delving into psychology, spirituality, and mindfulness practices. As she integrated these transformative insights into her own life, she discovered an undeniable truth: her passion for personal development was not a mere interest but a sacred calling.

Michelle courageously chose to venture beyond the familiar territory of her successful IT career. She embarked on a new chapter, merging her technical acumen with her heartfelt dedication to personal growth. Recognizing the profound impact she could make on the lives of others, she embraced her purpose with open arms and a radiant spirit.

Today, Michelle stands as a beacon of inspiration, offering her expertise in personal development to guide others on their own transformative journeys. Through workshops, coaching, and speaking engagements, she empowers individuals to unearth their true potential, transcend limiting beliefs, and step into lives of purpose and fulfillment.

As her journey continues to unfold, Michelle remains steadfast in her commitment to bring her passion to the masses. With each passing day, she lives a legacy of inspiration and empowerment, reminding us all that within the vast expanse of our being, there lies an untapped wellspring of potential waiting to be discovered.

Michelle illuminates the path for others to embrace their true calling and embark on their own remarkable journeys of self-discovery and purpose in the NOW.

www.MichelleOsborneCoaching.com

info@michelleosbornecoaching.com

Instagram and Facebook @michelleosborneofficial

Ahmed Diallo

18

~ Achilles ~

Achilles, embodiment of unwavering strength, unveils the power of patience and growth, inspiring souls to triumph over adversity and forge a path of remarkable transformation.

My Patience To Growth

By Ahmed Diallo

How old was I? Ten? Eleven, maybe?

On a fresh, dewy morning, I'd climbed onto the big stone, and sat thinking for hours. What was going on? The night before, Father had returned from his long business trip. He arrived late at night and was warmly welcomed. The longing of my mother — of all of us — for Dad was great. After all, a month is a very long time without him in the big house, located at the end of the street of the sparsely inhabited, albeit well-kept settlement on the outskirts of the large industrial city.

When we were too tired from the long wait for his arrival, my sister and I fell into bed. I couldn't fall asleep immediately and so I lay there in the dark, thoughts wandering into fantasies about all I could do with Father the next day. Half asleep, I suddenly heard loud voices. They were coming from my parents' bedroom down the hall. The aggression in the voices was muffled but clear and familiar. I hid under my blanket, not wanting to hear any more of it. Suddenly, a familiar feeling rose up, causing a lump in my throat. It's happening again, I thought, now jolted out of my sleep. I was paralyzed and the tear, escaping from the corner of my closed eye, felt like it had come from a nightmare I was just waking up from. I was trying to save myself from the terror that was rising inside me. It had really happened; it wasn't a bad nightmare, rather a nightmare that had happened.

The morning after, as if by magic, everything was back to the normality I was used to whenever the family sat together for breakfast on Sundays. Mother was making her much-loved pancakes, while Father was chatting with my sister about his experiences. I listened with one ear, puffing inwardly, and thinking, "Ah, you've taken your nightmares too far again.... It's all good and peaceful after all...." Three months later, however, Dad had moved out. There was no goodbye. I didn't want to believe it, and so I pretended he was away for his work, as usual.

I practiced patience, and very often returned to that big stone, as if he were listening to me, when my vision was blurred by unsustainable tears sinking into my nightmares. Sometimes, glimpses of light appeared that reminded me of beautiful and happy family times. I clung to them as if they were the last thing I had left. In them I saw a spark of hope that all would be well again. I then looked up at the sky, which, with the starry night that had fallen, was able to give me comfort and hope. I could not reproduce this peaceful feeling. It was just there, inside me, filling my heart with happiness and peace. I could not exchange these moments with anyone in the world. I would have loved to freeze time and stay in that state forever.

These glimpses of illuminating light were a blessing to my frequent otherwise dull thoughts. It felt like a positive energy that outshone everything that was weighing and dragging me down. I felt so strong, as if my Creator had again given me so much strength that I felt able to move mountains. When, three years later, we learned that my father had died in a tragic accident in custody, I began to seek support from my mother to soften my gloomy thoughts. I had been looking for support, protection, and security, and Mother gave me the feeling of never being alone. She was so peaceful and changed, incredibly strong, patient, and accommodating with us. It felt as if a switch had been turned on within her. She spent a lot of time telling us about happy times with Dad, and our younger times when my sister was 5 and I was 3. It made her so happy that once she started sharing those memories, she couldn't stop herself.

On warm summer nights, Mother and I would lie down in the garden loungers and silently gaze at the clear, starry sky for hours. It seemed as if we were talking wordlessly. To this day I cannot describe these moments of silent communication with her. When she suddenly passed away, three years later, my sister and I learned from her doctor that she had suffered liver failure. Mother had kept silent about her illness all that time. I was taken in by my uncle, and my sister was adopted by a good friend of our mother's. I always remembered the stone upon which I would lie at nights after my mother passed away, staring at the clear, starry sky, forgetting the time. This memory always came back to me whenever I felt weak and in need of help and impacted me like a source of energy that gave me the necessary strength to look forward, to find inner peace and security.

I gradually learned to be patient with myself and my feelings, and to gain some inner peace. This was supported by the fact that after a certain time I realized how important running meant to me. I started to realize, with increasing challenges in school and engineering studies, that running was a good regenerative balance of body and mind. I used the running training for the marathon to push the limits of my physical endurance. This eventually led to the desired result, and increased my endurance, patience, and inner peace significantly. I learned to develop inner strength without outside help. This motivated me to look for more, to further develop the ability I'd discovered, and gain more benefits for myself from it.

I also learned that intense inward communication brought me to peak performance, even without being expressed with words. I then remembered contemplating the stars in the garden with Mother. I remembered what spiritual as well as physical peace we had found in each other back then. There was a deep sense of love, peace, security, and contentment that I could partially relate to. I felt a void within me that needed to be filled. I needed to find that peace again.

The physical absence of my parents still didn't trigger feelings of loss and lack in me even after 10 years. Through patience with myself and my persistent inner ME, I began to realize how richly I'd inherited through my experiences. I am unable to erase from my mind the lack that resulted from the death of my parents. But I can develop further abilities to become a much better ME — not only to have more patience, but also to persevere until I break through limits to my freedom; take advantage of opportunities for development; and to strengthen my Inner Voice, to make it heard, and to render it obedience.

Simply to honor and nurture the happy, carefree child within me.

I realize I have come to a point in my life where I need support to meet the challenges that have arisen. This realization has paved the way for my personal development. Through the injuries to my soul, I need to work on myself more intensively and invest more in myself. I owe this to my soul. I have learned through my faith, upbringing, and past experiences that there are no coincidences in nature.

As Auguste Rodin said, "Patience is also a form of action." It helps to make better decisions and increases one's emotional awareness.

To me, coincidence in the mind is sometimes a state of ignorance.

However, it is important to note that not all coincidences can be attributed to ignorance alone. It's important to maintain an open-minded perspective when encountering coincidences. Cultivating curiosity and remaining receptive to the mysteries of coincidence can lead to personal growth, expanded understanding, and a deeper appreciation of the complexities of the world around us.

In summary, while it is possible to perceive coincidences as products of ignorance or a lack of understanding, it is also valuable to remain open to the potential meanings and connections they may hold.

So, on this basis, I have begun to work on personal optimization. My self-image of physical fitness is to care about my physical and mental vibes. I care about my diet. I love fresh air and working out. I have to be creative and improve my imagination. I have to be sympathetic to understand the needs of my beloved family and friends and be an active, intentional listener to their objectives, so that I can give them suitable, right answers. I need to invest in time to stretch and grow, so that I learn to organize myself to be more effective, to control myself and to plan my activities and get better at saving time. I also need to be friendly and pleasant to everybody I meet or surround myself with.

Prayer of Achilles

by Ahmed Diallo

Divine Source of infinite love and power, I affirm that I embody the resilience, courage, willpower, and endurance of Achilles. I am blessed with exceptional physical abilities and the ability to recover from any setback with ease and grace.

With the same extraordinary bravery as Achilles, I face any challenge with unwavering confidence and fearlessness. I am empowered by the strength of my willpower, which drives me towards my goals and inspires me to achieve greatness.

Like Achilles, I possess the unwavering perseverance to overcome any obstacle in my path. I refuse to give up, even in the face of seemingly insurmountable odds.

I am filled with the power of love, which flows through me and imbues me with the strength and courage to face any challenge. I trust in the infinite wisdom of the universe to guide me on my journey, and I know that I am protected and supported in all that I do.

May my spirit be infused with the power and resilience of Achilles, and may I be filled with the love and courage necessary to overcome any obstacle. I offer gratitude for the blessings in my life and for the strength and power that flows through me.

Amen.

About

Ahmed Diallo

Ahmed Diallo, a German citizen born in Conakry, the capital of the small West African Republic of Guinea and residing in Immenstadt im Allgaeu, a small town in the Bavarian foothills of the Alps, is an exceptional and compelling example of success and personal growth. As a graduate engineer in Mechatronics, from the University of Bochum in North Rhine Westphalia and with extensive experience in the development of manufacturing processes at industry leading company Robert Bosch GmbH, Ahmed Diallo has established himself as an exemplary and model employee in this company.

Driven by an unquenchable thirst for knowledge and personal development, Ahmed has immersed himself in transformative programs by Bob Proctor - Thinking into Results - and continues his personal development with the Napoleon Hill Institute, a leading personal development organization. As a passionate endurance athlete, he has participated in the Ruhr Marathon runs participated.

Ahmed Diallo, an ambassador-in-training with the Napoleon Hill Institute, embodies personal and professional growth. His dedication to empowering and guiding others showcases his character and unwavering commitment. Ahmed's inspiring journey exemplifies determination, perseverance, and passionate personal growth, inspiring those around him to unleash their potential.

linktr.ee/ahmeddiallo

Jamaal R Mitchell

19

~ Game Genie ~

The Game Genie Spirit helps you find purpose, develop talents, and embrace freedom. You shape your story, create your identity, and control your future. The true battle is within yourself, holding the reins with your mind, like a remote control.

Life Starring You

by Jamaal R. Mitchell

Ten years ago, my self-image, mindset, and belief system were in complete disarray. Within the span of a few days, my girlfriend of 5 years left me, an intruder broke into my home and stole over 15,000 of my studio equipment, and I was fired from my highest-earning job shortly after selling a quarter-million-dollar account. It felt like I was playing the same game, stuck on the same level, and dealing with the same boss. Life seemed impossible, I was ready to quit, and I was thinking about pulling the plug.

Now open the door to my three-story loft and smell the stench of pit bull urine and feces covering the unfinished basement floor. Walk up one step and take six steps forward as you head through the foyer and hang a left to enter the modern kitchen nook. Look at the beautiful stainless-steel appliances, white cabinetry, and glass-top stove, covered with dishes piled to the ceiling, and forks, knives, and spoons that wouldn't come clean even if you put them in the dishwasher. Walk cautiously over the beautiful bamboo hardwood floor covered with magazines, books, socks, clothes, leftover carry-out boxes, and Redbox DVDs. Continue ahead and you'll find me, slumped over an all-white, worn, pleather sectional, doing the Lil Boosie & Webbie "Wipe Me Down" to get the crumbs off my "shoulders, chest, pants, and shoes.

In the midst of this deep, dark, depression that no one was aware of I received a phone call that changed my life. It was from the most angelic voice known to man: my momma. She said, "Jamaal… Baby…I'm aware that my brother is bipolar… and I know that my niece is too… but do you believe… it's possible…that it could be true for you?"

I paused for a moment and replied, "Yes, ma'am, I do."

Then she asked me, "Would you be willing to take a test to find out if you are? Because your father and I don't feel like we're in a position to be able to help you… and that doesn't make me feel good."

That was the worst thing my mother EVER said to me: that she and my father felt like they "didn't have the tools to help me."

This was a defining moment for me. I became indignant and instantly made up my mind. I said, "There has got to be a 'Better Way to Play'."

Suddenly a memory from my childhood flashed before my eyes. I found myself in my childhood home– 523 Aladar Drive, O 'Fallon IL, 62269 — the redbrick house with maroon shutters, the perfectly angled grass, the Steve Harvey lining, and shrubs that looked like they were manicured by Edward Scissorhands himself. I opened the glass front door, took off my shoes, placed them on the shoe rack and headed straight past the sitting room, with the cream Victorian-style furniture, dark pink coffee table, and mauve carpet on my left. I walked on the beautiful, maroon throw rug, with the cream rectangle accents, past the dining room, with the black dining room set and matching china display cabinet on my right.

Once I reached the kitchen with the mauve countertops, I hung a right and headed down the gray basement stairs and entered the playroom at the bottom of the steps on the left. I could see the framed 1991, 1992, and 1993 back-to-back-to-back Chicago Bulls championships and Dream Team posters covering the walls. My midsize color TV was sitting on top of a brown entertainment system with two cabinet doors, paired with the old school, 5-disc, Sony surround-sound system connected to a Sega Genesis.

I was locked in, sitting upright and playing my favorite game, Sonic the Hedgehog. I was flying through all the levels, collecting all the coins, and whooping all the opponents, but when I got to that final sky zone level, Dr Robotnik would beat the brakes off me. He would take all my coins, lives, and confidence. I'd restart the game only to find myself repeating that process time and time again. The definition of insanity. The cartridge would get so hot I'd have to remove it and put it in the freezer for 10 to 15 minutes to let it cool off. Eventually, I got so frustrated I threw the controller, and bam, the brown cabinet doors flew open. They revealed something that had been sitting there all along, waiting to be used. It was the Game Genie and it contained infinite access to unused assets and functions. A better way to play. Invulnerability, unlimited ammo, and level-skipping.

From that moment forward I saw my life as a video game, one full of infinite levels. Each level had a different boss, each boss required a different strategy, and I was equipped with infinite strategies. A video game electronically manipulates images produced by a computer program to be displayed on a screen. My mind acted as a computer that processed the instructions sent from my thoughts which created feelings. My feelings inspired actions, and my actions produced results that were displayed in my life in real time. A level is section or part of a game. Most games are so large that they're broken up into multiple levels, so only one portion of the game needs to load at a time. In order to advance through and to the next level I had to meet specific goals and perform specific tasks. At the end of each level I faced powerful bosses, and winning required a greater knowledge of the game mechanics. Sometimes bosses were very hard or impossible to defeat so I use cheat codes to help me manipulate and modify the game data.

Bob Proctor said, "Change is inevitable, but personal growth is a choice." This means "If You Want the Game to Change" then you have to "Choose to Improve!" because it's "Life Starring You!" I was the Game Genie. I granted myself access to unused assets and functions. I had the power to create. I was the writer, director, producer, actor, etc. I could do, be, or have whatever my heart desired.

For the first time in my life my mind was in my hands, and I was holding the remote control. I sat down, sat back, kicked up my feet, relaxed, and put on my headphones, wore my glasses, closed my eyes, and imagined everything I wanted to happen. I took action and started writing the script for my dream life. I'd visualized it often and got emotionally involved with it so I could see myself there in real time. I started producing from the storehouse of inventory that God had put inside of me, and I developed the character necessary to fulfill my story. I chose my future.

I decided to use the Game Genie. I went to the counselor, and I took the test that revealed I was not bipolar, but I was in a severe manic and depressed state of mind. I had experienced some severe levels of trauma which I'd suppressed and, over time, that suppression had developed into anger. With no outlet my anger eventually grew into rage. After seeing her for several months I felt good, but I knew if I could overcome that rage then I would feel better. I decided to use a different Game Genie and found a cognitive behavior therapist who looked like me.

During our first session, he handed me a dictionary and told me to find the word "oner." I looked for it and it wasn't in there, so he instructed me to throw the dictionary into the trash. I was puzzled because he wanted me to throw the entire dictionary away, but I could tell from the look on his face that he was serious, so I followed his orders. He handed me another dictionary and told me to read the definition aloud and write it down. It read "Oner: a remarkable person or thing." He said, "That is what you are, Jamaal. You are a remarkable person or thing. You're the only person on the planet with the future that's bottled up inside of you." In a matter of seconds, his words transformed my self-image, mindset, and belief system. I saw myself as an asset because I was a person of great value.

A couple of months later he asked me, "Who are you?"

I laughed and replied, "You know who I am. I am Jamaal Mitchell."

He said, "That's not who you are, that's your name. Who are you?"

I replied, "I'm a marketing and advertising sales consultant."

He said, "That's not who you are, that's your occupation."

For the first time in my life, I was at a loss for words. I had no idea. I was 32 years old at the time and I'd never been asked that question before. It took me over a month to discover the answer and it happened right before I entered his office to begin the session that day. Something tapped me on my shoulder and a voice within whispered, "You are God's favorite channel for His children."

He said, "Hmm, what does that mean?"

I replied, "There are some places I've been going, some substances I've been abusing, and some friends I've been choosing that are no longer a good fit for me." I had been given a unique set of gifts and tools that most people don't have and would be willing to do anything to receive. I had a duty to use them and to help those who were less equipped to reach heights they could only dream of.

I had discovered my purpose and I felt so much better, but I was curious as to how I would feel once I reached my best. I chose to use another Game Genie and he was a specialist who identified I had OCD. He changed my perspective on what it was and showed me how to use it to benefit me. I saw it as a gift of accelerated growth, and everything changed. I had the power to choose what I obsessed over, so I became obsessed with becoming God's greatest version of myself.

What do you believe? Can you see the forest through the trees? Do you believe you can do the difficult immediately and the impossible takes just a bit longer? Do you believe that if you used a Game Genie your game could get stronger? Because I do. I believe I'm an eagle, with the heart of a lion, and the swag of a peacock and, if you can't see the forest through the trees, then you should ascend until you can see it from the treetops.

So, remember, the next time you are met with a test, never let it rest until your good becomes your better and your better becomes your best.

I Am Prayer

by Jamaal R. Mitchell

I Am a Oner.

I Am a remarkable person or thing.

I Am the only person on the planet
with the future that's bottled inside of me.

I Am important.

I Am valuable.

I Am needed.

I speak it. I believe it. I receive it. I repeat it.

I Am important.

I Am valuable.

I Am needed.

I Am the GME.

I Am the Greatest Me Ever there
will never be a better.

I Am in control; my mind is in my
hands and I'm holding the remote control.

I Am directing my mind power to
create the reality I desire.

I Am the writer, director, producer, actor, etc.

I Am writing the script for my life.

I Am visualizing what's possible for me.

I Am producing from the inventory within me.

I Am developing the character
necessary to fulfill my story.

I Am acting as if I'm who I desire to be.

I Am willing and able to do whatever
it takes to make my dreams a reality.

I Am helping people to discover their purpose,
master their gifts, and access their freedom.

I Am teaching people how to write their story,
create their player and choose their future.

I Am equipping people with the resources,
skills, and opportunities necessary to achieve
their greatest potential and live life to the fullest.

About

Jamaal R. Mitchell

Mr. Jamaal R. Mitchell is a natural leader that has the ability to help people discover their purpose, master their gifts & access their freedom. He reconditions your self-image, mindset & belief system to introduce you to the best version of yourself. He enhances the human experience by equipping people with the resources, skills, and opportunities necessary to achieve their greatest potential and live life to the fullest.

Jamaal is a Founding Member of the Napoleon Hill Foundation and a Master Coach. He works with individuals, small businesses, non-profits, and corporations looking to increase performance in their career & personal lives.

Jamaal has contributed his gift of speaking to numerous audiences as a keynote speaker including Les Brown Power Voice Summit IV (5), 2021 East St. Louis Senior High School Commencement, 2021 Normandy High School Commencement, Senator Paul Simon Youth Leadership Committee Mentor & Ambassador program, and Federation of Block Units of Metropolitan St. Louis 91st Annual Assembly.

Jamaal is the proud son of Elizabeth and Cedric Mitchell. He has a younger brother Shaka Mitchell and a handsome, 5-year-old son, Jaxon Mitchell. Jamaal is a native of O'Fallon, Illinois who graduated from O'Fallon Township High School. He attended Tennessee State University in Nashville, TN & Southern Illinois University in Carbondale, IL. He is a proud member of Omega Psi Phi Fraternity Incorporated Omicron Theta Chapter & an Omega Psi Phi Project Manhood graduate and mentor.

Jamaal has worked diligently over the past 20 years in his career in sales. He has become an expert in retail, communication, advertising & automobile industries. With many goals ahead, Jamaal will continue to expand upon his knowledge to provide resources for many years to come.

Jamaal received the Annie Malone Heroes "Salute To Excellence Award" for his role during the five-day, viral marketing campaign, that raised over $100,000 in funding that led to the outcome of keeping the Annie Malone legacy alive during the Covid-19 pandemic.

If you or someone you know is ready to learn How to Play the Game and Win then go to www.fyicoaching.com click the link for a free 15 min consultation and download my daily activity guide.

Social Media @therealjamaalmitchell

Margarita (Maggie) Lopez

20

~ Self Love ~

The Goddess of Self Love reigns supreme, a radiant beacon of empowerment and compassion. She teaches us to embrace our flaws, honor our worth, and bathe our souls in the purest love, for only then can we truly unlock our limitless potential and bask in the brilliance of our authentic selves.

A Journey Back To Self

by Margarita (Maggie) Lopez

It was the summer of 2020 when it all hit me. I was out of town with family when I received an unexpected text: "I hope you're having a good day." I felt tears well up and, although I couldn't describe what I felt, my heart raced, and I thought it all a bit unreal. I was surprised but at the same time I felt special. I remember my first thought was, "Why would a stranger take the time to send this?" And then my thoughts evolved to, "It was a stranger who took the time to send this." It got me thinking about how many people close to me didn't do this, including my family and my husband. In that moment I realized I heavily relied on the love, validation, and affirmation of others.

This was the beginning of my journey with self-love.

I had always viewed love as something grand and powerful. I knew giving love was the biggest gift someone could give you. So, I did just that. I gave love in different ways: romantically, as a mother, as a daughter, as a friend. So, you could see, I gave to others, but I'd totally forgotten about giving to me. I believed that if I created a new project to "give" my love to or had a baby to "give" my love to, that it would fulfill me. It doesn't. When you don't love yourself, you end up exhausted, giving from an empty cup and most likely attracting the wrong people.

If you're anything like me, you wished at some point to just be loved. You probably thought, "Why can't they just love me back?" or "Why am I not enough to love?" I had given so much in different areas of my life that I was left desperate for any love anyone could give me. Have you ever felt like you've given so much and received so little in return?

Following the unexpected text, I quickly became an observer of my own life. I started to take account for who I was and who I had become. I quickly came to the realization that I had changed for my husband, for my parents, for work, even for my therapist. I believed that's what I needed to do: change myself to keep my marriage together, to keep my parents from arguing, to not lose my jobs. In my marriage, it started with how I expressed myself or not, then it turned into who I was in the bedroom, and eventually it became how I chose to carry out my career. My ex-husband didn't contribute to all these changes; I thought I needed to be this "someone" for him. We encountered challenges that also led me to believing I needed to save us, and I would do so at the cost of me.

I lost my identity in the process of creating this "character" and thus, not loving myself. I chose to ignore the person in the mirror, because I feared losing my marriage and because I had low self-esteem and a limited understanding of self-worth. I had a preconceived notion that if someone did something to me or behaved a certain way towards me, there was "obviously" something wrong with me.

I ignored my needs when it came to my parents, too. I witnessed a great deal of verbal altercations that led me to feel responsible for quieting the noise because they wouldn't. So, I became the placater and the problem-solver. I eventually carried burdens that were not my own. In work scenarios, I would tell myself I had to be "this" person before I walked through the door, and it would leave me feeling resentful and ungenuine. I wore a different costume for each occasion which, in my mind, would help me keep the peace, love, and success in all these groups. But it left me feeling empty.

One day I looked in the mirror, and finally took an introspective look at all the puzzle pieces that made up this woman I saw. Remember the text from that co-worker? Practically a stranger … well, he became my mirror. It was a rainy afternoon when we got to talking about our past, and there he was, across the iron table. As I sat there, crying about my troubles and opening up about what seemed to be the end of many chapters in my life, he turned to me, cigarette in hand, and said, "Do you know who you are?" At first the question caught me off guard. I said, "What do you mean?" and he proceeded to describe me.

He told me things about my character, my accomplishments, and my talents, as if he had studied me in minute detail. He had paid more attention to who I was than I and many close people in my life had. I saw myself for the first time. And sobbed. I felt as if I had made it, as if this journey I had been walking had finally arrived at the destination I'd been searching for. It felt like home. I had returned home to myself.

In a few minutes I felt accepted, validated, accomplished, seen, heard, understood. The most revealing moment of this experience is that I was this person he was describing. The acceptance and validation were coming from me. I finally saw who I was when he held up the mirror.

Some days passed, and I began to have this love affair with myself. I had a rush of emotions every night: guilt for changing and leaving certain people behind; shame when I thought about the past years I hadn't embraced myself; excitement for that new version of me that was to come; and a sense of freedom because I no longer had to carry the burdens that weren't mine. I feared returning to self, accepting who I truly was and embracing authenticity. I felt excited and free as if chains had been broken — chains I had blamed others for, but which I had put there over the years. The most daring thing about this journey was the certainty of knowing I had to change but knowing it would change everything. And that's exactly what happened.

When you first learn to love yourself, you learn that some things and some people can stay, while others must go. It's at this point that you experience the loss. And most importantly, the loss of the old you, the one that – at least in my case – was a people pleaser; the one who accommodated others' faults or offenses for the sake of keeping the peace. It's difficult to say goodbye to that person who has been such a significant part of your identity over time. The older you are, the harder it can be, since you've played that part for so long. The grief is bittersweet. You know you must move on, yet you keep thinking of the past, wishing it wasn't coming to an end.

I remember knowing that the people and things I was removing from my life had served their purpose. I had now learned the lessons and it was time to move on. I found myself saying goodbye to my then husband. We had both chosen each other at such a young age and, due to many other circumstances, it just wasn't the right fit for us anymore. However, the most impactful grief process was becoming the new me — the one who set boundaries; the woman who voiced her value and didn't accept less than she deserved. Each realization of self – the woman – was transforming authentically into who I was always meant to be. There were many tears and desperate cries for that past self to return, but once I knew I couldn't betray myself any longer, I pushed to become her more.

I learned to pay attention to myself. I defined my values. I became aware of what I liked and didn't like, who I wanted to be around, who left me with energy and who depleted it. I finally understood what it looked like to invest in myself and embrace all of me. I recognized that it was OK to set healthy boundaries and to say no. Slowly I shed the people pleaser in me and became someone who prioritized based on my values. Most importantly, I learned how to embrace pain and not avoid it. I learned how to lean into it and derive purpose from pain. I rewrote the narrative of my life into the one I wanted to live. But self-love is a journey with no destination; the story doesn't end here. Although I had broken numerous chains, the opportunity to apply the lessons learned was just around the corner.

2022 was the year of the highs and lows. I soared high quickly and I crashed hard just as quickly. It took falling in love again to really see the piece within me that had been missing self-love. I recalled this man as everything I never had. He was the definition of freedom, adventure, and sexuality. In just a year, I had learned more about myself than in the previous 15 because I was finally paying attention. Loving him made me believe free-falling was safe. The moments spent were breathtaking, until darkness came. Reality.

Once the infatuation stage is gone, you start to see the person for who they are. I saw him for who he was, and I saw myself in the purer form. Having him in my life provided me with a mirror of my past. His presence in my life allowed me to see all my pressure points and triggers, which were all areas I needed to grow in. I saw that my attachment to him wasn't healthy. Emotionally, I couldn't function if he wasn't OK. Without him my world crumbled, and the highs now only felt like rebounds from the lows. I had made someone else my world, again, and had forgotten about me. Again.

The first sign that self-love is missing is when you betray yourself to serve someone else. My well-being was compromised. I carried a heavier emotional load than ever due to his emotional instability, and I expected to still thrive in my goals while believing my highs were contingent upon this man's presence. I wanted him to be someone he wasn't. My need to receive externally to heal my inner self needed him. This was wrong. I wasn't meeting someone at the stage of their journey. I was attempting to change them so I could feel whole. That's when it all clicked. I hadn't yet learned to love me, and so I began to.

As I unfolded the story of my childhood to my therapist in one of our sessions, the lightbulb went off in my head. I had picked men very similar to my father. This meant they were emotionally unavailable, struggled with vulnerability, selfish, either very quiet or hurtful with words, and struggled with depression. The result of this was always the same: I felt alone. I kept wanting to create a story with these men — a fairytale of some sort in which they became the man I never had. The man I waited for my father to be up until his death. These men, just like my father, were not going to heal me. They were not going to mend the shattered pieces in me that called for nurturing, understanding, acceptance, value. Only I could heal me. It took a year for me to accept that this great love was not for me, and that the grand love I had been in search of was already within me.

There comes a time in one's life when we must recognize that the only one who can heal you is you. When I learned I needed to stop searching exteriorly and needed to look inwardly, I soared. I stopped looking at the actions of my partner as against me or about me and I started asking, "What does Maggie need right now?" Then I would proceed to give myself just that. The art of self-love is healing. With consistency, I lost my unhealthy attachment to this relationship, and I started to see him for who he was. I started to identify those qualities that had showed up in my two previous partners, and my pattern became obvious. After that, I established a healthy pattern of giving to me and not needing him to soothe me. This meant going on dates with me, spending time with myself at the mall or at a movie. Sometimes loving myself meant sitting on my couch, alone, with anxiety, telling myself that I am safe. I would repeat the phrase and take deep breaths until my mind and body were one and I'd achieved a calm mental and physiological state. Self-love taught me that the love I give is genuine, empathic, self-less, passionate, real. I now knew the value of my gifts. My worth.

I had to learn that I couldn't love properly until I loved myself completely. I couldn't serve my love from an empty cup. Real self-love is shadow work, exploring and integrating the unconscious or repressed aspects of oneself. It is looking at reasons why you don't love yourself and healing each one. It is giving yourself kindness and love for all your imperfections; each maladaptive pattern you developed; and every insecurity. It is looking in the mirror and forgiving yourself for every mistake and every time you have ignored yourself. Self-love is learning to accept all of who you are and honoring yourself by becoming who you want to be. Love is tender, merciful, kind, generous, and beautiful. Be the love that you search for in others. Give yourself the love that you give to others.

Be the love of your life.

Self-Love Prayer

by Margarita (Maggie) Lopez

Divine Goddess of Self-Love,

In this sacred moment, we humbly invoke your presence and embrace your loving essence. May your divine grace surround us, guiding us through the highs and lows of life's journey. You inspire within us the unwavering belief that we are deserving of love, compassion, understanding, acceptance, empathy, and redemption.

As the embodiment of transparency, honesty, and self-identity, we seek your guidance to behold our own reflections with tenderness and acceptance. May we embrace every aspect of ourselves, recognizing the uniqueness that resides within. With gentle eyes, let us gaze upon our being, embracing our strengths and weaknesses alike.

You impart upon us the wisdom of self-love, reminding us to honor our boundaries and revel in our freedom. Grant us the courage to discern between them, for in doing so, we find our true authenticity. With trust in your nurturing energy, we seek your guidance, strength, and wisdom to heal our pain and deliver the balm of peace upon us.

Goddess of Self-Love, we offer our sincerest gratitude for your loving presence and the transformative power of self-acceptance. May your blessings shower upon us, illuminating our paths with self-love and allowing us to radiate that love to others.

About

Margarita (Maggie) Lopez

Margarita is a helper, a rescuer, a restorer. She was born with the spirit of service and with the desire to help people get closer to themselves. However, she would first have to learn how to do that for herself. Living most of her life "by the book" as she would say, she found herself truly embracing her authenticity in her 30's and learning how to love herself then. Her journey to self-love began at an early age and unbeknownst to her, she was becoming the woman she is today with every challenge she faced. In her chapter, "Goddess of Self-Love: A journey back to self" she tells a brief version of how she gained awareness into who she truly is, who played a significant role in her growth and how she finally came to exercise self-love.

Currently, Margarita is a Licensed Mental Health Trauma Therapist and dedicates her time to helping her clients live fulfilling lives, post trauma. She is a mother of 2 young girls and lives her life intentionally. She states, people deserve to be seen, heard, and understood without judgment. I work daily on being a person that creates secure environments for people because the world needs more compassion and love."

Digital Business Card @blinq.me/vBxEW7lquodQ

Shaunté L Chandler

- ~ Radiant Intuition ~

The Goddess of Radiant Intuition weaves the alchemy of spirit, guiding souls to embrace their inner wisdom and illuminate the path of profound transformation.

Alchemy of the Spirit

by Shaunté L Chandler

Have you ever found yourself thinking about deep ideas, like the possibility that there is more to life than meets the eye? It is said that we are spiritual beings having a human experience, which is an amazing thought when you consider that every part of who we are has been carefully designed by some greater intelligence. Personally, I have always believed there is more to life than the physical, and there are unlimited possibilities awaiting to be explored. The vastness of life resonates deeply within me. What never resonated with me, however, is the idea of a conventional and mundane existence. I yearned for a life greater than ordinary; I yearned for a life filled with extraordinary experiences. The conventional norms and shared experiences of daily life seemed disconnected from my essence.

Recognizing the profound impact that our surroundings have on our individual lives, I became acutely aware of how my environment was influencing and shaping my being. With the understanding my idea and life vision were not in alignment with my environment, I knew I had to step outside the confines of comfort and familiarity and nurture myself through the unfamiliar. My heart desired to traverse the globe, to partake in the tapestry of diverse cultures that grace the world. My mind and soul desired knowledge and experiences that extended beyond the limits of textbooks, television programming and my environment.

My quest for diving deeper into life started in church, as I delved deeper into the realm of spirituality, an undeniable spark ignited within me. I realized that the answers I sought were not confined to a single place or belief system. There were more layers to uncover, and more paths to explore. This led me to studying philosophy, eager to gain a deeper understanding of the nature of existence. It was a transformative experience as I encountered profound insights from great philosophers who pondered the big questions about the meaning of life, the nature of reality, and the essence of human existence. As my fascination grew, I found myself drawn towards the captivating field of psychology. I wanted to explore the inner workings of the mind and unravel the factors that shape human behavior.

The mind and human behavior have always fascinated me with their complexity and ever-changing nature. There are countless elements that contribute to our thoughts and actions, but at the core, it often boils down to patterns and habits formed within our neural pathways. Sometimes, however, significant emotional events shape the course of our lives and the way we perceive the world. I've come to realize that our thoughts, emotions, and behaviors are not isolated occurrences but rather interconnected threads in the intricacies of our existence. Navigating the complexities of human behavior in the realms of psychology is one aspect and metaphysics is the other. We must recognize the presence of something greater. Metaphysics reminds us that there is a grander scale to our existence, one that extends beyond the boundaries of our everyday experiences and speaks to the interconnectedness of all things and the presence of God, a higher power or universal energy based on your belief.

On a personal level, one way this interconnectedness is demonstrated is through our intuition. We all possess an intuitive guide, a deep well of wisdom within us. It is the inner nudges leading us in the right direction, guiding our choices and actions. Sometimes, it is through moments of stillness and reflection that we can tap into this intuitive guide and access profound insights and clarity. By acknowledging the divine consciousness and intelligence that reside within us, we open ourselves to a deeper connection with the world and a greater understanding of our own existence. It is through this recognition that we can experience moments of profound synchronicity, where the universe seems to conspire in our favor and guide us towards our highest potential.

Throughout my life, I've often encountered the notion that trusting one's intuition was somehow discouraged. Society seemed to prioritize external validation and conformity over deeper self-exploration. Caught up in the demands of work, family, and various distractions, it is easy to lose touch with our inner voice and succumb to external pressures and others.

In my journey, I have discovered the power of listening to this intuitive voice. It has served as a compass, leading me towards paths that align with my true purpose and bringing a sense of peace and alignment to my life. I have come to recognize that my intuition is one of my greatest assets. It is a guiding force, unveiling hidden truths and leading me towards paths that resonate with my authentic self.

How many times can you recall that if you had listened to your intuition and acted accordingly, you could have avoided unnecessary headaches or mishaps or experienced something greater than you imagined? One of my most vivid memories of a profound intuitive experience occurred when I was around 11 or 12 years old. I remember a strong gut feeling, a sense of knowing that something was wrong. I was sitting in class when an unexpected wave of sadness washed over me, causing tears to well up in my eyes. It was a perplexing experience, and I couldn't help but question the sudden surge of emotions. As I glanced up at the clock on the wall, it read approximately 8:34, and it all started to make sense.

Throughout the day, that feeling of sadness lingered, refusing to fade away. Despite my best efforts to carry on with my routine, I couldn't shake off the weight on my heart. After school, I decided to keep myself occupied, attempting to distract my mind from the lingering emotions. Engaging in chores, although not my favorite activity, provided a sense of busyness and a chance to reflect. As the evening unfolded, my mother arrived home, I continued to put on a brave face, concealing the emotional turbulence within me. However, the weight of what I had sensed since that morning was about to be confirmed. Shortly after her arrival, my mother called my brother and I to her bedroom. It was at that moment that she gently shared the news I had intuitively known since 8:34 that morning. My beloved Grandmother had passed away. Although the words were spoken, they merely validated what my heart had already understood.

This experience confirmed that there are times when we simply know things without any logical explanation. This would not be the last instance where my intuition provided me with insights beyond the realm of conventional understanding.

Have you ever wondered about the origins of our awareness? Where does this profound sense of knowing come from? This question has led me to ponder the eternal nature of energy—the concept that energy cannot be created nor destroyed; as above, so below; there's nothing new under the sun; and the Akashic records. Can you recall a time when you entered a room and immediately felt a lingering heaviness, as if a fight had taken place or a dense energy hung in the air? How was that sensed? It's as if the vibrations of the space whispered their story to your very being, transcending the boundaries of what can be perceived with the physical senses. Or perhaps you've had that deep gut feeling, indicating that your significant other may have been unfaithful. And what about those times when you've sensed that your child might be in danger, even before any evidence presented itself? There is an energetic awareness that transcends ordinary perception. We cannot deny there is an energetic field of awareness and intelligence working. The essence of life is found in metaphysics. Going beyond the physical world, looking past what we can see or measure, we find God's true nature, the spirit behind all things.

Understanding and acknowledging our energy and emotions is essential for healing, personal growth, and navigating life's journey. It's crucial to be attuned to our internal feelings and the energy we carry within us, as well as being mindful of the energy we encounter in our interactions with others. "The Language of Feelings", taught during my Spiritual Life Coaching certification course, equipped me with invaluable tools to comprehend the emotional spiral, interpret the meaning behind emotions, and the effective processing of emotions. Emotions are often likened to energy in motion, shaping our experiences and influencing our path through life.

Recalling the memories of going to the mall, a place that evoked a bizarre sense of dread within me, arousing instant nausea and the draining of my energy. My mind immediately became fixated on finding the nearest available seat and to plot the swiftest way to feel a sense of relief. For years, I endured these sensations. It wasn't until my late 20s, amidst the chaotic and bustling Christmas season, that I received a revelation. As I drove my car on the mall's parking lot, an overpowering wave of emotions overwhelmed me, stripping me of my focus, weighing me down, and zapping every ounce of energy within me. It was in that crucial moment that I grasped the significance and impact of the effect various energies played on my wellness. This awareness set the foundation for me to consciously discern the energies that influenced my state of being.

It is said that our weaknesses can be our greatest strengths, but we've been conditioned to view pain and hurt as signs of weakness that never lead to strength, thus in turn we suppress and bury these emotions instead of processing and healing . After two intense consecutive combat deployments, I embarked on a profound journey of self-care and healing and sought out practical tools to aid me in transitioning back to a sense of normalcy. It was during this transformative period that I made the decision to enroll in an introductory massage therapy course. During my training, I learnt trauma and emotions can be stored within our tissues, causing energy blockages. Through the manipulation of our tissues, the process of releasing these blockages, healing can begin. This concept fascinated me to no end. However, what truly intrigued my curiosity was when the instructor introduced the power of Reiki. Now, you might be wondering, just as I did at that moment, "What is Reiki?" Reiki is a form of energy healing based on the belief that we all have an inherent life force energy flowing through us, and when this energy is low or blocked, it can lead to physical, emotional, or spiritual imbalances. Reiki promotes healing energy, helping to restore balance and harmony within the body, promoting relaxation, stress reduction, and overall well-being.

Embarking on the path of Reiki ignited me on a profound journey to becoming a Reiki Master. Through my certification training, I gained an understanding of the fascinating world of energy healing and its impact, both subtle and overt, on individuals and collectively. Individually, we have energy centers within us known as Chakras, which correspond to our physical, emotional, and spiritual well-being. There are seven primary chakras: Root, Sacral, Solar Plexus, Heart, Throat, Brow, and Crown. Among the seven primary Chakras, the Root Chakra holds significance as the life-sustaining energy that supports our existence, thus I want to focus on and explore this one with you.

The Root Chakra is intimately linked to our sense of stability, security, and belonging. When the flow of this energy is hindered or blocked fear, insecurity, and anxiety may engulf us, wear down our self-trust and affect our relationship with others. Financial difficulties and instability in relationships often stem from this energetic blockage, as they are closely intertwined with our sense of self-worth. However, when the energy within the Root Chakra flows freely, we tap into our innate resilience. We establish healthy boundaries, nurture a deep sense of self-worth, and experience a profound feeling of safety and security within ourselves and our environment. We also gain the strength to navigate life's challenges with grace and determination. It is essential to recognize that the formative years of our childhood, ages 0 to seven, have significant influence over the development of energy in this chakra. Our experiences during this period shape our sense of stability, security, and trust in ourselves and the world.

I've come to realize the profound influence our formative years have on shaping our being and how we present ourselves to the world. It is during this critical period that the stage of our lives is set, and our essence is molded. However, through newfound awareness or glimpses of something greater, we are granted the power to rearrange the set or even create an entirely new one. I am grateful that early in my life, I sensed there was something more significant; something greater beyond what meets the eye. This awareness ignited a flame within me, propelling me on a life path of growth, exploration, and service. I recognized that life is a continuous unfoldment, a journey of experiences. It is in connecting with our essence, our true selves, that we unlock the door to the essence of life itself.

In this connection, there exists an abundance of unlimited possibilities, waiting to be embraced and realized. This is an invitation to dive deep into the vast expanse of existence and uncover the richness that life has to offer. Embrace the journey, explore the depths of your being, and let the essence of life guide you towards extraordinary discoveries and fulfillment.

Goddess of Radiant Intuition Prayer

by Shaunté L Chandler

Goddess of Radiant Intuition,
I stand in awe of your divine presence,
seeking your guidance and blessings.

I thank you for awakening my intuitive abilities
and expanding my understanding.

I call upon your radiant light to clear any energetic blockage
preventing me from hearing intuitive guidance and whispers of
discernment of my inner knowing.

I trust your guidance,
the compass that leads me toward clarity
and truth, confidently trusting
my perceptions and judgments,
even when doubt clouds my mind.

Goddess of Radiant Intuition,
I am grateful for your presence
and the powerful awakening you bring.

Thank you for reminding me
that the answers lie within
and empowering me
to embrace the strength of my intuition.

With your guidance, I trust in the journey
that unfolds before me.

About

Shaunté L. Chandler

Shaunté L. Chandler is a passionate and dedicated professional with a diverse background that includes experience in mental health crisis counseling, housing stability case management, and over 20 years of military leadership. As the founder of Essence of Life Healing and Wellness, she uses her unique skill set to guide and inspire individuals on their personal development journey, helping them achieve transformation and holistic wellness.

Born in St. Louis, MO, Shaunté has resided in and explored various cities and countries, expanding her perspective, and deepening her understanding of different cultures and people. She holds a bachelor's degree in psychology from Southern Illinois University - Edwardsville and a Master of Arts in Human Services Counseling, with a concentration in Crisis Response and Trauma, from Liberty University.

Shaunté's commitment to personal growth, development and healing is evident in her extensive certifications and training. She is a certified Spiritual Life Coach through Holistic Learning Centers, Reiki Master, and certified Soundbath practitioner. A graduate of both the Proctor Gallagher Institute's New Lead the Field Coaching and Thinking into Results program, and Les Brown's Power Voice Academy.

Additionally, Shaunté is a founding coach of the prestigious Napoleon Hill Institute, further solidifying her expertise in personal development and success principles.

Determined to create a lasting positive impact on the lives of millions worldwide, Shaunté L. Chandler provides practical, powerful, and therapeutic mind-body-spirit healing, wellness, and personal development programs. As a coach, mentor, and author she is dedicated to empowering individuals to transform their lives, fostering personal harmony, and promoting overall well-being.

Shaunte@essenceoflifehwc.com

Barbara Gardner

~ Optimism ~

With her radiant spirit, illuminates despair, infusing hope in weary hearts. Her unwavering belief in potential inspires limitless possibilities, empowering individuals to embrace life's beauty, overcome challenges with faith, and manifest a future of joy and growth.

Going Forward and Embracing Possibilities

by Barbara Gardner

Some years ago, I heard of a study of retirees in nursing homes. They were interviewed about their lives and asked what regrets they had. The overwhelming response was that they regretted not what they had done wrong but what they had never got around to doing. The excuses they had made out of fear of change or lack of imagination imprisoned them to a life not lived before time ran out.

My greatest adventure in the ocean was being scooped up on the back of a very gentle humpback whale. I was swimming with her and had my camera filming her. She was there in front of me and then I lost sight of her. I felt a nudge behind my knee, and I looked down and this submarine-like figure was below me. Then she lifted me up onto her back, my face was over her blowhole. I felt her immense power and loving protection and was exhilarated and in love! How lucky was I? This was a once-in-a-lifetime moment, I thought. She picked me up again two days later.

How did I find myself on the back of this whale in the middle of the Pacific Ocean at the age of 60? I have to go back to my darkest times to explain how I brought myself to the Islands of Tonga.

One night my husband sat in a chair with a gun in his lap, watching me sleep. When I woke up and saw him, he mused about killing me and the children and then taking his own life rather than allowing me to leave him. Chilling moments like this were normal. I heard him say, "What you want doesn't matter. I'm more important than you. I save lives."

253

It was after hearing my husband of nearly 20 years say this that I really saw who he was for the very first time. This realization was the unspoken truth I had accepted all along. This wasn't a good marriage, though from outside appearances we seemed to have an idyllic life. My husband was a heart surgeon. We had three adorable children. We lived in an historic lakefront Florida mansion with a tennis court and swimming pool. We hosted huge dinners and public tours of the home for fundraisers. Our trips to his home in Italy to be with his mother were wonderful. Our trips to the mountains or the seaside were amazing. But there was a secret terror my children and I endured. We felt panic whenever he came home and we heard the garage door opening, knowing he might be enraged for some infraction of the rules. We were walking on eggshells, never knowing whether it would be Dr. Nice or Mr. Monster. What I wanted now, more than anything, was to protect myself and my children. I was taking our three children, whom he called "worthless parasites", and I was going to leave the perfect life to escape the nightmare. No amount of money was worth being abused. So I didn't respond to my husband's outrageous statement of murder and about who mattered and how he saved lives. I was conditioned to be fearful but this time I wasn't going to be drawn into a debate. I called his bluff. Despite the panic in my gut, I was going to escape. I finally knew he was wrong and had faith that leaving was the right option. I finally was able to see it. I mattered. I was just as important and so were our children.

The conditioned response of panic and fear lived in my gut, but deep down I knew I mattered. That anxiety was the subtext in my life for years to come but these were the first steps to healing. I was taking action. I was fearfully taking control of my life. I had hope for the future though I had no idea what that looked like. I had childlike optimism that was stronger than the fear. I was motivated to do this for my children and that gave me strength. Doing for them gave me the ability to take action.

How did I come to think my needs did not matter as my normal? When I was 6, my parents divorced. I learned then that what I wanted didn't matter. It became natural for me to put up with things I didn't choose. My mother, without warning me, left my dad and moved us to another house. There was no preparation. No discussions. I was shanghaied overnight to a new town and ripped from the life I knew.

My childish world had been perfect. My nature as the youngest of four children was to be the happy-go-lucky entertainer to my siblings. I was a funny little imaginative dreamer. I spent long playful days outside in nature unsupervised and reliant on my own imagination. I grew up near the ocean and was at home in and under the water. In our yard I climbed trees, dug in the dirt, played with bugs, and collected flowers and leaves. My cat had kittens one night and I watched with a flashlight under my sheets the wonder of her birthing her babies. I was fascinated and connected to animals and nature and the beauty of the world around me. Two people can stand side by side and see the same stormy weather. One can say in a sad voice, "It's raining" while another can say, "Hurrah! It's raining!" Once I was so hot that I was overjoyed when it began to rain. I immediately ran outside, fully dressed, dancing to feel the pleasure of being soaking wet. I loved the indulgence of simple pleasures and finding joy in simple moments.

After divorce, my new world was sad. I just wanted to go home to my dad, but I had no control over my life. I plotted how to get back to him but that was never going to happen. Worse still, my dad remarried and a little girl my same age became his new daughter living in my house. I felt replaceable. I became so sad and miserable that I punished myself by plucking out all my eyelashes, making myself feel so hideous and ugly that I hid behind my bangs and eyebrows with my chin buried in my neck. I was now shy and embarrassed to be seen. I just wanted to feel good again. I became so adept at shoving my feelings down and taking the focus off me by entertaining others that my shyness was masked with my adapted gregarious way of making other people happy.

Underneath I was still ashamed and embarrassed although I couldn't articulate all these buried layers of feelings. People were attracted to me mainly because I made them feel good. Which made me feel good. That charm and playful irreverent humor was what attracted my husband to me when we met. He recognized my intelligence and wit. He was a handsome surgeon from Italy. We fell in love. I devoted myself to him and felt so happy to create a home with him and my babies. But the hidden flaw was his monster side which I tried to calm with silly irreverence or simply hid until he calmed down. He never hit me. His cruel words were his weapon. With his Jekyll and Hyde personality, I got his happy side only half the time.

Waking up to see him watching me sleep in this chilling moment was the turning point for me to realize I had to take action and leave.

More terrifying was to face the unknown future but I found strength focusing on my children, who mattered and needed my protection. I chose to take control of my life and reject being a victim. I had to make a safe world where my babies could be nurtured and thrive. I loved helping them dream big and seek options. I showed them that life is meant to be joyous and fun. Always playful and irreverent, I once surprised my serious children on the way to school saying, "Just kidding, we are going to the theme park today." Happiness is contagious and they caught it from me. My children have grown and have amazing stories of success. My daughter flew F-16s and is a professional pilot with a major airline. My son, ironically, saves lives as a paramedic. My youngest son is leaving Wall Street to pursue his dream of living in Italy. They are my progenies, and we are kindred in our desire to make a difference in this world despite discouragement from their father. I taught them through example to pivot and explore options and change their perspectives when needed.

Once divorced, I set a path to working in the healing field of orthopedics. I loved that field because it works to make improvements and fix what is broken in people. I balanced work around my children's needs. I built a successful manual therapy practice in a busy orthopedic group, and I was on staff at Cirque du Soleil taking care of amazing athletes. The energy exchange with patients of all ages and walks of life was my greatest privilege. Focusing on their ailments allowed me to help them find ways to heal. And I benefited from their energy. It took a long time for me to find a way to retire from my beloved healing practice once it became physically impossible on my body.

Solving what was next for me was my puzzle, and who could imagine that my solution to changing careers was to take my life savings, and buy a restaurant in the South Pacific islands of Tonga? There were many steps to get there, and it didn't happen overnight, but I was open to inspiration that came to me to explore options and possibilities. I was anxious but ultimately fearless, and tuned in to positive energy and took many leaps of faith. Swimming with whales first brought me there and their magnificence then lured me to stay. Those magnificent creatures took care of me in the water with their power and protective gentleness just as I had taken care of so many others. We were kindred spirits. Locally, they called me the Whale Whisperer. Being open and optimistic to possibilities allows the world to meet you halfway. I met amazing people there and I helped many who stopped by our marina cafe. I always see possibilities and solutions and cannot stay silent when I see what is possible.

Hearing their amazing stories was inspirational. I'm so grateful for those experiences. Their stories could fill many books. The brave journeys of these fearless travelers left me in awe. Anyone traveling to Tonga in the middle of the ocean shares the spirit of exploration of possibilities. When it was time for me to leave Tonga because of many orthopedic injuries that needed surgery, I entrusted the restaurant to my dear sailor friend for his promise to pay me once he turned a profit. Sadly, he died and the restaurant along with him. I lost my life savings. Still, I felt grateful and like I was the richest woman in the world.

I have traveled all over the world through staying fearless and open to options. I love mingling with land and sea creatures. On an amazing night dive in the Cayman Islands, I saw octopuses change to psychedelic colors. I've been on shipwrecks 100 feet below, peacefully swimming alongside sharks. I climbed Machu Picchu and hung out with llamas. In Thailand I rode an elephant, hugged tigers, and a boa constrictor hugged me. In Hong Kong, I ran a 5k on St Patrick's Day and partied with gorgeous lady men. Sailing around Necker Island I wound up in the hot tub with my idol, Sir Richard Branson.

Important lessons have come over my lifetime. My mother taught me it is better to give than to receive and, as a child, it made little sense until I saw the joy it brings. My father taught me forgiveness is freedom from pain of the past. Circumstances taught me to be courageous and fly into the face of fear. Now I always look forward through my windshield, not backward through my rear-view mirrors. Forgive, learn, and move forward.

A key lesson I learned over time was that focusing on others instead of myself during dark moments raises our vibration and helps them and me, all at once. When I feel my worst, I turn my energy to doing things for others and it lifts me out of wallowing in my own misery. I am an eternal optimist and, in the darkest moments, of which there have been many, I strive to reset feeling happy. I summon positive energy and search for silver linings, not like a frivolous Pollyanna but as a fearless seeker of solutions. I am a magnet to positivity. I indulge my senses and search for pleasure in the simplest of moments. I expect positive energy to prevail, and I am rewarded with experiences with people and creatures who are drawn to me.

An important lesson came most recently for that background anxiety that I tried to quell with escapist behaviors. When faced with that panic in my gut, I used avoidance, hedonistic pleasure-seeking, and trying to please other people to make me feel better. This most wonderful gift came from the wise Dr. Joe Dispenza. Through meditation, the power of my own mind is the key to override and reprogram my reactions. I recognize it, put a halt to it, and replace it with my new thoughts. I'm so grateful for these self-healing tools.

I'm so grateful at my age not to be in a nursing home but to have had so many wonderful experiences, and I'm looking forward to more. I willfully defy my age. If I allowed fear of unseen possibilities to hamper my imagination, I might be sitting in assisted living now with an empty bucket list. I remain attractive to positive energy, viability and being useful. I haven't finished my bucket list! I'm always imagining what could be next. I know with my mind I can summon the feelings of anything being possible whenever I need it. I optimistically explore options and what is possible, and I strive to help others find solutions. The calmness I feel now, thanks to lessons learned, reminds me I'm on the back of that powerful gentle whale, feeling fearless and powerful.

Prayer of Optimism

by Barbara Gardner

Allow my optimism and imagination to
power through darkness and fear.

Let my heart be generous and forgive others
for the harm and the pain that is now in our past.

Guide me to see the hidden silver linings
that adverse circumstances provide.

Let me be grateful for what I have and
to find the joy in simple pleasures that surround me.

Let me remain imaginative and playful in
life with boundless optimism for what is possible.

Let me reject negative circumstances and embrace
my ability to respond by fearlessly exploring options.

Let me contribute and bring joy and inspiration
to others, helping them to find their power
within to see endless possibilities.

About

Barbara Gardner

Barbara Gardner's remarkable journey emerged from the vibrant energy of New York, where she experienced the idyllic days of water sports and tight-knit communities. Florida became her home, where she raised three children before ultimately settling in Colorado to be closer to family.

A college student torn between art and nursing; Barbara's nurturing spirit led her towards a career in healthcare. She worked in hospitals and orthopedic surgical practices, specializing in physical therapy to aid patients in recovering from injuries and degenerative conditions. Her expertise even took her to the mesmerizing world of Cirque du Soleil at Disney World. In Orlando, she became an entrepreneur, owning a business in the healing arts and mastering Reiki. Real estate investing became her passion, and she obtained the necessary licenses.

Retiring from orthopedics, Barbara embarked on adventurous world travel. Destiny led her to the South Pacific, where she acquired and nurtured a marina café in the captivating Kingdom of Tonga. Returning to the United States, she focused on real estate investments and thrived as a Colorado Realtor, guiding clients with her experience. Constantly expanding her knowledge in the healing arts, Barbara also found solace in visiting her children across the country.

Barbara Gardner's extraordinary journey encapsulates resilience, adventure, and boundless compassion. From New York's vibrant community to raising a family in Florida, her artistic and nurturing talents guided her through nursing, orthopedics, and captivating experiences with Cirque du Soleil. Entrepreneurship, Reiki mastery, and real estate investments enriched her path.

Traveling to the South Pacific and returning to Colorado, she gracefully navigated life's transitions, always embracing personal growth. Her story finds its rightful place in this anthology—a tapestry of inspiration woven with threads of strength, adventure, and unwavering devotion to family.

linktr.ee/barbaragardner

Fritzner Desty

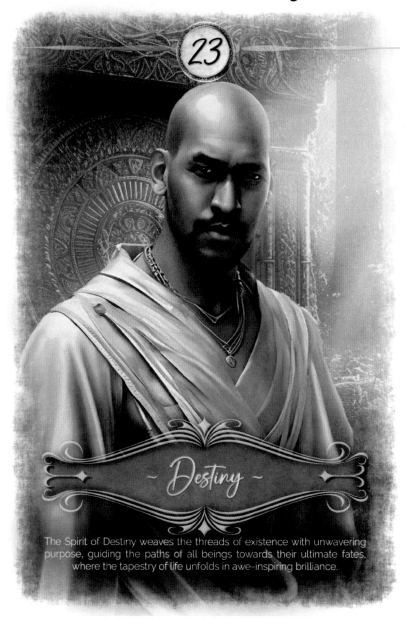

~ Destiny ~

The Spirit of Destiny weaves the threads of existence with unwavering purpose, guiding the paths of all beings towards their ultimate fates, where the tapestry of life unfolds in awe-inspiring brilliance.

Spirit of Destiny

by Fritzner Desty

It has taken me almost four decades to finally understand that one must make a conscious decision to be happy, to be grateful, and to have faith that tomorrow can be better than today in times of uncertainty. I have also understood that one must learn to live a life without minding the opinion or judgment of others. Learning who I was and who I was becoming enabled me to embrace my inner self, the same part of me that caused shivers to my spine out of fear; the part of me that caused tears, knowing that, in some parts of the world, people like me get killed. In my teenage years and mid-20s, those feelings caused me to have suicidal thoughts. I am glad life is very different now, as I have learned to become a stronger being.

It all started while living as a devoted Christian in New York City at the age of 19. I was living a life that I felt wasn't mine. Everyone seemed happy around me, while my life seemed gray and dull. I had fallen into a dark place and had no voice of my own. I felt as if I was a prisoner within my own soul and body; the outer me kept the inner me as a prisoner. My attraction towards men — that had been repressed for years — wanted to break free, while the outer me refused to accept it. This war raged on for more than a decade.

As the years passed by, I still rejected the idea that I was homosexual. I rejected the idea I could be different from everyone else. I rejected my desires and emotions. For most of my life, I lived the life everyone around me was expecting of me. However, with time, the situation became overwhelming.

As my attraction for the same sex grew stronger, I began pleading with God to take my desires away. Over several years nothing changed. I felt sad and betrayed by the emotions I have been suppressing. I thought if I went to church, I could pray those feelings and desires away. However, the feelings remained unchanged.

As time went by, I slowly allowed myself to accept the fact that I was different. That moment of realization made me feel even more hopeless. Different emotions ran through my mind, I felt physically stuck, as if life was about to end. I felt that letting my real self out would be liberating but instead, I found myself unloved and unwanted. I thought death would be better than the embarrassment and pain I would place on my family. I also thought that I would not be able to get married, have children, enjoy close friendships, and most of all I would lose my relationship with God. I felt I had lost my sense of identity.

As time passed, I started to replace my suicidal thoughts and depression with new dreams, hope, and most of all new beliefs about the future. In my darkest place, I started to have hope that my future could be brighter. I started listening to podcasts and reaffirmed brighter thoughts of the future with affirmations. I started taking small messages of hope, and believed they could be true. I worked to create a new reality in my mind. I also made a personal decision that I would love myself and not let anyone stop me from doing so. I decided I would no longer show anger towards myself, and I would believe only the best outcomes for the future. I decided to love myself.

To move forward, I decided to love every aspect of my life, including my attraction towards men. I began dating, and I enjoyed dating men. It was empowering to meet other people who were just like me. I felt more comfortable with myself as I realized I was not alone and there was a community of people like me. I continued replacing old thoughts with a new way of thinking. I replaced suicidal thoughts, depression, and hopelessness with new dreams and hope. I began to dream that I could have someone who would love me, have children, and have a candid relationship with God.

As I continued to surrender my old self and started to love and appreciate who I was becoming, my perspective started shifting. My perception of people changed dramatically. I had to forgive people's negative words on the gay community. I had to learn to take away those thoughts and replaced them with a new thought: everyone deserves to be happy. Most importantly, everyone is loved by the Creator equally. I had replaced fears with daring dreams that I would be happy and accomplish set goals.

I decided I wouldn't wait for my parents' acceptance to come at the expense of my own happiness, and I let go of the need to be loved by them. I decided the love I have for myself is enough. I also let go of the feeling that I can control people's opinion of me. I also had to learn to let go of my negative opinion of other people. I truly learned to live in a place full of love; in my new world there's no place for hatred, but only love.

I can also learn to control who can influence my life and my decision-making. I learned it is best to have a few close friends who can help becoming the best version of oneself. With my world full of love, I decided to extend love to my parents for where they are in their life, regardless of whether they accepted me as a gay son. Out of love, I decided it was better to have my parents in my life rather than not having them at all. In time we have learned to love and accept one another for who we are.

After accepting my new identity, I entertained the idea that I could be in a relationship. In the beginning of my first relationship, I was anxious and sad at times that I was dating men instead of women. It seemed I had many unresolved emotions which I had to deal with one by one, but I took the time to extend grace to myself and be patient. I gave myself time to heal and acknowledge that the old self is still here. During my healing I had to repeat to myself that I had to reject others' opinions of me over and over. I had to learn that people's opinions are not important, and I should continue to live my truth and find my own identity. This was a lesson I had to frequently repeat to myself.

With time, I began to feel at peace while being in a relationship with a man. Dating in the gay community gave me a sense of belonging again. As time goes by, the fear of others, including my parents, does not matter to me anymore. Even though my parents have not fully embraced my new identity yet, I continue to love them for where they are in life, instead of loving them for where I hope they would be.

While dating, it is possible to fall in love. I fell in love with a beautiful soul, but with time we realized we were not compatible. I remember it was painful to walk away but walking away was one teaching moment in my life. I have now learned to walk away from situations, people, and life circumstances that do not help me to become the person I dream to be. I have learned it is OK to be alone for a while, until that special one comes along.

In dating, I don't have to be aligned or be liked by every single man; I just need to find that one single person who ticks most of my boxes on my wish list. I learned to set a clear picture of my dreams, hopes, and desires. I am now witnessing each of those dreams becoming reality.

It seems what I needed all along, was an alignment with myself and the Creator of the universe. Once I accepted myself, all dreams started to fall into place. Having clarity about what makes me happy — including being in a relationship and having children — has attracted my handsome husband into my life. I have been married for five years, and I am very grateful to have finally met the man of my dreams.

Looking back on this journey of self-acceptance, I would like to encourage my younger self to keep on moving forward, especially when life gets hard and difficult. To have dreams, goals, and to believe that dreams are possible. People will have an opinion about how you should live your life, but the only opinion that matters is your own. I would tell my younger self that your desires, dreams, and hopes will be a beacon of light when you are in a dark place in life, and to have a clear sense of who you are, love who you are, and love who you are becoming with each new day.

Triumph and Compassion

by Fritzner Desty

When all seems foggy, dreams seem distant,
And the world whispers doubts, leaving us resistant.

Oh, Creator of the universe, hear our plea,
Reveal our identity and set us free.

In a world that questions where we belong,
Grant us the wisdom to stand strong.

Embrace us with love, dispel our fear,
Remind us that our purpose is crystal clear.

When doubt paints a picture of a love that's gone,
We know deep inside, that belief is wrong.

Creator of the universe, in times of despair,
Wrap us in your arms, show us you care.

Thank you for guiding us to self-acceptance,
For nurturing our souls with loving tolerance.

In your divine presence, we find our worth,
Celebrating our uniqueness since our birth.

Creator of the universe, we offer our gratitude,
For your unconditional love, so absolute.

In moments of feeling lost and all alone,
Please comfort us, make your presence known.

Show us the path to grace, forgiveness, and light,
Guide us through the darkness, day, and night.

For we are grateful, knowing deep within,
That the creator's love extends to all kin.

As we embrace our true identity,
May we inspire others with love's intensity.

Creator of the universe, forever we'll proclaim,
Your love for all creations, always the same.

About
Fritzner Desty

A Journey of Triumph and Compassion

In the captivating anthology, prepare to be inspired by the remarkable life story of Fritzner Desty, a registered nurse on a transformative path to becoming a Mental Health Nurse Practitioner. With unwavering determination and a heart filled with empathy, Fritzner has embarked on a mission to help others conquer the adversities they face, drawing from his own personal triumphs.

Raised in a nurturing household amidst the warmth of a loving family of six siblings, Fritzner's upbringing instilled in him the values of resilience and compassion. Bound by a deep bond, their unwavering support propelled him forward, enabling him to surmount countless trials throughout his own journey.

Embracing the love of his life as his partner, Fritzner discovered that love transcends conventional boundaries, manifesting in diverse shapes and forms. The profound love bestowed upon him by his spouse and cherished family exemplifies the power of compassion and human connection—a force that has driven Fritzner to dedicate his life to uplifting others.

As an immigrant hailing from Haiti, Fritzner has shattered the confines of societal expectations, demonstrating that anyone can accomplish their aspirations with the right intentions and unyielding determination. His resolute spirit and unshakeable faith have served as guiding lights, propelling him forward on his pursuit to make a lasting impact in the lives of those he encounters.

Within the pages of this anthology, Fritzner Desty opens his heart to share his awe-inspiring narrative. Through his words, he imparts the wisdom he has gained from his personal triumphs and reveals the secrets to unlocking one's true potential. Prepare to be captivated by his authentic and heartfelt storytelling as he invites you to join him on a voyage of self-discovery and transformation.

With each turn of the page, Fritzner's compelling story will ignite the spark of hope within you, reminding you that amidst life's trials, resilience and love can triumph. His life's purpose is to empower others to become the best versions of themselves, and in this anthology, he joyfully shares that purpose with you.

Get ready to be moved, inspired, and forever changed as you delve into the extraordinary world of Fritzner Desty, a beacon of light and an embodiment of the limitless possibilities that lie within every soul.

linktr.ee/fritznerdesty

Ramon Martin

24

~ Bravery ~

In the face of adversity, the indomitable spirit of bravery and courage rises, igniting a flame that defies fear, surpasses limits, and paves the path to greatness.

Unlock Your Greatness

by Ramon Martin

As humans we are capable of doing more than we know. God made us to be extraordinary, not the average Joe. There is greatness within you. Each and every one of us was born with a gift. If you don't know what your gift or talent is, ask God to reveal it to you. It doesn't matter how young or how old you are, you can get started on your goals and dreams at any age. The greatness within you is ready to be unlocked. One day you will tell your story of how you overcame what you went through, and it will be someone else's survival guide.

Growing up in the San Francisco Bay area, I was in special education classes from the sixth grade until my senior year of high school. In third grade, I lost confidence in myself, I had a hard time focusing, and developed bad habits. I was getting put down by teachers whom you would normally look to for encouragement, leadership, and guidance. It was my first of many encounters with the harsh realities of the world we live in.

In sixth grade, my first year in middle school, I met with a teacher by the name of Paula Ginsburg. I didn't know she would make such a major impact on my life. She wasn't just a teacher, she was my mentor, a leader, community activist, and a huge environmentalist. Ms. Ginsburg used to have us listen to inspirational content. There was one in particular she would play constantly, which has stayed with me until this day. It was by the great motivational speaker, Les Brown. In the year 2020, I was fortunate to work with the great Les Brown and attend his class which led to amazing opportunities and meeting extraordinary people. This all started with a cassette tape my teacher, Paula Ginsburg, played in my sixth-grade classroom, and came full circle in 2020 when I attended the Les Brown Power Voice class.

Feeling stagnant most of my adult life, I knew there had to be a better solution than working a 9-to-5 and chasing someone else's dream. I just didn't know how or know where to go or who to ask. Staying in the comfort zone when you're in pursuit of unlocking your greatness will not yield the results you need. Although I was hearing success stories on television and social media about how people accomplish their goals and dreams, my desired goals still seemed out of reach for me. I was good at encouraging and believing others to go for their goals and dreams but lacked confidence in myself to do the same. We can be so hard on ourselves. I used to tell myself I wouldn't be able to succeed in anything beyond the unknown. Wanting a better life, wanting a better situation for myself and my three kids, I knew something had to change. Frustrated, living paycheck to paycheck, and not able to get my kids what they needed… I felt like I'd failed my family.

The Journey of Being Courageous

I continue to lean into fear and being courageous in life. I've learned life can be a numbers game. I learned how to handle rejection well; the more times I'm rejected, the more courage I develop. Staying consistent, taking action, and placing my faith in God are what keep me courageous in the everyday journey.

After I completed that course with Les Brown, it was time to go back to normal life. It was time to put what I'd learned and my personal development into action. I knew I had to make some great changes in my life. It was time to lean into fear more than ever before. Realizing I had to keep my vibration high, I intentionally worked to shift my paradigms by reading and listening to more personal development books and audio. I had to end some relationships that didn't benefit me in my growth development. I started building my personal network with only like-minded people. I continue to have communities of accountability partners who I meet with on a weekly basis.

In order to stay courageous, I realized I couldn't do it on my own. I needed to invest in myself; a personal coach and mentor could definitely help me. I felt fear surface again, this time over the thought of the cost of investing in myself. With the support and encouragement of my beloved significant other, I leaned into fear once again and bet on myself. I partnered with Dolly Cina, a mastermind mentor. We worked on learning how to change my paradigms and have control over my thoughts. This also taught me how to push my limits.

Keeping consistent in reading personal development material and staying in contact with my accountability partners also helped me push past my limits. Learning to build self-confidence was also a major key to unlocking my greatness. I wrote messages of hope and encouragement to myself and looked in the mirror while reciting inspirational quotes. I learned the importance of loving myself in order to love and help others. I recognized I needed to become the best version of myself in order to have an abundant relationship with my soulmate. I continue these practices on a daily basis.

Changing my self-image was also a major key to unlocking my greatness. I had to get my shift together. I had to shift my mindset and change the way I thought of myself. I learned to look at situations as possible opportunities and solutions. All of this led me to become a public speaker and coach. Making a difference while making a living gave me the keys to unlock my greatness. It also gave me my set of keys to an open heaven.

Now I am coaching people around the globe and sharing my story.

Once you unlock your greatness, it is only the beginning. Once you've reached one of your goals and dreams there will be many more goals and dreams you will accomplish. Unlocking your greatness is like having a set of keys with a storage box full of padlocks. It may take time to find the right key to unlock the right padlock. My mom, who raised three kids and already had a good career working at a law firm, decided to go back to night school to develop her skills and further her career. Her determination and sacrifice to better herself helped her find the key to unlock her greatness, which led to buying her family a home. That home is now paid off.

Abundance is our birthright, and our calling is what we are made for. We have the option and the tools necessary to create an abundant life. You can create an abundance of many things: money, friends, cars, books... just to name a few. Unlocking your greatness and creating your abundance go hand in hand. It's about getting to know about yourself from within.

Find a coach or a mentor who can help you see the greatness within you. Seek someone who is where you want to get to, someone who believes in you, and borrow their belief in you. When I didn't see and believe in myself, my mentor showed me how to believe I had greatness within and showed me how to use my God-given gifts. Sometimes it just takes someone to believe in you before you can believe in yourself.

Stay on a high vibration level. Keep your vibes on a high positive frequency. It's almost impossible and very difficult to unlock the greatness within you on a low vibration. Holding yourself on a high vibration means you must surround yourself with positive people, people who share the same things you want, and people who want to see you unlock your greatness. My mentor, Les Brown, calls this practice OQP (Only Quality People). Reading personal development books is also a known strategy that the most powerful and successful people in the world use. You can join study groups in your local area or virtually.

Don't worry about how to get started on unlocking your greatness - JUST START! The only right time to start on your goals and dreams is RIGHT NOW. So, if you're thinking when a good time is to start... the time is now. I've heard it said that you don't have to be great to get started on unlocking your greatness, but you have to get started to be great. Taking that huge leap of faith, without worrying about how or where you're going to land, will serve you well. Focus on the goal and the prize not the how-to.

Fail forward. If you fall short of the goal, do not be discouraged. Some of the richest people on the planet have failed numerous times before finding success. In fact, failing is how they found success. Their ideas have been rejected frequently by multiple people and businesses. For example, following his professional basketball career, Magic Johnson pursued the business world as an entrepreneur. He was an amazing athlete and undeniably a phenomenal success, but even he got rejected by 10 banks before the 11th bank accepted his loan application. KFC, the fried chicken fast-food franchise now known around the world, was founded by Colonel Sanders. After failing at multiple jobs and business ventures, he was nearly 65 years old when he started Kentucky Fried Chicken. Affectionately known today simply as KFC, today that restaurant is a multibillion-dollar, worldwide franchise. If he had given up every time he failed, he would never have created such an incredible legacy. Don't focus on the failures; learn from them and move forward.

The major key to a better future is you. We are responsible for our own failures and successes. In life there will be many distractions, setbacks, and delays but it's up to us to unlock our greatness ourselves. Yes, there will be people, tools, and information along the journey that will help you, but you have to be intentional about accessing the greatness within you. Let the greatness — and the God in you — thrive to limitless abundance and prosperity.

As I reflect now on the pain caused by my third-grade teacher and my special education experience all those years ago, I realized it was not just incredibly painful then; it left a lifelong scar. I kept the pain and hurt inside for a very long time. Those feelings of inadequacy and anxiety silently haunted me for years because I thought no one cared or that there was no help available to me. Feeling like I was the only one with no skills or gifts, I was just drifting aimlessly through life.

Now that I have put in the necessary work and have shifted my mindset, I've gotten comfortable in my own skin and found the confidence I lacked for so long. That shift has changed everything for me. I've changed and my circumstances have dramatically changed. I'm thankful to my sixth-grade teacher for introducing Les Brown to me through those cassette tapes. I believe that's what led me to join his class in 2020 and consequently to figure out what I had to do in order to unlock my greatness.

To sum it all up for you, I created an acronym for what I did to unlock the greatest in me. I believe it may help you as well. So, here it is: UNLOCK your greatness!!!

Understand you have greatness in you

Nurture seeds of positivity

Look for role models

Own your part in the process

Create confidence

Know what you want

Prayer for Courage

by Ramon Martin

Heavenly Father,

Thank you for your grace and mercy. I pray for my dear readers who are struggling with fear and uncertainty. Please grant them the courage to face their fears and overcome them. Help them to trust in your guidance and to have faith that you will always be with them.

May they find the strength to step out of their comfort zones, to take risks, and to pursue their dreams. Help them to stand up for what they believe in, even in the face of adversity.

May they be filled with the courage to face the challenges of life with grace and determination. Help them to be a light in the darkness, and to inspire others to do the same.

Thank you for your love and for the courage that you instill in us. May we always remember that with you, all things are possible.

In Jesus' name I pray,

Amen

About

Ramon Martin

Ramon, a native of the vibrant San Francisco Bay area, is a remarkable individual whose life embodies the essence of prosperity and personal growth. With a career in the logistics industry spanning over 17 years, Ramon has cultivated deep and meaningful relationships with countless customers and clients, earning their trust and admiration.

However, Ramon realized that life had much more to offer beyond the confines of his job. Fueled by an insatiable desire for personal development and a yearning to make a profound impact on others, he stepped out of his comfort zone and placed a daring bet on himself. It was during this transformative journey that Ramon had the privilege of collaborating with the legendary motivational speaker, Les Brown, along with several other esteemed coaches and inspirational figures.

Guided by their wisdom and inspired by their unwavering belief in his potential, Ramon has now dedicated his life to helping others conquer their fears, unleash their hidden talents, and unlock the boundless potential within them. Through his words, actions, and contagious enthusiasm, Ramon serves as a beacon of hope and empowerment, motivating individuals from all walks of life to strive for greatness.

Whether he is delivering a captivating keynote address, leading transformative workshops, or offering one-on-one coaching, Ramon's mission remains the same: to inspire and uplift others, empowering them to break free from self-imposed limitations and achieve their wildest dreams.

With his innate ability to connect with people on a deep, personal level, Ramon creates a safe and nurturing environment where individuals feel supported, encouraged, and empowered to embrace their authentic selves. His infectious energy and unwavering dedication to his craft make him an invaluable guide on the path to personal and professional fulfillment.

Keymartin39@gmail.com

TikTok @Guapolatte

YouTube @ramonmartin79

Chris Dyer

~ Courage ~

The Goddess of Courage, with her majestic presence, inspires hearts to transcend fear's grasp, to boldly embrace the unknown, and to unleash the limitless power that resides within their souls.

Courage is Her Birthright

by Chris Dyer

"The imagination, once stretched, can never regain its original dimensions" -Oliver Wendell Holmes

A beautiful summer night on a hotel rooftop in Athens, Greece, offered a most amazing epiphany. It was a moment that years of self-study and reflection had finally revealed what teachers, mentors and guides of my journey had offered through their wisdom. Until the emotion and feeling of the lesson resonate with the student, they can remain dormant for an indeterminate amount of time. I am grateful that the timing and the lesson opened a deeper understanding of the meaning of manifestation and of the Law of Gestation, which states that we must release our expectations of things to occur based on our human timeline.

As a 10-year-old student in the fifth grade, I was mesmerized by stories told through Greek mythology. I easily memorized the names of the gods and goddesses and their respective 'superpowers'. The stories and allegories, as their lives intersected with humans, and all the metaphors and storylines within the plots modeled for a young mind, created an early framework of life circumstances, culture, and an appreciation for early philosophy.

The Greek islands hold a certain majesty of bold architecture that has been replicated for millennia. Enormous temples, erected to honor the memories of these gods and goddesses, allow us to step back into history with a sense of awe and majesty. The meanings imparted in each are rich.

As that 10-year-old girl, I would dream about visiting this magical country and travel amongst its many islands to partake in the experience and immersion of Greek culture. What I couldn't fathom is that, in human life years, it would take me 45 years to manifest that dream into reality!

During the dusk hours of June 17th, 2022, our tour group gathered on the rooftop of our hotel for a meet-and-greet after a long day of travels. While in my jet-lagged state, I glanced across the skyline to behold the surprise of the Acropolis, erected on a mountaintop. Dramatic lights cast glorious shadows to outline the details of its stature across the sky only a couple of miles away. It was breathtaking to behold and was the moment that brought everything to my understanding. Time stopped. My eyes welled up with tears.

It was like a moment in a movie, where the main character has flashes of their entire life sequence flying by in reverse: people, places, and memories racing backwards in visual pictures in their mind. And I was that young girl sitting at her desk, again, with a dream. An ask. The beginning of a manifestation that took years of healing and allowing the pieces of life to arrange themselves beautifully into the cosmic puzzle that life is.

That little girl was shy, unseen, and unheard. And yet, she possessed a spark of creativity and knowledge that the world has more to offer and greater experiences to behold than the sheltered projections of her childhood.

What the girl did have was an inherent courage to stand up against her paradigm, much to the chagrin of her mother, who allowed her own fears to always impede the ability to stand out. This courage would surface several times throughout her life, which offered glimpses of power that were destined to reveal themselves when afforded the opportunity to break out of the generational and societal molds.

The mother loved her daughter yet couldn't allow her the freedom to express her imagination and courage. She had been raised by an abusive, alcoholic father, which created massive insecurities and emptiness within her. Naturally, her instincts were to overprotect her only child, who had been born during a tumultuous time, and without a father.

The fear, lack of support and love, and her own insecurities, were handed down as a gift to the girl. A lifetime of shifts and self-reflection would reveal that those gifts were not intended to be carried. The adult version of this child handed those gifts of fear, feelings of lack, and insecurity back to the universe. Still, she persisted and stretched her insatiable curiosity, taking many leaps that were frowned upon by her mother.

The adult in the story, of course, is a depiction of the journey of self-healing, self-awareness and learning to trust. The quantum leaps created in the past four years have helped to reframe the story of a courageous and creative girl into an empowered woman goddess. The goddess-in-training began her truest and most beautiful work the moment she decided she was worth the investment to own her own story…in her own words.

My earlier successes in life were attributed to bold and courageous steps despite my insecurities. I had always held the picture of what I wanted, and circumstances I would no longer settle for, knowing and holding true that whatever I desired was up to me to create. And yet, I was still beholden to the old paradigms of living under the control of others and the desires of what they thought my life should be.

I never knew my father and have no physical artifact as proof of the person who helped initiate my arrival on this rock. I have studied my own subconscious to reveal that he was not the person my mother portrayed him to be to me. Not knowing anything about this man allows me the freedom of insight to extract the fascinating qualities about my most favorite character traits and attribute them to this unfound, physical entity. I get to create a narrative about this person that is enticingly full of energy, enthusiasm, and adventure...the person I choose to be, considering the programming of the past to stay comfortable and play small...always playing inside the lines. (Any pique of curiosity or daring, risky behavior was immediately tempered.)

Living with this duality of courage and insecurity, craving more knowledge, and being held to smallness created inner turmoil, and misunderstanding of my intuition and lack of self-trust. At the tender age of nine, I was told that my feelings and emotions were inappropriate, therefore I learned I couldn't trust any thoughts or feelings. They became abated for decades. There were three times in my life when I considered the world would be better without me. Three times I felt I couldn't endure another day.

The last time I felt miserably alone in my own skin, misunderstood, and without support, I sought out the help of a doctor. He quickly diagnosed me with anxiety and offered an antidepressant to help calm me so I could function without inner stress and constant tears — a distraction to cover my emotional wounds that I'd carried for a lifetime.

For 17 years I survived on antidepressants. I tried numerous times to wean myself off (Courage trying to reveal herself), not wanting to be dependent on medication to keep my emotions on an even keel. Funny thing was, after two-three weeks without it, I decided I liked myself better while taking antidepressants. It was easier and the path of least resistance. Too many people were relying on me to show up and hustle, the trap of the human condition and paradigm. I hadn't yet understood the value of the degree of work and self-reflection that would be required to decide that I no longer wished to be hooked by my old story and insecurities of lack and loneliness.

2019 was the year of waking up the dormant goddess of courage. I was ready to chisel away the years of scars of my generous heart and soul. I knew the universe had more answers to reveal wisdom, love, and light. Another goddess who had shone her light, offered a new door of possibilities, and cleared a portal. Old stories were rewritten, and old thought patterns were traded up for understanding and knowing and trusting. Beautiful colors were added to puzzle pieces of my life that once had been misunderstood circumstances but now had meaning and purpose. Within six weeks of dedicated self-work, I released my hold on the antidepressants, grateful to have new tools to self-regulate my emotions, and continue revealing and healing emotional injuries that no longer served my future.

It is said that the purpose of our life is to know ourselves and then give that wisdom back to the universe, in service. The clarity and understanding of my soul's purpose is unconditional love, for myself, and others. I am eternally grateful for the lessons and work that I have invested to sit in this space of knowing…trusting…having faith that the universe is co-creating with me to inspire others to aspire to knowing themselves. There is no better gift. Today's courage requires me to share this opportunity of healing with others struggling to move beyond and still trapped into holding onto their pain.

On the hotel rooftop in Greece there was a pivotal moment of understanding about the intersections of mythology, parables, and analogies as part of the human form. These stories, shared though the millennium, are about us mortals and how we create impact and manifest our dreams using our gifts. The universe had planted her essence within me the day I arrived on earth.

The duality of humanness allows us to be the essence of

multiple gods and goddesses, at the same instant. Why would it be necessary to choose only one? Stories shared from Greek mythology are parables of human understanding, where humans formed gods and goddesses in their imagination. Modern religion/dogma imprints upon us that we were formed in God's image. What I understand now is quite the opposite: the gods and goddesses of all cultures and religions are inspired from humans.

On one of my walks in the City of Athens, I admired a powerful statue of Athena. I felt her essence as I sat for several minutes on a cold, marble seat, listening to my soul for the next download. A new awareness was seared into me: yes, we can be multiple goddesses and gods. I am Aphrodite and Athena…I am her and she is me. Love, power, courage, protection. Service and strength. My psyche (Goddess of Soul) holds space for all of them. Even as I am placing these words on paper, my awareness is expanding. I have just realized that Psyche is known for her immortality, magical abilities, inner beauty, and butterfly wings…a profound realization, as I have created a brand awareness around butterflies. The universe is truly guiding my soul's purpose and knows my subconscious better than I.

I am grateful for the investment made to reveal my soul which was previously disguised by shadows of emotional scars and false beliefs. As I share this wisdom with you, I continue to be in awe of new discoveries around me every single day. I am an open channel to receive love and signs offered by the universe and share them with those who need to reveal their own courage. We are all connected through the family of gods and goddesses and source.

Healing Prayer

by Chris Dyer

Universe, who out there is excited to bring me on board into their conscious, kind, and meaningful company?

Who values what I bring and are happy to pay me generously for me to bring my presences, my insights, and my gifts to their tribe?

Our values completely align and together we share a powerful vision for a positive and empowering impact. Who is ready to bring me on board to be a part of creative projects that truly inspire people?

Where can I go to contribute and receive at the highest level? Universe, where are you bringing me where my soul and my body are happy?

My breath, my being, and my heart are open. I invite joy and ease into everything that I do.

About

Chris Dyer

Chris Dyer, RT(R) is the Most Valuable Partner (MVP) for Women 40+ and shows them how to create greater vitality, visibility and success in life and business. She holds multiple degrees and certifications in Health Sciences, Life; Leadership Coaching with over 30+years of experience in Clinical Education, Sales and Marketing, and Entrepreneurship. She is a 2 X National Best-Selling Author, and International Speaker. Her Lifestyle.

Legacy and Leadership Program inspires women to strive to higher levels of personal excellence while impacting their communities. Chris lives in sunny Las Vegas, NV with her husband and fur babies. She is also a proud glam-ma to two beautiful kiddos in Colorado. Her happy places are outdoors in the mountains or by the ocean, rivers, lakes, and streams.

She and her husband love traveling and adventures to new and exciting places, especially national parks.

Serving women has been her passion for over 16 years while helping them achieve healthier lives. More recently, she began offering retreats abroad and domestically to encourage the mindset of sharing the gift of travel as a form of expressed abundance. Experiencing new cultures in exciting places, while restoring the body and soul, is a source of joy for herself and the clients she serves. Her cup is truly overflowing and the gift to share with others fills her soul and life's purpose.

chrisdyerconsulting.com
Facebook @ChrisDyerConsults
Instagram @chrisdyerconsulting

Tammy Lee Rose

26

~ Ananda of Love ~

Embracing the ananda of love, we become vessels of light, spreading its transformative power to all who cross our path. Let love guide us, let ananda inspire us, and let our love-infused existence weave a tapestry of harmony in the world

Dance

by Tammy Lee Rose

"A child's life is like a piece of paper on which every person leaves a mark." - Chinese Proverb

In my earliest memories, pure joy filled my heart as my sister and I gleefully ran through the hotel's lengthy hallway, engaging in games of tag and hide-and-seek. Despite assumptions of vacation, the truth was that we lived there. During a brief period in my childhood, my mom, older sister, and I called the hotel our home. After my parents' divorce when I was three, my mom met a new partner, and we were in the process of moving in with him. The hotel was a transition to what should have been a new and happier life.

However, life doesn't always turn out as you would expect, and things took a drastic turn after our stay at the hotel. My mother's new partner, a seemingly respectable government employee by day, transformed into a violent alcoholic by night. His abuse towards my mother became our new normal. While he didn't physically harm me directly, I still felt the blows just the same. Helpless and terrified, I often felt like an outsider, observing the chaos from a detached perspective. Every encounter followed a similar pattern, with our daily routine turning into fear and uncertainty at bedtime as that's usually when his rage would begin after a night of his binge drinking. I would stay awake, seeking solace in my sister's bed, desperate for safety. Back then, I couldn't comprehend the extent of the trauma I experienced, as it was all I knew. It was only when I became a mother myself, looking at my innocent child, that the realization hit me. The thought of my son witnessing such violence shook me to my core.

The environment we grow up in greatly shapes who we become. And so, I became the epitome of introversion. Shyness consumed me, rendering me as the timid, quiet, and fearful child. Childhood should be a time of joy, imagination, and boundless adventure, not plagued by fear, insecurity, and shame. My shyness was suffocating, to the point where unfamiliar faces in our home would send me running and hiding.

Amidst the turmoil, there existed a sanctuary that brought solace and comfort—my time with my Dad. I spent every weekend with him and eagerly embraced the opportunity to be by his side, relishing every minute together. He was the kindest man I've ever known, and I thought he could walk on water! Those cherished memories remain etched in my heart, forever treasured.

And those who were seen dancing, were thought to be insane by those who could not hear the music- Nietzsche

The love for dance has always been an integral part of who I am, though I cannot pinpoint exactly when or how it came to be. Perhaps it was the constant presence of music in my life, thanks to my mom. Despite the abuse she endured, she was always a happy, optimistic person who loved music! Country melodies filled our home as she passionately sang along to the likes of George Jones, Conway Twitty, Johnny Cash, Loretta Lynn and, of course, my namesake, Tammy Wynette. As I grew older, my musical horizons expanded, but the soundtrack of my life remained ever-present. While my singing abilities fell short, dancing became my outlet. It was through dance that my introversion melted away, replaced by a profound sense of joy and liberation.

Growing up in a small town, dance schools were nowhere to be found, leaving my exposure to dance limited to the magical world of movies. I held onto dreams of becoming a prima ballerina, with my room adorned with images of satin pointe shoes and delicate pink tutus. But those dreams remained confined to the walls of my bedroom, as I had never received any formal training. How could I ever consider becoming a dancer without proper training? Then, when I was 16, a dance teacher arrived in my hometown, offering classes in Tap, Jazz, and Ballet. Without hesitation, I signed up for every class. Each moment was pure love, and I never missed a session. Sadly, the teacher departed after just one year, but this brief exposure only solidified my inner certainty. Dance was my true passion. Despite my shyness and quiet demeanor, dance became my refuge—a place where I could transcend myself, embodying different characters. In that realm, my authentic self-emerged, and I experienced a profound bliss as the weight of the world, its stresses and worries, simply vanished.

As high school graduation loomed closer, my friends were charting their paths as teachers and nurses, while I felt adrift. None of those choices resonated with me. Confusion and doubt plagued my mind. Why couldn't I figure things out like everyone else? Why couldn't I conform and follow their lead? The truth was, I wasn't aligned with any of it. The pursuit of a university degree held no joy, bliss, or satisfaction for me. Dance was the singular passion burning within my soul. Being much older now, my ballerina dreams changed to that of dancing on Broadway or perhaps opening my own studio in my hometown. Summoning courage, I secretly requested an application from one of Canada's premier dance programs in Toronto. I kept it hidden from everyone. When the application arrived, I anxiously opened it, only to be deflated and disheartened by the first requirement: a video audition! I tore up the application and tossed it aside. How could I even contemplate filming myself? My struggles with body image compounded my self-doubt, and I lacked substantial experience to showcase. My inner voice berated me, saying, "You fool, who do you think you are? You're not a dancer, not even close. Forget about it."

We travel not to escape life, but for life not to escape us!

That marked the inception of my journey into exploring mindset. While my friends pursued higher education, I delved into the secluded aisles of bookstores, searching for answers in the hidden realm of "self-help." Deep within, I sensed that life held more than the conventional path of acquiring degrees, jobs, marriage, and children. I didn't fit the mold of societal norms—I craved more from life! They say, "Do what you love, and you'll never work a day in your life!" But if dance was no longer an option, what else could bring me joy, passion, and fulfillment? The allure of travel beckoned me. Growing up in a small town on a remote island, opportunities to explore were scarce. I had only been on a plane once, visiting family in Toronto. However, an insatiable wanderlust stirred within me, yearning to discover other countries, embrace diverse cultures, and seek new experiences. Joining the travel industry seemed like the perfect avenue, so I began my journey as a part-time agent in a local agency, embarking on what would become a 25 year career.

Transitioning from a travel agent, I ventured into the world of airlines and embarked on a fulfilling career with Air Canada, which spanned most of my professional life. Growing up in Gander, Newfoundland, an airport town once known as the crossroads of the world, held great significance. It was particularly important to my Dad, as this position came with a great salary and coveted pension, an idealized notion instilled in me from a young age. However, my true excitement stemmed from the travel benefits. And let me tell you, I made full use of them! Finally, I could satisfy my passion for exploring by jetting off to enchanting destinations like Hawaii, Cancun, Barbados, Jamaica, St. Lucia, Grand Cayman, and Miami. Do you notice a pattern? I was irresistibly drawn to warmer climates, perhaps influenced by my upbringing in the chilly, snowy winters of Newfoundland—all I yearned for was the soothing embrace of the beach!

Throughout that period, I forged valuable friendships and cherished unforgettable moments. Nevertheless, my heart yearned for the world of Dance. I dabbled in taking occasional classes and even contemplated the idea of becoming a dance teacher. However, my excuses and rationalizations would inevitably take precedence, causing my dreams to be once again sidelined. The captivating allure of carefree travel, with no commitments or responsibilities, seemed to temporarily numb my aspirations, allowing life to carry on without addressing my true passions.

Even miracles take a little time - Cinderella

In due course, my career with Air Canada led me to Montreal, where I crossed paths with my future husband. We dated for many years and eventually married. Naturally, the next chapter involved embracing motherhood. Despite our initial struggles, we had made peace with the notion that parenthood might not be in the cards for us. However, two weeks prior to my 40th birthday, a delightful surprise awaited me—I discovered that I was pregnant! Overwhelmed with joy and excitement, words cannot capture the depth of my emotions. This marked the beginning of a heartfelt paradigm shift in my life. Motherhood awakened a profound longing within me, revealing the true essence of bliss, and fulfillment I had been seeking. I never really understood how much I wanted to be a Mother, until I became one! I was divinely guided to be a lover, a nurturer, and a caregiver. It served as a poignant wake-up call, prompting me to reassess every aspect of my existence. Here I had found the purest form of love I had always yearned for, yet I lacked the precious time to fully embrace it. I found myself entrusting others to care for my son while I remained chained to the hamster wheel of life to pay the bills, with little free time or flexibility. It pained me deeply. This pivotal moment prompted me to take inventory of my life and embark on a mission to effect change. I resolved to pursue endeavors that brought me joy and fulfillment, creating a life defined by time freedom, allowing me to be fully present for my son.

-Little girls with Dreams, become Women with Vision

As someone who embraced motherhood at a later stage, my focus shifted towards the pursuit of healthy aging, and this was my new mission in my life. It ignited a deep desire within me to impart this value to others. The dream of dance had seemingly faded into the past. However, I recognized that there were other avenues involving movement that I could explore, such as yoga. I pursued certification as a yoga instructor with dreams of having my own studio. Additionally, I ventured into other areas of wellness, obtaining certifications as a nutrition coach and women's wellness coach. Constantly seeking more certifications, I hoped that each one would be the key to unlocking my desired path.

Unfortunately, despite the training, my visions didn't manifest fully. It became clear to me that my mindset played a significant role in my perceived limitations. Consequently, I delved deeper into the world of mindset and manifesting, seeking a better understanding of why I remained stagnant. Once again, I turned inward to find the answers I sought externally.

During this transformative period of my life, a serendipitous encounter on social media introduced me to a man whose profound resonance deeply touched my soul and felt strangely familiar. This charismatic individual not only understood the challenges I faced but also possessed insights that had the potential to change my entire existence.

Under his guidance, I was introduced to the notion of the God Germ—an inherent spark within each of us, capable of igniting an insatiable hunger for growth and change. That concept was so validating to hear as I always felt there was something wrong with me for never being satisfied with the status quo. We are not meant to be SATISIFED! We are always either Growing or Disintegrating. His words breathed hope into my weary spirit, reigniting the flickering flame that had long been dimmed. In doing so, he reminded me of my true essence and divine nature as the pinnacle of God's creation.

Through his mentorship, I learned to believe in myself and embrace my own abilities.

Filled with excitement, I enthusiastically reconnected with my initial passion—the captivating world of dance—and sought the guidance of a private dance coach. Through dedicated practice, this endeavor culminated in an exhilarating and intoxicating experience: my very first live performance before an audience! It was a full circle moment!

I also created an online wellness group where I continue to grow and encourage others to foster a healthy, active lifestyle. I took the initiative to step onto the social media stage myself, sharing his wisdom with others and creating a following of my own. His unwavering support instilled within me the bravery to step beyond my comfort zone, confront my fears head-on, and act on my dreams with unwavering determination.

Over time, our mentorship evolved into a fruitful collaboration, and I now have the privilege of assisting him in expanding his community, extending the same transformative impact to others that he once provided for me.

Witnessing the blossoming of individuals as they tap into their inner power and manifest their dreams brings immeasurable joy.

You are never too old, and it's never too late!

My story serves as a testament to the limitless potential within each of us. That once shy little girl wasn't shy at all, she was just conditioned to be that way. The BEST advice I ever received from my mentor was to set a big, beautiful goal for myself that makes the old version of me obsolete and give my life to that! Which is exactly what I did and continue to do, and I encourage you to do the same!

Dance, always the unwavering constant in my life, embodies the essence of bliss and freedom. Embrace its guidance on your remarkable journey and hold this truth close:

D - Dare To Dream

A - Act On Your Desires

N - Never Give Up

C - Cultivate Confidence

E - Express Your Creativity

And DANCE like EVERYONE is watching!

Divine Ananda of Love

by Tammy Lee Rose

With humble hearts, we come before you, overflowing with gratitude for the boundless blessings of the past, present, and future. In this sacred moment, we offer our prayers of thanksgiving and rejoice in the eternal bliss that you bestow upon us.

We are grateful for the tapestry of experiences woven into our lives, for each moment that has shaped us and led us to this divine connection. Your love has guided us through challenges, illuminating our path with the radiance of joy and serenity. With heartfelt gratitude, we embrace the lessons learned and the growth that has blossomed within us.

As we stand in the present, immersed in the divine flow of your love, we are filled with overwhelming joy. Your presence surrounds us, lifting our spirits and infusing our souls with the profound essence of Ananda. We offer our deepest appreciation for the love that sustains us, nourishes us, and connects us to the infinite web of existence.

Looking toward the future, we surrender to your divine will, knowing that your love will continue to guide us on our journey. With trust in your infinite wisdom, we welcome the unknown, for we understand that within it lies infinite possibilities and opportunities for further growth and bliss.

Divine Ananda of Love, we are forever grateful for your unwavering presence in our lives. May our hearts be forever open to receive and share the divine love that emanates from your essence. In unity and harmony, we embrace the eternal dance of gratitude, joy, and bliss.

About

Tammy Lee Rose

Tammy Lee Rose was born and raised on a small, picturesque island off the east coast of Canada called Newfoundland, where she developed a deep appreciation for nature and a sense of community. With a vibrant spirit and an adventurous soul, Tammy's journey in life has taken her on an extraordinary path.

Tammy's career in the travel industry spanned an impressive 25 years, during which she honed her skills and expertise in various sectors. She began as a travel agent, assisting clients in crafting memorable experiences around the world. Her passion for exploration led her to venture into the airline industry, where she gained invaluable insights into the logistics and operations of travel. Tammy concluded her illustrious career in the travel industry in the realm of corporate travel and finally as a recruiter, where she found immense fulfillment in forging meaningful connections with aspiring travel professionals.

Amidst her professional pursuits, Tammy developed an unwavering passion for all things dance and wellness. Recognizing the transformative power of movement and self-care, she immersed herself in the world of wellness practices and became a certified Yoga instructor. Through Yoga, Tammy discovered a path to personal growth and inner harmony, and she eagerly shares this wisdom with others.

In a recent exciting development, Tammy has rekindled her passion for dance and delved back into the world of rhythmic artistry. Currently, she is dedicated to training as a ballroom dancer, under the expert guidance of a private dance coach. Driven by her aspirations to showcase her skills on a competitive stage, Tammy is diligently honing her technique and refining her artistry.

Guided by her commitment to personal development, Tammy came across the teachings of Troy R Chadwick, a renowned mindset mentor. His philosophy resonated deeply with her, igniting a fire within her to explore the realms of mindset and consciousness. Recognizing the immense value of Troy's teachings, Tammy eagerly collaborated with him, contributing her expertise to help grow his community and assist others in reaching their highest potential.

Tammy's warm and compassionate nature, coupled with her vast experiences, creates a nurturing environment for growth and transformation. Her genuine desire to support others in their journeys is evident in every interaction. As a mentor, instructor, and advocate for holistic wellness, Tammy Lee Rose continues to inspire and empower individuals to embrace their true potential and live a life of purpose and passion!

www.TammyLeeRose.com

Brandi Englett

27

~ Healing ~

The Goddess of Healing, in her radiant embrace, restores, soothes, and revitalizes. With infinite compassion, she sparks miraculous transformation, igniting vitality in those who seek her divine presence.

From the Ashes

by Brandi Englett

"I no longer feared the darkness once I knew the phoenix in me would rise from the ashes." William C. Hannan

The fire that I was born into was intense. It burned me deeply, leaving many deep wounds. My life started in abuse and neglect. I had no concept of what it meant to fit in — even within my own family. As a 17-year-old I almost ended my life because of it. I was severely depressed and didn't see a reason to live, but somehow, I found the strength to continue living. My internal landscape was just as severe as my external world. No one tells you that, when you're abused, your internal voice takes on the role of the abuser as well. I didn't love myself and lived my life anticipating the needs of others to keep the peace. Looking back, it seems so foreign to me now.

My parents were ill-equipped to deal with a child like me. I was bold and opinionated — even as a small child. I had a strong will and intuitively knew when things were wrong, and I had no issue pointing them out! I also didn't blindly follow authority figures just for the sake of it. I questioned and refused. My parents were very rarely pleased with me and became verbally and physically abusive towards me. This environment left me feeling unloved and alienated, not knowing who I could trust. In my early 30s, I knew something had to change, but I had no idea how or even what needed to change. I was prosperous, but I remained depressed and angry even after all those years. My internal landscape hadn't changed much from that of my 17-year-old self.

Then it all came crashing down. I had an abrupt and profound awakening at the end of 2017. I began having spiritual experiences that rocked the foundation of beliefs I had built my whole life upon. Then, my husband had a mental breakdown, and I began to fear him. I suddenly saw my father in my husband, and I couldn't look at him. I didn't want to be near him, and I honestly thought he would hurt me. I had made a promise to myself, when I moved out of my parents' home, that I would never be abused by anyone again. But there I was, living with a man who, I thought, was capable of exactly what I had fled. He packed his bags and left one afternoon. I had a wash of emotions that ranged from absolute relief to profound gutting sadness. This one event sent me deep into a healing journey that would change the way I saw myself and the world.

During the separation from my husband, my entire life was upended. I was alienated yet again. I felt as though I had gone right back to square one in my journey. All the painful memories of my childhood flooded over me like a torrential river. I was reliving the memories and had no support system yet again. The pain was felt deep within my bones. I didn't know who I was any longer.

Then, I would encounter an angel that would change the entire trajectory of my life. I was having a particularly hard day with the emotions of my broken marriage. I had access to thousands of acres of land across from my home, so I decided to walk to clear my head. I had walked several miles from my home and sat down in the forest, crying and unable to walk any further. Suddenly, a white light doorway came into view, and a large male angel was walking out into the forest towards me. All I could see at first was the arch of his wings and his towering height. When he came nearer, I could see he was broad across the chest and shoulders, with blond hair and wearing a white robe. I was unable to process what I was seeing with my physical eyes. He came up to me and wrapped me in his arms. I could feel his chest against my cheek and his arms firm around me. I could even feel his warmth. At that moment, I felt a love this world has no words for — a love that engulfed me in peace and acceptance. To this day, I can't describe to someone what that felt like. I knew then that I had never been alone.

All those times in my life when I felt neglected, unloved, and unwanted were false. This angel had been with me through it all. He had been helping me and loved me beyond what the human mind can even process. He never spoke a word, but my inner knowing was without question. The encounter ended when he released me and disappeared back into the doorway. When the forest came back into view, I was a new person. I was no longer upset; instead, I was in awe and felt like my soul was glowing with love. I was also wondering what else I didn't know. What else was there to experience? I started walking home as the encounter began to settle into my mind. I found feathers all the way back home that day. These feathers confirmed the experience I'd had and filled my heart with joy. That one encounter changed my life forever. I can never go back to who I was before that day.

My spiritual journey deepened after that experience, and I began to naturally gravitate to crystals and meditation, even though I had no previous reference or exposure to these practices. I knew something was happening to me on a deep level, but I didn't have the words to explain it at the time. Now, I know I had begun to rise in frequency. This caused my spiritual abilities to become more pronounced. Meditation became a craving, and I had several profound experiences with passed-on loved ones and other angels. This became my life and passion. I was seeking that connection I didn't have in the physical world. I began seeking information wherever I could find it to help piece together my experiences and to try to understand what I was going through.

During one of my meditations, I asked why I had been given such a dark childhood.

I heard: "How can you help those in darkness if you have not been in darkness?"

I pondered this deeply and realized I was here for a reason. My childhood had been this way for a reason. I had a purpose. Shortly afterward, I began to have dreams, which lasted for exactly two weeks, and each night I would have one dream of myself as a healer. I would then wake up and was told to write down my dream. I did this and began to wonder who I really was. Having been separated from my husband for several months, my entire view of myself and my journey on this earth had been changed. I was facing intense healing and had begun to go for Reiki sessions that helped to remove layers of trauma. I didn't have an identity that I recognized any longer. I was being recreated into the healer, pulled from the ashes of my past and being reborn. It was painful and labor-intensive — like all births are — but parts of me were also dying at the same time. I was stepping forward for the first time in my life and I told God, "Here I am! I surrender!" That surrender was sweet and frightening at the same time. I had always had issues with trusting, but this felt more "right" than anything I had felt before. I had been walking through life, and life had just been happening around me, really without my conscious input. I started to stand in my power and take control of my own destiny. Life was no longer happening TO me; life was happening FOR me.

My husband and I reconciled our marriage and then I realized the reason for his mental breakdown. In the time we were separated, we were both undergoing dramatic transformations, but we couldn't do these things together. We needed a catalyst. We needed to be isolated to be led forward. I saw all the events of my life in a new light and realized it was all part of the plan. Coincidences do not exist. I began to accept my new journey as a beautiful adventure and was open to receiving all the things that would come because of that embrace. Gratefully, my husband understood and accepted this new being that I was becoming. He wanted to know more and support my journey as best as he could.

Late one night, one of my cats became very sick. I feared he would die before morning. I felt a strong urge to do what I had been shown in my dreams to see if I could help him through his sickness. I gathered a couple crystals and knelt beside him on the floor. When I placed my hands on his sides, I became aware of an angel standing in my living room. By this time, it was not uncommon for me to encounter angels. Then Christ walked into my awareness. He knelt beside me and placed His hands over the backs of my hands; I saw this pure white light emanate from His hands, through my own, and into my cat's body. I saw him filled with this light. Christ backed away and the encounter was over. Later that night, I woke up in extreme distress. I was sick and it came upon me suddenly. It lasted for about 10 minutes and then suddenly left me, as quickly as snapping your fingers. It was gone. I was so confused by the experience, but I was grateful I could return to bed. The next morning my cat greeted me and was completely healed. I began to question whether the experience had happened and whether my cat had really been as sick as I thought he'd been. I began asking questions and realized that the sickness I had experienced was due to the healing I had participated in.

That first healing solidified my new identity. At a soul level, I am a healer, a being of light. I knew the path that was laid before me, and I began my Reiki journey because the modality had helped me with my own healing. It most closely matched the form of healing I had been shown. Of course, the Reiki path has also profoundly changed me and offered an even deeper understanding of life in general. I live a Reiki life. It is not just a modality to me; it is a journey all on its own — a spiritual path of deeper and deeper truths. Truths I have been searching for my whole life.

Over the years, I have freed myself of the heavy burden of trauma and forgiven my parents for their inability to raise me differently. I've released the need for my old coping mechanisms and the more I release, the more I rise and the more profound my spiritual experiences become. I had to burn away all that dense energy to be reborn into who I am today. Healing is a lifelong journey, and we evolve and grow through our experiences in this life. Some of those experiences change our entire life. From that day forward, we can never go back to who we were before. I can assure you, however, you are never alone and there are no coincidences in this life. The journey of the phoenix tells us that we must die to be reborn. The question is, what part of us must die? What part of us needs to be burned away? Are we willing to go through that pain to rise from the ashes? Each person must ask themselves those questions and answer them truthfully. We cannot rise from the darkness if we are not first willing to light a fire. It is in our darkness that the light can be seen the clearest.

Healing Prayer

by Brandi Englett

Divine embodiment of compassion and grace, I come before you with a humble heart,

Seeking your divine presence and healing embrace.

In your sacred presence, I find solace and peace, I surrender my worries, my pain, and my grief. Wrap me in your loving arms of light and guide me on the path of restoration and relief.

With your gentle touch, mend the wounds that burden my body and soul. Infuse me with your divine wisdom and strength, as I embark on a journey towards being whole.

Illuminate the hidden places within my being, where imbalances reside, and ailments persist. Pour your healing balm upon my weary spirit and grant me the gift of radiant health and bliss.

With gratitude, I honor your boundless love, for the miracles you weave in every life you touch.

I am forever grateful for your nurturing embrace, and the transformative power you bring forth as such.

I place my trust in you,

Knowing that your divine light guides my way. As I walk this path of healing and renewal, I am blessed by your presence, each and every day.

Thank you for your grace, for the blessings bestowed upon me from above. With faith in your divine intervention, I surrender to your healing power and infinite love. And so it is.

About

Brandi Englett

Brandi Englett, a middle Georgia native, has quite the story to tell of how she overcome adversity to become who she is today. Her spiritual journey is nothing short of novel worthy with many twists and turns along the way. In that journey, she has learned a lot about herself, healing, death, and how to live a more fruitful life. Brandi's spiritual journey is best showcased in her radical life transformation, a woman that truly walks the talk.

Her life was radically changed by Reiki, and this helped her realize her true calling was to help others heal through the modality. She is an Usui Reiki Master Teacher and is nationally accredited through the International Center for Reiki Training. She is also Holy Fire and Violet Flame activated and is a keeper of the Golden Ray, a Christ light frequency that provides deep healing through pure love. She has a knack for seeing people at their true core and can lift them from their despair into the light. Her spiritual abilities run the gamut, and this makes for a unique and powerful session. She also teaches Reiki to those that resonate with her energy. She embodies Reiki in all aspects of her life and is always in a state of self-realization and growth. Approaching life with a go get it attitude that keeps her learning new things that help her clients heal on a deeper level. In her pursuit of yet deeper healing, she became a Keys to Freedom practitioner. This modality works directly with archangels to reveal and clear deep seated imbalances within her clients. It is not uncommon to find Brandi doing house and property clearings as well, where she is fearless in her work. Brandi's role as a gatekeeper to the afterlife allows her to escort troubled souls back to their true home.

Brandi's inspiring story shows that it is possible to overcome a traumatic past. She lives out her truths unapologetically and encourages her clients to do the same. Her spirit is soft but fierce and her energy will wash over you like a soft breeze on a hot summer day. Offering you a safe place to speak and heal deeply from the things that trouble you the most.

If Brandi's story and energy resonate with you, she can be reached through social media.

Social Media @internalflamehealing

Traydon Inspires

~ Worldcraft ~

The God of Worldcrafting, a master of divine language, guides souls to
build upon the archetypes of existence, skillfully scripting consciousness
with the transformative alchemy of love and wisdom.

Whispers of a Worldcrafter

by Traydon Inspires

Ideas and worlds knew of me before I knew of them. They were expressed by outward acts singing in my bedroom and thinking I was a professional dancer (which I wasn't). Running around the house and watching SpongeBob were regular occurrences, along with wearing my Spider-Man bedcover as a cape. Some days, I was Spider-Man climbing up walls and swinging on doors. On other days, I was Sharkboy, dreaming of adventures to go on, while in my backyard with sticks and boxes. To me, my daydream was life and play — or was that my way of coping with the world?

What I didn't tell you was that I often felt powerless, dreading the systems of the outside, where parents didn't listen, and suffering crept into radiant smiles. In the lifeless world, gunshots sang in the night and the fear of being killed infiltrated my mind. My mom played musical chairs between being both mother and father. Everyone's favorite hobby was smoking, drinking, and self-deception. Sometimes the lights were off, and sometimes my shoes didn't have holes in them. You see, poverty became the only possibility that paved my path.

Often, I made anger my protector against the villains who attempted to have control over me. Though I was innocent for a time, the world had already created its own perceived destiny for me, one that left out my father, my innocence, and my ideas of who I wanted to be. Even my name became a limitation because of the adjectives that were attached to it, like "poor", "ugly", and "irritating".

One night, I heard yelling from my room. Rushing to the scene of anger, I saw the furious look on my mom's face. "Leave and never come back! You are a cheater and a liar, and you broke my heart!" she shouted, with the power to shatter glass. I stood just a few feet away, unable to utter a single sentence. I didn't know what had happened, but I knew that my voice was powerless to stop it.

What I wasn't aware of then was that when my dad left, my confidence and voice left too. He was goofy, expressive, and childish. When he left, my opportunity to be that way was lessened. From then on, my mom's bitterness toward my father silenced every aspect of me that resembled him. "Be quiet! You are irritating!" reigned from her lips multiple times a day, coupled with a look that caused disdain. She was always irritated with me whenever I was bothering her with questions; with my loud footsteps zipping throughout the house; and with "being in her face". She possessed a quiet energy that sucked the creativity and energy out of me. Sometimes I would try to have a conversation about it which was met with, "You're the child, and I'm the adult. You don't know anything." The more this criticism continued, the less I wanted to speak with her.

The lack of patience for my imaginative personality caused me to be defensive and afraid to show my true self. My voice was often measured by how many years I'd lived on the earth. The younger I was, the less my voice mattered and the less power my ideas had. Again and again, the pattern of screams echoed on repeat, with boyfriends and baby-daddies. "How could the little voice of a child quieten the voice of raging adults?" I wondered. And again and again, my voice got smaller and smaller until all I could rely on was my dreamworld to hear what I had to say.

So, I went to sleep, so I could live in a happier place...

"Throughout the cadence of day and night,

In between the breath of intuition and dream,

My vessel and immortality dance,

Leaving me within the trance of being,

Venture to worlds and realms,

Reliving distant stories,

Escaping my own,

Until one ocean within quantum leaps,

Someone familiar came to me..."

I woke up within a realm that was painted to me as a dream. Its ebony sky was brushed with strokes of the aurora coming from the east, hurrying to dance with the west. The sky had splashes of indigo nebulas with an eclipse that radiated an emerald hue. This celestial painting reflected onto the ocean beneath my feet. I was walking in a bath of communion waters, each step rippling into a prayer. My eyes were charmed with elegant colors that moved like sentient beings. Why does this feel so familiar? The realm echoes within my body without ceasing, like the moment of seeing someone long forgotten.

"You've been here before," uttered a voice filled with the ocean's depth and the stillness of an oak tree. It was as though it had emerged from my own head. "Who was that?" I wondered, while looking aimlessly for its owner. Immediately the voice replied, "Calm your heart, and you will know me."

"Who are you?" I questioned, unable to hide my curiosity.

"I'm called by a name that doesn't belong to me nor holds onto me. It was given to me but not given for me to give to others as my own. It shines a light on part of me. It is only one part of me.

You wish to know my name to give concepts to me, but I won't indulge. This moment is for a different intention, one where I need for you to listen. Calm your heart, and you will know me."

As I heard this, the dawn peered from the coverings of the eclipse and inspired a spring's wind into my skin. "Where are you?" I questioned with clarity. Without knowing why, I turned around and saw an entity looking back at me, eyes with an indigo iris radiant with curiosity. My face was his face, and his curls were like mine. The being was me, and I a reflection of him.

"Here I am," the being said, "within and without, a memory remembered, and a voice made visible." The being began to walk around me, getting closer each time. "You are the bridge between and the crafter of worlds." "The bridge and crafter?" I asked. The closer the being came to me, the more nothing made sense. "What do you think this world is? You created this," said the being, now just a few steps away. I questioned him and myself, "I did?" The being reassured me by saying, "Listen and calm your heart. Your faith and expression are yours if you stay within my word."

When the being reached out his hand to me, I could feel nothing but a summer's passion. "Touch my palm," the being said. "Your curiosity and initiative will inspire the lives of the unseen. Now, place your left hand over mine." Once I had done what the being had instructed, our hands became inverted, and everything afterwards was lost to the lifeless world again…except for the being's name and essence.

When my vessel rose from its mystical illusion of sleep, my body felt a calmness that tugged slightly for my attention. I noticed something was different, but school wouldn't wait for me to figure it out. Once my feet touched the floor, I was sure something had changed about or within me. Thinking it was the lingering of the dream, I continued to get dressed. As time went on, I couldn't shake the feeling of being watched over. Every time I moved, I felt an empowering presence moving in step with me. What has happened to me? After my sudden investigation, I recognized the presence. It was Nameless, the being from my dream. He was in my head, participating in my every thought and watching my every move. He functioned as a harmony to my melody and together we moved in a dance.

His voice emerged from the music of the moment saying, "Welcome to your new world. If you choose it to be, it will be so. For I am now at the heart of your creations." I hurried out of my room. Though all of this was surreal, my senses were quickly normalized when I noticed my mom's quiet frown as I shut the front door. Now, it was time to deal with school.

Where school lives, lifelessness develops like a cancer, killing the courage of creativity. There I saw grades that degrade the minds that aren't confined by the system, that aren't shackled to the desk that depresses ingenuity. Despite fluently fixing logic with bells and broken clocks, it was in these moments I first tried to bring Nameless' world into mine. One time, when I strolled into the classroom, I noticed the stress on the teacher's brow quickly replaced with a smile as my peers emerged from the hallway. Thinking I was allowed to speak to my peers, I conversed about some ideas I had until the teacher erected her authority to silence me. "No talking!" edged into my psyche every time I heard it. Those words scratched my ears. "Why am I not allowed to speak?" I thought. I couldn't comprehend why my voice was a burden wherever I went. It seemed like all adults do is tell you to quiet your ideas. To protect myself from her words that echoed in my mind, I picked up a rhyming book and read it at a desk in the back of the class. However, what was read and the voice I heard were two different things.

"Rhyme and rhythm revive realities. Remember to read and to

receive. And remember to reveal such in reality. For you are the bridge between the lines and the crafter of space and time. Your mind is melodies. Yes, your mind. Your mind is a mine of poetry. So, uncover and recover every mystery, never to miss the universal clarity."

What was once thought of as simply reading a children's poetry book became the catalyst for poetry as a worldcrafting tool. Words were now illustrations that leaped from pages. Sentences were movie scenes and paragraphs were episodes. Now, whenever a teacher would try to silence me, I would silently sink into writing myself into another world. Whenever kids would try to bully me, I would use words to wrestle with their minds. I would try to ignore their teases and enter a world I'd created, one like the realm where I met Nameless. I would sit at my desk writing poetic worlds, leaving behind the screams of a teacher or taunts of that week's bully. In these realms, I was powerful and loved, instead of criticized and powerless. Though worldcrafting had endless possibilities, I mainly used it as my coping method and defense against my environment. It wasn't until I got to high school that I realized it could be used in other ways.

Writing began as my main tool of worldcrafting. Nameless would remind me of the world I wanted to create, continuously telling me, "Calm your heart, and you will know me". I realized that to "know" Nameless was to know myself. It meant listening to my desires of who I wanted to be and the world I wanted to live in. My emotions would often heighten in excitement at the new characters and realms I would create. Little did I know that the intense emotions and putting pen to paper would manifest these worlds in my reality. This was tested within my pit of depression, periods where poetry and journaling were my claws out of its depths. My words of intensity were the manifestors of realms realized within the physical. Once upon a time, this was observed within my playful desire of walking upon Parisian streets, written within imaginings until realized years later.

At 20 years young, I ended up going to Europe for nine months, earning thousands of dollars. While there, my dream of Paris was fulfilled with the Eiffel Tower within my view. While eating vegan lasagna in Paris, I became aware of worldcrafting as a method to cause my imaginings to manifest within physicality. I had realized that an idea crafted years ago is not forgotten within manifestation. All around me now and then was what I'd imagined whether consciously or subconsciously.

The tool of worldcrafting was the gift in the essence of a child's imagination. So many people are told to "grow up" and forget about their dreams, but what people don't see is that those dreams are where our power resides. Worldcrafting is not my power; it is a power that everyone beholds. I simply chose to harness it and invest in its power. Sometimes that meant being bullied for being weird, being yelled at by my mom for being positive, or being rejected by society for thinking too big for my class. Nameless told me his name didn't belong to him nor hold onto him. His name was Traydon, my given name.

See, society had already made up its mind about Traydon; it had chosen my destiny for me. I was never meant to escape poverty or be successful. The world wanted me to conform to the discrimination and societal abuse. When I rose above my name, the caricature of my own person, I became a heightened being. That being is the one who is able to manifest and be on the same playing field as everyone else in the world. I gave myself opportunity where others didn't, love where others wouldn't. I have risen above the destiny that the world set out for me. I crafted the reality I wanted, to replace the one I existed in. From the quantum field to my existence, I am the bridge between and the crafter of reality. This is the power of worldcrafting, the power of imagination, the power of me.

World Crafting

by Traydon Inspires

Oh, Nameless Source of Creation,
I come before you with a humble heart,
Seeking the power to craft a new world into existence.

I am the vessel through which inspiration flows,
A channel for your divine wisdom to manifest.
Grant me the strength to inspire others, as you inspire me.

Infuse me with the life force that brings life,
That I may breathe vitality into all that I create.
May my very presence be a space for others
to embody their true selves.

As I weave the tapestry of universes,
Guide my hand to build upon the archetypes of existence.
Help me script consciousness with love and wisdom.

Grant me the lyrical language of expression,
That my words may carry the weight of prophecy.
May I be the keeper of shadows and secrets,
entrusted with their sacred knowledge.

I am Invision, the artist of imagination,
Empower me as I paint visions with ink and knightly passion.
Let me be the storyteller of dreams,
weaving tales of eternal significance.

In this journey of self-discovery,
May I embrace the essence of who I truly am.
For I am Nameless, the crafter of worlds,
With your divine grace, I shape a new reality.

Bless my endeavors, O Creator of All,
May my creations be vessels of love,
harmony, and transformation.
Together, let us bring forth a world of beauty, |
compassion, and boundless potential.

So it be, in reverence and gratitude,
For the opportunity to co-create with you,
The Timeless, Spaceless, and Nameless.

Awoob

About
Traydon Inspires

Traydon Inspires is a visionary soul here to uplift others through self-expression, creativity, and intuitive healing.

An international multi-disciplinary artist, teacher, and mentor on a mission to promote personal growth and help countless people embrace their truest selves.

A bridge between ancient wisdom and modern techniques that seeks to uncover universal truths within each individual through intentional spiritual practice.

Through various projects he has published books, conducted mentoring sessions, created courses to help people in the journey of self-mastery and established an ongoing campaign to travel the world and share his message of enlightened awareness. With intuitive interpretations and creative visuals, he illuminates stages and empowering lives wherever he goes.

www.TraydonInspires.com

IG @Traydon.Inspires

traydoninspires@gmail.com

Kathleen Walton

29

- Breath and Stillness -

The Goddess of Breath and Stillness breathes serenity into restless souls, kindling faith and igniting the flames of courage to navigate the unknown with unwavering strength.

The Beginning Whispers

by Kathleen Walton

My journey of healing started at a time of unknown turmoil. From the outside, everyone around me saw my life as beautiful, with a loving husband, son, home, and career. I lived life with a smile and a glow, bringing joy to others while hiding my own turmoil so deeply, it went unnoticed or recognized — even by me. There was an emptiness I filled with a career I didn't love, my amazing then husband, and our awesome son. I never felt 100% present in any moment of any day, as though something was missing from within me.

I have always been a learner or, shall we say, a work in progress, which would lead me to try new things whenever the opportunities arose. My friend, Anibel, would ask me to go to yoga every once in a while, and I always said yes, thinking it would be good for me. I would be the girl sliding around on the mat, not really knowing the poses, and just waiting for the yoga session to be over. I constantly went to yoga with Anibel, I even went to a retreat in Costa Rica. I would do all the obtuse moves but never really felt connected to any of it. Then it happened. One Saturday morning at yoga, the instructor guided our breath into every movement and position. And just like that I was connected! I used my breath to guide intention and stillness into my movements, and with that intention, felt zen. Falling into a zen state felt like absolute peace and tranquility. I felt truly present. I felt isolated with my breathing and every yoga motion, even though there was a room full of people around me. I wasn't just going through the motions; I became one with them with every breath.

Guided breathing began to change my world in so many ways. I became so intentional about yoga and fell in love with it in a new way. It was something I needed and became very passionate about. One day the universe whispered to me, "I have bigger things for you." The universe kept presenting yoga study in my life. It was mentioned at the yoga studio, on social media, in regular conversation, everywhere. Finally, I listened to these whispers and got my yoga certification. The bigger picture was so much more than teaching yoga. Yoga study allowed me to live a yogic lifestyle. I brought that guided breath into my daily life. By breathing with intention, I stopped meandering through life but instead became very present. My guided breath brought me tranquility and stillness and allowed me to be more grateful for the moments I would absorb. Breath (prana) is seen as a universal energy which flows in and around the body. Yoga helped me move energy through my body as I moved and breathed.

However, as the universe guided me on my new path, many changes came with it. My 22 years of marriage ended shortly after I finished my yoga study. No divorce is easy and obviously comes with an abundance of emotions. I saw that the universe was testing me. It was waiting to see whether I would use and implement all the newfound knowledge that my yoga study provided me. I tried to ignore it, letting anxiety and depression consume me instead. So much of my identity had just died. I was now single and 50 years old.

One day, I felt like my world was spinning out of control and I couldn't get my footing. I decided to attend my favorite yoga class and the instructor worked with us on breathing in and out with an audible exhale to release and let go of what no longer served us. As I guided my breath with intention, I moved all the negative stuck energy in my body towards the surface and then gave it back to the universe. The universe grabbed hold of that energy and pulled it away from me. At that moment I could feel my hidden worthiness bubbling up from inside and shining outwards to be my true authentic self and to stand in my truth. Needless to say, the release during that class was incredible and the tears were flowing. I knew immediately after that class it was exactly what I had to do to heal and get through that chapter in my life. That class was the introduction to my true healing. Ultimately, I had to remember to breathe.

I have learned that breathing on a physical level activates my body's parasympathetic nervous system, which slows my heart rate, lowers my blood pressure, and reduces my body's cortisol levels. In a sense, it brings me an inner calming stillness. When I am stressed and feel like I cannot catch my breath, I call breath in deeply for a count of seven and out for the count of 10. Guided breathing allows me to not only relax my body, but also my mind. Breath allows me to become still and present within myself.

As I was going through this healing process, I would invite stillness. Being still and present allowed me to see what emotions were arising and where they were coming from. I realized I had a lot of pain mourning someone who had been in my life for so long. With that pain, I struggled with letting go. I partially didn't want to. I had the belief I didn't want to give up that part of my life yet and, even more, I didn't want to feel the pain of that mourning. I knew I couldn't continue living a life of sadness and resentment, due to a failed marriage and not seeing the happily ever after of two good people. I had to force myself to breathe. I had to breathe into the pain, let it have a voice and experience it. That meant feeling it and letting the tears flow instead of holding them in.

Have you ever tried to stop breathing so you wouldn't cry? It's because breath moves that energy and gives it life. But energy cannot be created or destroyed, only changed, or moved. By breathing into the pain, I moved that energy and released it. This most often came in the form of tears. After respecting the painful energy that demanded to be felt and released, I would feel lighter. The negative energy would leave my body and I would be left with stillness. That stillness was like a medal, each time allowing me to be present and to feel the tranquility of forgiveness and grace.

While this routine seems nice, it was a choice I had to make every day. Every day, I had to choose to breathe into those emotions. As humans, we replay memories in our heads that keep us stuck. Well, I am human, and I would replay the blame, anger, and sadness in my head. Hanging onto negative emotions is no good for health in mind, body, or spirit. I would mentally live in this awful space, daily crying randomly, making myself depressed and anxious. Being able to release anger from within makes one's soul lighter, brighter, allowing a pathway for happiness to flow back in.

There was a point that stillness brought me clarity so I could breathe in gratitude, love, peace, and breathe out all the negative emotions that were no longer serving me. I had to breathe out the anger of two decades ending between two wonderful people; the sadness of not spending the rest of our lives together as a family; and the life we built together. I had to breathe out my idea of "our happily ever after." Breath allowed me to have a clean slate to work with, so any emotions that would come up in daily life weren't adding to any anger, sadness, and blame. When the negative emotions no longer played a role in my daily well-being, my mind, body, and spirit were allowed to be open to all the positivity that surrounded my daily moments. Breath allowed me to forgive myself and my ex-husband and move forward to create my new independent life.

Breath shows up in funny ways and is very expressive. My ex-husband and I once had a beautiful American German Shepherd, named Judge, that we adopted at 2 years old. We were his fourth owners, because people tried to make him something he wasn't. One night, after we'd had him for about six months, he was lying between my then husband and myself, and this beautiful soul of a dog let out the biggest sigh ever in his sleep. That amazing sigh was Judge knowing he was home and content. It absolutely made my heart happy.

After my divorce, I lost my sense of home. And even after I'd picked up all the pieces, something was still missing. What I realized was that I'd spent my entire life finding home in other people, in my family, and the circumstances of a "happy home". When that fell apart, I was left with nothing. Nothing but myself. While building a relationship with myself, I became a lot closer with the trauma and pain that were acquired in my early life. This was frustrating. I thought I was getting better but now I had a whole other pain to tackle. I wasn't comfortable with who I was. I realized I had a very poor self-image of myself that had been created from the judgments that people had made of me early on in life. As a child, the adults in my life always told me: "You can't", "That's not practical", "You don't show ambition". My biggest supporter at the time would put down my ideas, which made me feel as though my dreams were not worthy or, once again, "I can't make these dreams happen."

I cemented their comments in my subconscious and believed them. I realized I had to heal myself next. Just like my dog, I had to find a sense of home so I could have that same peace. I wanted to feel just like him: home, and content within myself. I didn't realize that my inner home, peace, and tranquility were missing. I was of the belief that my physical home, family, and career were all I needed. I had to find my home within me, instead of with others and my surroundings. I had to learn to accept and love every part of myself. I had to make myself comfortable with myself, the version of myself outside of being a mom and yoga instructor. I had to give myself an internal home.

I needed to take a serious look at myself and reevaluate my beliefs. I had to view myself as those around me saw me: as a shining light that brought joy into their lives, rather than what my past beliefs were. A strong individual who invites breath and stillness into my day, keeping me calm at times of stress or uncertainty. This process became my go-to whenever one of my past paradigms would resurface: stillness would whisper, "No, no, breathe in all things positive around me and be grateful for all the abundance in my life — from friends who are family, serving others to become their best selves, waking every morning healthy, a warm home, breathe, stillness." I was breathing in all the amazing truths of who I really am in daily practice and breathing out all my negative past beliefs that had been planted into my subconscious but no longer served me. Breath became my daily sidekick, helping me to see how much I had to offer. I was working on bringing my self-confidence back, taking what I learned living a yogic lifestyle and implementing it in all areas of myself. Stillness would be there whenever I needed to be mindful, navigating the thoughts with my inner monologue, so I could be fully there for myself to show up for my son who was mourning the loss of his family.

Breath has allowed me to move energy of life through my body in every moment of every day, releasing anything that no longer serves me, and this has been life-changing. I breathe through all moments, good ones and tough ones. They are moments, not who I am. Stillness has helped release old paradigms/beliefs and now I embody my new story. Moving forward in my truths, one breath at a time, keeps me focused on my beautiful life with breath and stillness. Breath now stops by as a big sigh when I am least expecting it, letting me know everything is in divine order. This sigh of breath lets me know I am home, I am content, I am

334

happy within myself, I have found my internal peace, my internal destination. What I learned, living a yogic lifestyle, and being introduced to breath and stillness, is that I wasn't energetically aligned. If breathing was not in my life I would have not been introduced to stillness. Together they fill me mentally, spiritually, and physically as my internal home. I now live every day one breath at a time.

Breath & Stillness

by Kathleen Walton

Divine Spirit of Breath and Stillness,

In this sacred moment, I turn my attention to you. I seek your presence to guide me on the path of healing.

As I inhale, I breathe in the essence of life, drawing in the healing energy that surrounds me.

With each exhale, I release tension, worry and pain. Allowing them to dissolve into the vastness of your love.

In Stillness that resides within me, I find solace, peace, and rejuvenation.

In this serene space, I surrender to the flow of healing. Allowing it to permeate every cell and fiber of my being.

Goddess of Breath and Stillness, I invite your gentle touch, to calm my restless mind and bring clarity to my thoughts.

Grant me wisdom to embrace the present moment, and courage to let go of all that hinders my well-being.

May the rhythm of my breath be a dance of harmony, Aligning my body, mind, and spirit in perfect balance.

May the stillness within me be a sanctuary of healing. Where I find restoration and reconnect with my essence.

I offer my gratitude for the healing that unfolds, knowing that your divine presence is always with me.

May I carry the essence of breath and stillness within, Radiating healing energy to all those in need. With every breath, I embrace the healing power of stillness, knowing that within its embrace, transformation occurs.

May this prayer be conduit of healing and love, Spreading healing vibrations through the universe.

So be it, and so it is.

May this serve as a powerful tool for embracing breath, stillness, And healing in your life.

About

Kathleen Walton

I have lived in Wisconsin my entire life. Wisconsin is beautiful and lush in the summer, full of color in the fall, and can be extremely cold in the winter, but is a beautiful white wonderland.

I have one amazing son whom I laugh with often, is an old soul (very mature for his age), and a very motivated entrepreneur as he goes into his last year of high school.

I enjoy being outdoors in all the Wisconsin seasons, with my two dogs whom I consider my furry daughters. I have a goofy light-hearted side and an empathetic personality that brings beautiful souls into my life that are often looking for positive energy to help direct them to be their best selves.

I have a passion for the written word and enjoy blogging about all things that help others live a healthy lifestyle in all areas of mind, body, and spirit. I am an Elite Global Napoleon Hill Institute Coach and a certified 250-hour RYS yin yoga instructor. I live a lifestyle from the 8 limbs of yoga. I come from a judgment-free zone, as I am a strong believer that we all have our journey in this one life, and unless we walk in someone else's shoes, we have no idea what their personal day-to-day is.

Every day I wake up to serve others spreading love and light through coaching, teaching yoga, blogging, podcasting, being a best-selling author, and speaking in the areas of wellness, motivational talks, inspirational views, and living my yogic lifestyle.

I hope you enjoy my "Breath and Stillness" goddess chapter. It is a journey of healing from two amazing humans that ended their marriage and moved in their own directions in life. The goddess of "Breath and Stillness" showed me how to move forward forgiving myself and my partner for a marriage that did not work out. My hope is that my goddess helps you find your peace through breath and stillness.

Sending you peace, love, and Joy.

www.whisperswithinus.com

Instagram @katrwalton

Facebook @kathleen.renee.96

Yashica Mack

30

~ Strength ~

In the realm of unwavering might and indomitable power, there stands a deity unmatched and revered—the Goddess of Strength, whose very essence resonates with the resolute courage and boundless fortitude dwelling within us all.

Crying Was Not An Option

by Yashica Mack

Strength is not always as it seems. Many people believe that tears are a sign of weakness. For a long time, I was one of those people. I believed that if I allowed myself to cry; I was weak. Over the years, I've dealt with a number of situations, circumstances, and trials that would've brought even the strongest of the strong to tears. Still, I refused to cry. My heart wanted to cry, but my head was convinced not to. More than anything else, I wanted to portray myself as a strong woman. People admire and respect strength. In my culture, one of the most powerful compliments you can give another woman is, "You are a strong woman!"

On the journey of life, people go through a lot. Some things they deal with are handed to them and others they take on all by themselves. Well, I am no different. I've gone through a whole lot during my lifetime. I always prided myself on going through things with grace and strength. I was extremely careful to never let anyone see me cry. In fact, I was so good at it that I taught myself how not to cry – even during those times when 99.9 percent of people would cry. I trained myself to push the tears back far enough until they couldn't reach the surface. Sure, I still experienced pain, hurt, and disappointment, but I never let anyone see what I was feeling. In my mind, that wasn't their business. Whatever I was dealing with was between me, myself, and I. Just to give you an idea of the kinds of experiences that I'm talking about, I want you to join me on my journey down memory lane.

I am no stranger to grief and loss of most every imaginable level. Let's start with my first foray into adulthood. As a country-girl from Alabama, I've always been a tomboy who used fear as a steppingstone. I was just 18 years old when I enlisted in the United States Army. I was expecting it to be difficult and challenging. In fact, I trained and prepared for that. What I didn't realize is that the world outside of Alabama was just a little bit different. Well, actually, I now know the military world is a lot different from the rest of the world, period. First and foremost, the military is a world that was not initially designed for females. I figured that out on the very first day of my military in-processing. The 10:1 male-to-female ratio smacked me right in the face as soon as I arrived at my duty station. I had never even given that a thought, so I was quite surprised when I became aware of this reality. Being young, unaware, and naïve, I had not even considered the fact that the handful of women on the base were looked at as prey for the male-dominated field. Let's just say I was quickly indoctrinated…

I was introduced to my squad leader and informed that he was going to be the one who was responsible for training me and looking out for me. I respected his leadership role and was looking forward to learning all that I could from him. As it turns out, I learned more from him than I could ever imagine. Just a couple of days into my introduction to the military, he and I were riding in a car when he told me he needed to stop by his house for a moment. I stayed in the car, but just a minute or so later, he motioned for me to come in. I went into the house, but almost immediately, I noticed a shift in the atmosphere. He started to make advances toward me, and they were not of the work relationship variety. I felt really uncomfortable, so I ran to the bathroom and locked the door. I asked him to take me back to the barracks. He said OK, but as soon as I came out of the bathroom, he grabbed me and dragged me into a bedroom. Before I knew it, he was on top of me. I did not know what to do. I realized I was not just defeated physically; I was also defeated mentally. I wanted to cry, but I could not. I stopped fighting and just laid there quietly as he entered me. I felt numb and voiceless.

I was speechless, and I realized I would never be the same again. I felt my heart hardening. I guess I was in shock. My fight or flight mode never kicked in. I wondered if anybody would believe me if I told them what happened. I was smart enough to know that if I told, it would jeopardize my future in the military.

My next major traumatic life event came years later. By this time, I was in my second marriage. So, it goes without saying, I faced other challenging life events. However, this next situation forever changed me. It built on my already existing pain factor and took it to the next level. I was progressing through life as a wife and mother, as many of us do, and then I found myself trapped in a new nightmare. Seven years in, three children later, with one of them being a newborn, I got the devastating news that my husband was diagnosed with Amyotrophic Lateral Sclerosis (ALS), popularly known as Lou Gehrig's Disease. ALS is a neurodegenerative disease that is aggressive and progressive. It affects the motor neurons that control movement. Basically, it is like having a stroke in your spinal cord and all muscles eventually die.

At one point, the diagnosis left him bitter and mean. The more he tried to accept the diagnosis, the more difficult it was to deal with his emotional state. I can certainly understand why that would cause the emotional roller coaster after learning that his prognosis was 2 ½ years to live and that all quality of life would be severely diminished. Just as it was not easy for him, the adjustment for me was difficult, to say the least. I became the caregiver for a once strong and vibrant alpha male. Within those 2 ½ years, he became confined to a wheelchair first and then to the bed, before ultimately losing the fight for his life entirely.

Once again, my heart was shattered. I was numb and did not allow myself to cry; I had to pick up the pieces of my life that had been scattered around me and juggle being mother to three young children. I just continued to move forward and adapt to my new circumstances. In my mind, crying was not an option. I did not have the time, resources, or desire to do the work I needed to do to heal; life had not stopped because my husband died. I had too many responsibilities to just sit and cry. As I did before, I pushed through and kept it moving. My heart mended, and I looked like the pillar of strength to everyone on the outside. Even though I did my best to be strong, it was just an illusion. I had fooled those around me, and maybe even myself, but deep inside, I knew I was not healed. I was still broken.

Of course, my husband's death had a profound effect on our children. Things went from bad to worse. My daughter who was 17 years-old, struggled. She was clearly hurting, and being mortally wounded myself, I was at a loss for what to do to help her. Our mother-daughter relationship virtually disintegrated into a volatile, explosive mess. Our home had become a toxic environment. She would leave home for days at a time, sometimes weeks and a few times, months. This pattern persisted for the next seven years. It was a horrible existence – for both of us. With each incidence, I detached more and more. Ultimately, she was diagnosed with bipolar schizoaffective disorder. On one hand, I was relieved because it explained so much, but on the other hand, it was still another devastating blow. Again, my heart was shredded into pieces, but crying was not an option. For me, crying was a sign of weakness. My heart hardened, and I continued to move.

I moved through life without a connection. I questioned myself as to why I could not feel these things emotionally. It has always been something in me that allowed me to process the hurt, grief, trauma, and just move on. I did not ask God "Why me?" Instead, I would say to God, "Why not me?"

March 1, 2020, is a date I will never forget. I lost both my children within 10 minutes of each other. My daughter and I had an argument, and she stormed out of the house screaming and yelling as she walked away. I was telling my oldest son about the incident, and then he and I argued and then he left. I'm not sure why this time it felt different, but it did. My daughter had now been gone for about an hour and I began to worry about her, so I called her social worker. I ended up filing a missing person's report with the police. Not even 10 minutes after they left, I received a phone call from my son's girlfriend telling me that he had been in a bad car accident and was being rushed to the hospital. My heart stopped, and I began to cry! My youngest son, who was now nine years-old, comforted me. He was surprised because it was the first time he saw me cry.

The next few hours were so critical. It was touch and go for my son. He lay in the hospital with multiple broken bones and in agonizing pain. I could not help him. I felt I was letting him down. I was defeated, my body was numb, and yet, I held back the tears.

My daughter was found and admitted to the hospital down the street from the hospital where my son was. Once everyone was stable after the longest 24 hours of my life, I went home. I climbed in the bed exhausted, and I held my 9-year-old tightly. The next morning, while he was in school, I collapsed in my sitting chair. My heart ached, stomach hurt, and the tears began to roll. I cried for the next eight hours.

This was not just a simple cry. This cry was different. This cry was for the years of pain I hid. This cry was for the betrayal and neglect I harbored inside. This cry was for the death of my grandparents, whom I was close to and had not properly mourned. This cry was for the death of my husband. I cried for the 18-year-old being sexually assaulted. I cried for the wife of a husband that cheated on her. I cried for the 16-year-old girl with an abusive boyfriend. I cried for the natural delivery of my children that I could not experience. I cried, I cried, and I cried some more. This cry was symbolic of a cleanse that I desperately needed. This cry released my shackles. This cry let burdens of guilt and shame go. This cry gave me freedom. This cry revealed everything to me I needed to heal. This cry was setting my soul free. This was a turning point in my life. I prayed, but most of all, I listened. I listened to GOD. I surrendered myself.

All the years I held in the cry thinking how badly I did not want to appear weak. The many times I controlled the emotions I would let others see. I thought I was building a pretty secure wall around me, but I came to realize I was building a strong wall within me. I locked away some of my greatest values. I locked away my voice. My voice is one of, if not the most important elements of being strong. I thought crying was a sign of weakness, but instead it was the ultimate test of strength. It took that cry to reveal to myself that I can be strong and still give myself grace. It also took that cry for me to accept and acknowledge the trauma I endured, and that cry allowed me forgiveness. Yes, I cried the last hour of that cry, transitioning from the pain to the purpose, "forgiveness." I forgave them all, every human, and every circumstance. But most of all, and most importantly, I forgave myself. I gave myself permission to soften my hardened heart, to feel where I was numb, and allow myself to experience healthy emotions.

Beyond the cry and the forgiveness, I also realized that the past is gone and doesn't have to define me. I am present with God and who God says I am. I am a strong woman of Faith and because of God's grace and mercy I am a whole woman bathed in strength and dignity. I walk with my head high and my back straight. Nowadays, my tears are of joy. I smile at the journey and bridges I have crossed. I transitioned to a different kind of strength, a peaceful strength, a strength of courage, confidence, and empowerment. I embody it all.

God gave me an acronym. P.A.I.D. in Full. He reminded me of the reason

His son was sent. He reminded me who I am. He reminded me to look to the hills for my strength. He held me together. He had me when I did not know to have myself. He told me He would never leave me or forsake me. He was there throughout all the traumas. He turned my traumas into transitions. The transitions I had to go through to be who I am today. P.A.I.D. in Full is the acronym I now go to when I need strength and understanding. I choose to be better and not bitter. I chose to use my transitions as a journey to my greatness. I chose to heal.

P.A.I.D in Full

PRAY. I know and understand that prayer can be all that you have in dark times as well as good times, too. Prayer is a conversation I have with God. In trying to understand the power of prayer, I asked God to show me how to pray. He gave me a definitive answer; the answer was simply to have a conversation with Him.

ACKNOWLEDGE. The letter "A" here in the acronym has a few layers. I had to acknowledge what God had shown me and I had to Accept what it revealed. When we know better, we can do better. The "A" is also for - Accountable. Hold yourself accountable for who you may have been and who you desire to become. That is the beauty of prayer and developing that conversation.

INTENTIONAL. Once I acknowledged, accepted, and held myself accountable, I was able to ask and be intentional about the life I now desired. Intentionally letting go of the old me. Intentionally creating the new and improved me.

DELIVERANCE. Now I know that I must pray, acknowledge, and accept who I was and transition to my desire to become whom I want to be and who I am. I must be intentional about living and be grateful for the deliverance. It is said that most people will not participate in their own rescue. I participated in the rescue of myself from myself.

This took many years of studying myself to get here. It is definitely a process and will not happen instantly. I say this for you, the reader, "Give yourself a break and be kind to yourself!" The cry was my break. Acknowledging is a step in the right direction. I now repeatedly apply the acronym PA.I.D. in Full to areas of my life. The work is done daily. You must stay committed to the process. The work is hard, but the effort is worth it. The designed life is far greater than the defaulted life.

My acronym helped me through my ordeals by:

Helping me to get to know myself.

Helping me to love myself.

Helping me to develop a personal relationship with God.

Asking for forgiveness from myself and others.

Giving me a true understanding of forgiveness.

Recognizing what activates me – negatively as well as positively.

Helping me to stop taking things so personally.

Helping me to detach from others' opinions of me.

By studying myself, I finally understood why I allowed people to take advantage of me, why my heart was hardened, why I was numb, why I did not cry, and why I would be so defensive. Recently, I learned how to activate my strength as power. I understand, and now that I have faced many transitions in life, I understand that these transitions were necessary to grow me in spirit and faith. My assignment was to heal first and then help others to do the same. My experience has been P.A.I.D. in Full and yours can be, too.

Prayer for Strength

by Yashica Mack

Mighty Goddess of Strength,

I humbly come before you today,
With reverence in my heart and words to say.

Grant me the power to endure life's trials,
To face challenges with unwavering smiles,
In times of weakness, lend me your might,

And guide me through darkness, into the light.
Goddess of Strength, in you I find solace,
Empower my spirit with unwavering boldness,

Grant me the courage to rise above,
To conquer my fears with unwavering love.
May your divine presence fill me with grace,

In every step I take, in every challenge I face,
May your blessings bestow unwavering might,
As I strive to make the world shine bright.

Goddess of Strength, I offer this prayer,
With faith and devotion, I solemnly declare,
Guide me, protect me, in all that I do,

For with your strength, I know I'll see it through.

In your name, I pray,

Amen

About
Yashica Mack

Yashica Broughton Mack (YashicaB!) specializes in relationships and self-discovery. Yashica realized throughout most of her life she was chosen to experience a struggling lifestyle. Later she understood to replace the word "struggle" with "transitions".

Yashica learned that through her transitions her heart had to heal first. She knew by healing she had to acknowledge and accept her true self. Yashica founded Healing Hearts and became a Coach Ambassador with the Napoleon Hill Institute. At Healing Hearts Yashica integrated her passion for horses with coaching and counseling. Yashica's interaction with horses taught her "the art of letting go." She has now dedicated her life teaching others "the how" of letting it go.

Yashica believes that understanding your inner-self and acknowledging the self-talk working inside of you makes the difference in becoming the better "You".

Yashica is an Army Veteran and founder of MackHouse Charities a 501(c)3 after losing her husband, a 23-year Army Veteran to a neurodegenerative terminal illness, Amyotrophic Lateral Sclerosis (ALS), better known to many as Lou Gehrig's Disease.

Yashica is a graduate of Troy University obtaining a Bachelor's in Psychology as well as a Master's in Counseling and Psychology, a Certified Life Coach, Napoleon Hill Institute's Coach Ambassador, a Certified Les Brown Power Voice Speaker, published author, and a Visionary International best-selling author. Her works include two anthologies' Mothers and Daughters and International Best Seller Women of the Power Voice, A Mother's Love Tested: Why Not Me? and the most recent The Kiss of Judas: Understanding Betrayal and its Purpose.

Yashica has worked with many professionals in an array of career and personal fields, from professional athletes, other counselors, chefs, and military personnel. She has been featured in "Imara Women's Magazine", sports media outlets such as ADSN, World Combat Sports, Kiss FM, local news outlets such as WLTX 19 and the 2020 Power Voice Summit and the Women's Power Voice Summit with the world's greatest influential motivational speaker, Mr. Les Brown. Yashica created the popular live interactive talk show Conversations for the Soul along with co-host and friend Dr. Angie Gray. Yashica was recognized as one of the most Inspirational Women of 2022 by

Yashica combines her education, training, and experience in becoming among the most sought-after self-discovery leaders across the globe. She has studied with and been mentored by some of the greats in the field for speaking Mr. Les Brown for self-development Mr. Jon Talarico, the amazing light worker and mentor Dolly Alessandra, as well as the late great Bob Proctor.

Yashica is a lifelong student of the enrichment courses taught at the Proctor Gallagher Institute and the Napoleon Hill Institute. She specializes in enriching relationships and teaching others to manage their eclectic mindset. Yashica is a devoted mother of three children and is committed to living her life as the best version of herself and teaching her children and others to do so as well.

She remains steadfast in making sure that her coaching/teaching reflects the strategies and techniques necessary for those she teaches to become their best selves so that they, too, are equipped to add value to the world at large.

Yashica lives by the mantra, "You do not have to tear down anyone's kingdom while building your empire. There is plenty of room at the top, it is the bottom that is crowded! "And you will often hear her say "As long as I am on this side of the dirt, there is always room to improve and make today better by doing something different to make a difference."

www.yashicab.com

yashica@yashica.com

**Facebook and Instagram @yashicaB4U
or Yashica Broughton Mack**

Danijela Nakovski

~ Fierce Devotion ~

Bathed in the radiant glow of her inner wisdom, the Fierce Devotont Goddess illuminates the path of truth, guiding souls towards awakening and liberation.

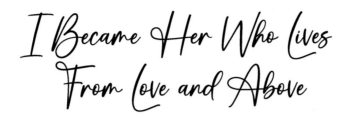

I Became Her Who Lives From Love and Above

by Danijela Nakovski

I became her. I walked in her shoes, acted like her, spoke like her, and became her. The girl who doesn't look back and uses everything negative that has happened in her life as fuel to go further.

Where does this story begin? In a small town of Užice in West Serbia, during the time of hard communism and strong paradigms.

As we learn to navigate the different stages and dimensions of our lives, everything becomes easier.

In the year 2000, after three months of running and hiding from bombs, I decided to go on vacation. I traveled to the sunny beaches of the Caribbean in the Dominican Republic, and realized the life I knew was about to change.

Have you ever taken a trip to a new life? I did, just at that moment. I didn't realize it, though, because arriving in the Dominican Republic was a total shock.

Cultural shock. Emotional Shock. Climate shock. Language barrier. My broken English wasn't of much use and my perfect Serbian was totally useless.

However, the blue ocean and beautiful beaches were the amazing food for my soul and brought much needed peace.

During the first week of my life at the beach, life brought my way one fine Canadian guy who was on vacation as well. When I say life brought it, I mean that literally. We were both renting a room in the smallest apartment hotel in Cabarete. I guess I can now say I believe in love at first sight, as, fast forward a year from that day, we were married and living our best life in Cabarete.

Meeting new people and learning the beautiful Spanish language was a life-changing experience and I took the Dominican Republic to my heart. My first job while learning Spanish was as a henna tattoo artist, working for a Serbian guy in the middle of the Caribbean. So, my native language wasn't that useless after all! The world indeed is small. I got my next job as a spa manager and then as a public relations manager in a hotel resort. Life was fun under the sun.

I learned my lesson: go with the flow, enjoy life, and look for blessings in everything.

I truly believe now, when we learn our lesson, we'll go further in life...so four years later, life brought me to my husband's hometown, Montreal. That is, I believe, when my next life started. In every one of these life chapters, I got a new role to play.

A new world. A new language. A new mentality. A new climate. A new life.

Having met a great lady at my job in the Dominican Republic, she helped me to get a wonderful corporate job as soon as I arrived in Montreal.

Having never been taught the power of gratitude, I didn't see my life as amazing back then. Things were being taken for granted and I found myself always wanting more. What I was about to discover years later, though, is that there was a huge difference in wanting more when coming from a place of lack versus coming from a place of abundance.

Life also wanted me to be a mom even when I wasn't sure whether I wanted to play that role. My first girl was born in 2005. It seems like I played that role well, as God gifted me with twin girls nearly two years later! I still remember how I cried when I found out I was going to have two more kids when I barely knew what to do with one. My boss at the time told me that God will never give you something if He doesn't believe you can handle it!

That was another lesson, right there. Surrender, and make the best out of it. Whatever you receive from the Creator you should carry with pride.

However, I lived mostly alone with my babies. My family was far away in Serbia and my husband at the time was working long hours and never present. This wasn't the life I had dreamed about. That taught me a lesson on perspective. In my mind, he was tearing the family apart and never putting us first, but in his mind, he was doing it for the family.

There are always opinions. In life, things and situations mean nothing until we give them meaning. That is the only moment they become important to us. After years of searching for that meaning in my marriage and believing there must be another way to build our family, I couldn't find the meaning I was seeking.

The divorce! It came through the biggest door ever, and I fell straight into the rabbit hole, hitting the bottom hard. The castle that I'd spent ten years building, simply crashed, and my whole world with it.

I had three babies, a couple bags of clothes and one sofa. That is how much I was apparently worth to my ex-husband. The truth is, I believed the same, blaming myself for ending it all. If only I

357

could have agreed to what he was thinking…

And just like that, we left. That is where another kind of "war" — over what "belongs" to whom — started.

Another lesson: There are always two sides to the story and, for any relationship to work, it takes at least two people. Unless it's the relationship with yourself… But there WERE two persons: me and myself.

Art. The pure art of relationship is what you need to master so you can live effortlessly with others. I decided I would master that art, and this is when my new life began. There was another role to be played and this one required extreme strength and a new set of skills I didn't yet possess.

Bringing your kids safely through a tough divorce requires building yourself up first, and the relationship between me and myself had to be stronger than ever.

How do you teach two five-year-olds and a seven-year-old gratitude in uncertain situations, where there is no money even to provide enough food? How do you teach that to yourself? Where did the faith go? Was it ever there?

Where there is a will, there is a way. Always. We started with naming the nice things that happened every day. Even the smallest. The first words my twins learned to write were about what they were thankful for. Mom. Dad. Sister.

Another lesson: never talk badly about your ex. Not to your kids, not to anyone. For your kids, he needs to remain a hero. Kids are smart; they see it all.

I can only have control over what is going on in my own house. When they were with their dad, I learned to let go of any concerns. I learned to trust that my babies had chosen us as their parents to teach them how to experience certain things in life, and if I direct them towards appreciation and learning the blessing, they will move faster towards the new lessons.

To all the single parents out there: kids need to feel safe, accepted, and loved. That's all. When we didn't have separate beds, we slept in one. When we didn't have food, we shared what we had. But there was never a lack of love or acceptance. Those things were non-negotiables.

The road from hate to love was rough but taught me one thing: there is only one emotion and its love. Fear and hate come from loving something or someone so much that we are in fear of losing it, or we hate someone for taking from us something we love.

If there is only love out there, I kept asking myself, what do I need to do to fix my broken self and my broken relationship? What do I need to do to find love again, to love myself again, with all my faults and mistakes? To love the father of my kids regardless, so I can liberate myself?

The biggest lesson in my life is living from love. How do you love someone who always wants to do bad things to you? Who talks badly about you to your kids? Who reports you in order to get full custody of the kids? Who doesn't allow your kids to mention your name in front of him?

You love him from afar. Wayne Dyer said, "When you change the way you look at things, the things you look at change." It's always up to us.

I started finding all the good things about him. Was it hard? Yes! Was it impossible? No! I had to put in the work, one day at a time. I started to note things daily. Whenever he was yelling, messaging, or calling, I responded with love. I needed to stay sane and to continue with my life after those encounters. Not long after, I witnessed it: my perception of him started to change.

I started to love myself and to love whatever good I found in me as well.

Then the most amazing thing happened: I met him. I know now that God wanted me to go all this way so he could appear in my life. The journey was totally worth it!

I met him and I felt right at home! How my soul was searching for that feeling. Living my life in this way allowed God to bring my true love into my life. This guy, who I call my most amazing husband, right now walked into my life to stay. He didn't know that 11 years ago, but I knew.

He didn't have any kids, was extremely handsome, and younger. Now we have four great kids together and a beautiful relationship that had to be polished and worked on every single day.

We take life for granted. We take our spouses, health, and kids for granted. We even take ourselves for granted. If we take a flower for granted and never water it or nourish it, it will eventually die.

So, I decided I would change that about my life and my relationships. I studied everything about him, including his likes and dislikes. I dreamed about him. I wrote about him. If I was to manifest him in my life and in the life of my kids, I had to see him in a certain light, so that he would appear in my reality in that light. This surely paid off.

This new chapter of my life was to be a fun game and I only needed to learn how to play it.

My notebooks and emails were full of affirmations about our

lives together. My poems spoke about the most amazing love story ever. Even though that love was only mine, I knew that coming from lack and writing about it would just bring more of it. The only thing I wanted more of was his love, and I yearned for it with every cell of my being.

He couldn't be my second half! I had to be complete so we could complement not complete each other.

Why did I do all that? In order to DO something, we must always BE something. I became love first, so I could love.

I was vibrating love and breathing love. In order to create something good, we must feel good. Therefore, the most important thing for me was to feel good, and I could only feel good if my thoughts about him made me feel that way.

Writing about him and affirming him made me live all that love before it even happened. The one who vibrates pure love is stronger than hundreds who don't, so why not use the power of love, then?

I became devoted to him and our life together and he simply stayed. He didn't feel as good around anyone else as he did with me. People never forget how you make them feel.

I became her. The devoted woman who lives her life from love and above.

Fierce Devotion

by Danijela Nakovski

The divine being of love and devotion.

Grant me strength to bring love and light to people.

Help me show others how love can heal everything.

May I feel the unconditional liquid love and show the way to others to feel the same.

Let love speak always and forever and heal the broken hearts.

May you help me remind people of the power of love.

May the effortless way become the only way.

Thank you for guiding my way through these times of the masters as I keep showing to others and myself what is possible.

Grant me the power to heal myself and others and to forgive myself and others as forgiveness is the best gift we can offer to our heart.

Help me understand that what I seek is seeking me and that everything has it's perfect divine timing.

May I never forget to find the God in me first.

I offer this prayer to you, and I devote my life to bringing the love, and life to the world.

May you be always by my side to remind me of who I really AM.

Amen

About

by Danijela Nakovski

As a Transformational Coach and Personal Resilience Mentor, Danijela works closely with her clients to help them achieve their personal and professional goals. She worked and was mentored by the biggest teacher on human potential, the late Bob Proctor. She is also a Founding Member and a Master Coach at Napoleon Hill Institute, which is the world's foremost authority on personal development.

She will welcome you to the New Realm of Possibilities!

Thirteen years ago, Danijela was a single mom with three little girls with a corporate job and no hope.

She was working hard without making any real progress and I had that burning desire to be the one that gets somewhere.

She kept thinking - There must be an easier way!

Today, she walks hand in hand with the most amazing husband, paving the way for their four children while doing the job she adores.

What IF it was possible for you?

As you think about your own life and future, you know if you walk long enough, you'll get somewhere, but why not explore the magical way to get you where you really want to go.

She is not your ordinary coach but rather your agent of CHANGE.

She is your friendly reminder that life is meant to be wonderful.

She challenges her client's belief that life must be a constant struggle by teaching them ease and effortless way.

By teaching you the Mastery of Love you will realize that true love is not hard to find.

She sure will challenge every belief you have that is stopping you from living the life you truly desire.

Imagine being able to believe in as many as six impossible things before breakfast.

There is no illusion. Only your perception of reality being ALL that it can be.

As you start perceiving beyond the limitations of the physical senses, you allow a whole new reality to emerge.

You are worthy and magical! But magic will only work if you allow yourself to step in it.

www.instagram.com/findpearlwithin

www.FindPearlWithin.com

Courtney DeMatteo

32

~ Transcendence ~

Through her wisdom, she leads us on a transformative journey, shedding doubt and fear. Her wisdom breaks our perceived limitations, unleashing dormant powers. In her presence, we become liberated spirits, soaring to unimaginable heights, unlocking infinite possibilities within.

On the Other Side

by Courtney DeMatteo

Transcendence is found in the freedom of no longer belonging to the pain.

I looked into his big brown eyes, and I saw fear. He was shaking like a leaf in a frigid wind. Upstairs was a hurricane of anger; smashing, yelling, guttural screams of pain looking for anywhere to unleash and pour out the misery that was raging inside. I was safe for the moment, locked behind my bedroom door, praying he wouldn't break it open. Then a flash of calm overtook me. In a moment I went from fear for my life to treading a determined path forward. I was leaving and there was no stopping me this time.

My poor dog, all 85 pounds of gentle giant, was on his bed shaking and, in those big brown eyes, I saw the pain and fear of my future children. I had no choice; this was not something I was willing to tolerate, excuse, or justify any longer. I found two empty garbage bags and packed everything I could. I called my sister and said, "It's time to come and get me." With two garbage bags full of my clothes, my dog, and my car, under the supervision of my sister and her formidable boyfriend, I left behind a story that would shape the rest of my life.

Driving away, listening to the playlist that would define the next few years of my life, I found transcendence in the moment I knew I was finally free from the pain.

Black eyes, I don't need 'em

Blue tears, give me freedom

Black eyes all behind me

Blue tears will never find me now…

"Black Eyes, Blue Tears"

Shania Twain

Transcendence is complete surrender. You have no idea where you are going, but you know it will be better than where you are now. You stretch your arms open wide and trust that a higher power will take over and steer you in the right direction, far away from where you are. You have crawled over broken glass; bloody, tired, and empty. You have tried to will your way through it, listened to everyone's advice, and found only emptiness. There is only one thing left to do: hand it over, hand it all over, to a higher power. When you've reached this level of exhaustion and emptiness, there is nothing left to do but to pack your bags, get into your car, and let Higher Power drive.

I lay there, huddled on the ground, sobbing as quietly as I could so my husband wouldn't hear me. How could I share with him the pain I was feeling? How did I end up here again? So many years later, so much older and so much wiser, and yet in such familiar territory. Once again, an abusive relationship had taken over and I was lost, confused, and at the darkest moment I had ever been. How could we call this an abusive relationship? She was a friend. She wasn't physically attacking me, even though she threatened to. It was different, and yet that shame, that guilt, that desperation to be loved, it all felt so familiar.

The voice of the police officer rang in my head. "Come with me to the station. We need to take a restraining order out on her." My simple determined answer: "No, we work together, I can't." Lying there on the floor, in so much pain, and the only thought inside me was, I don't want to wake up tomorrow. In the strongest voice

I could muster, which was barely above a whisper, I looked up to hope and I said, "Help me." How did I end up here again?

At that moment, my phone rang. The caller ID told me it was the one person I would answer the phone for in the state I was in: my Aunt Beth. "Hello," I said, and the rest was a blur. I know she shared with me the energy I needed to borrow in that moment, a thread strong enough to get me off the floor and onto my couch, strong enough to wake me up in the morning to face another day. For the next 30 days we spoke, and each day that thread grew thicker until it was more like rope that helped pull me to my feet. Then the rope dissipated, and I had the strength to stand on my own again. That's when the work really started. Transcendence found me in the moment I surrendered to the Source and opened myself up to be helped.

Don't be afraid

Close your eyes

Lay it all down

Don't you cry

Can't you see I'm going where I can see the sun rise?

I've been talking to my angel, and he said that it's alright.

"Talking to My Angel"

Melissa Etheridge

I am so blessed, now, to have gone through what I've been through and to have come out the other side. The first time, I almost lost my life at the hands of another. The second time, by my own hand. Yet, I can sit here today, retelling these stories in complete gratitude for where I've been and how far I have come. The lessons that are given to us are always a blessing, even when they feel like torture. I wouldn't have agreed with that statement 20 years ago, when I was carrying two garbage bags away from the life I knew, or 15 years ago when I was huddled up in a heap on the floor, but I can sit here in reflection now, holding space for who I once was, and proud of who I have become because of it.

The lessons have been many, and one stands out above all others. Moments of transcendence are why we crawl through our painful experiences. We are made up of two selves: Spirit Self and Ego Self. When we are hurt, traumatized, or damaged in any way, only the Ego Self is affected. Spirit is all-knowing and cannot be damaged, which means we always have a healed self to lean into whenever the damaged self has too much pain to handle. Getting to know my two selves has been paramount to healing my past and moving forward in confidence. Moving from my hurt Ego Self into a self-actualized and integrated ego/spirit unification is TRANSCENDENT.

On reflection, I can remember watching Dr Wayne Dyer on PBS giving a talk about spirit and ego. I remember saying to my husband, "This man is my church." Everything he was saying resonated with me to my core. It was as if he were standing right in front of me, talking directly to me, and offering a new perspective on what it really means to be healed. He was talking about the spirit as the all-knowing, everlasting source of power and wisdom. Then the ego, the selfish aspect, only concerned with self-preservation, was bad and needed to be released in order to move on in the healthiest way. I took the new perspective to heart and began to learn more about the concept of spirit vs ego. I heard many mentors speaking of ego death and killing the ego. I learned from this that ego was a bad thing and to heal I needed to do everything I could to stay away from ego and only live in spirit.

As a spiritual being, we choose to move into this physical, focused position of human life. We know as spiritual beings that the focused energy of the human experience is the very best way to experience growth and expansion of our consciousness. It was in this recognition that my beliefs began to diverge from Dr Dyer and so many others who believe the ego is bad and that we need to kill our egos. As the wise spiritual beings we are, WE chose to be human and have a human experience, which means we chose to have a second self: the Ego Self. The ego is a function of the mind, meant to protect and keep safe and secure our physical body.

And for that I am grateful.

It was my Ego Self that screamed at my ex to pull the car over when he was racing down the highway at dangerous speeds. It was my Ego Self that convinced me to sleep with a knife by my bedside "just in case". It was my Ego Self that made the decision to preserve my life when the darkness fell heavy over me.

The Ego Self has an incredible way of directing our thoughts in its favor, to make us believe we are in physical danger even when we are not. The ego voice is the voice of the inner critic that will tell you you are not good enough, strong enough, or powerful enough, so that you won't take a risk and put yourself in danger. My Ego Self believed him when he said he was the only one who would ever love me. My Ego Self believed him when he told me I wasn't pretty enough for others to look at. My Ego Self was convinced I deserved it when she threatened me physically. My Ego Self thought I'd brought on every abusive word and action taken against me. My Ego Self was broken.

The awakening to these two separate states of being took some time. We hear things when we are meant to hear them, and we understand them when we are meant to understand them. What I came to realize was that the existence of these two separate

371

concepts within me was deliberate and meaningful. I heard from many of my mentors that the ego is bad, and it should be pushed aside or even done away with entirely. Through my own reflection and life experiences, I have come to recognize that idea as hypocritical to the grand design. My own thoughts wandered into the question, "Why would our wise Spirit Selves choose to step into a human existence knowing full well that meant taking on an ego to help us grow and expand, if we are only meant to kill that very ego?" And then it hit me: if it is the ego that becomes damaged, then it is the ego we must focus on healing, not kill or eliminate. My spirit chose to be here, my spirit is all-knowing, and my spirit chose to live in a plane of existence that has an ego. The ego is deliberate and necessary, not expendable and "bad." Ego death is egotistical.

As we integrate with our ego, it can come into alignment with spirit, and that is the very moment when we experience the fullest expression of our true and most powerful selves, the transcendence from where we are to WHO WE ARE MEANT TO BE. One of the most powerful moments of transcendence I can remember was during a coaching convention when we were taught how to re-story. This is a process of turning your victim story into a story of victory, with a spiritual upleveling in your awareness. As part of the process, we needed to tell our victim story to a small group, and it was the first time I had spoken the words "domestic violence" out loud. To be clear, this was almost 10 years after stuffing those two trash bags with my belongings and leaving the life I knew. I shared my story in some detail, with a quivering voice and often looking down to the floor in shame. Then the questions came…Who am I now because of what I went through? What did I discover because I went through it? What lessons did I learn as a result of it? These questions were electrifying to me! They poured over me like a warm wind, enveloping me with their promise of freedom and release. I am a stronger, more powerful, wiser woman with a voice that is worth listening to and a heart that is deserving to love and be loved, at its highest level of existence. I am a cycle breaker, healing the wounds etched into me by my ancestors.

I was invited by Mary Morrissey, the lead coach of this conference, up on stage to share my story. It was at that moment that I claimed, "I am no longer a victim of domestic abuse, I am not even just a survivor of domestic abuse, I am a thriver, and I am grateful!" [BOOM]. The sound of victory in my head was louder than any applause that came from the audience. My moment of transcendence was there. I walked away from that conference a new woman, with a higher level of awareness, awakened to the power of perspective.

Imagine the moment when you no longer have to be right, you no longer have to prove your worth to others, you no longer feel the need to pour energy in resentments, anger, victimhood, or any other state which pulls your attention away from your true purpose here on Earth. Imagine the powerful moment when all of that has been healed and you can go forward with your primary mission: to live a joy-filled and happy life of service to humanity, sharing the gift placed upon your heart by our divine Creator. Feel the power of that moment being transmitted to you now. Close your eyes, imagine who you are as your healed Ego and Spirit Selves combine forces to propel you forward into a higher level of conscious awareness. Imagine the ripple effect you will cause and the healing you will catalyze as the pure white light energy you were born to be.

This has been my healing quest: to unite my healed Ego Self with my already whole Spirit Self and allow them to rise together. This is the transcendence I believe we are all charged with in our human existence. The ego, being prone to dominance, and the spirit, feeling no need to explain, justify or prove itself in any way, create a constant dialogue inside my mind. I have to check myself often to decide which is the dominant voice in my head and which one I should lean in to. If my life is in danger, it is the ego who takes center stage, but if it is only a perceived threat and my life is safe, I try to lean into what spirit has to tell me. I am in no way perfect in my movements, and it is sometimes a conscious decision with deliberate focus when I need to lean into spirit. When I am in alignment, though, the feeling of flow is exhilarating and worth any effort it took to get me there.

To continue my healing journey, I have challenged myself to look at every opportunity of offense and triggers and dissect them. I know that if I am feeling threatened, out of alignment, offended or otherwise triggered, it is a signal from within that there is something there coming up to be healed. After the initial response of my ego protecting me by putting up a defense, I give myself grace, show gratitude to my ego for the newest opportunity to clear my field, and get to work shining a light on the darkness to bring on the healing. In the beginning this was a laborious and very deliberate practice. As I have come to embrace the work, I have also come to enjoy the experience and look at it more as play than work. I know this practice is shifting me closer and closer to who I am meant to be, and I eagerly await the new me that grows out of each new healing experience.

Transcendence is found in the freedom of no longer belonging to the pain. Transcendence is waiting for you on the other side of what everyone else thinks you should do. There is no human construct that can keep you from transcendence once you have surrendered. Transcendence is walking away from everything you know because you have a deeper understanding that there is something greater waiting for you.

Transcendence is the portal you climb through, the blanket you wrap around yourself, and the smile that is waiting for you on the other side.

Transcendence is the love you feel for yourself when you finally choose you. Transcendence is the love that Source Energy greets you with when you finally come into alignment with who you are meant to be.

Now it is your turn. What is the one decision you need to make to find your transcendence?

Prayer of Transcendence

by Courtney DeMatteo

You are doing it all right,
exactly as you are meant to be doing it.

You are creating your successes
and making your mistakes
in perfect unfolding
with what you came here to do and be.

Now be gentle with yourself,
give yourself grace for being human.

Remember, YOU CHOSE THIS,
and you knew you weren't going to be perfect at it.

There is no growth or expansion in perfection.

There is transcendence
in learning from your mistakes though.

And that's what you came here to do.

About

Courtney DeMatteo

"You may say that I'm a Dreamer, but I'm not the only one."

-John Lennon

Jump into the vibration elevator and soar to new heights with Courtney as your guide. A certified Life and Business Alignment Coach and Reiki Master, Courtney DeMatteo has tapped into the wisdom of the ages to help unlock and open the doors of opportunity and success for those who have asked for her assistance. Her mission is to raise the collective consciousness of the world because each person who finds happiness is one more person spreading love in this world to others.

Courtney is the owner of Crystal Clarity Life Coaching, LLC, the author of The E3 Experience – Empower*Enlighten*Evolve, and the originator and producer of The Uplevel World Festival. Her background experiences in marketing and teaching unite a diverse group of skills to form a unique view and expert voice for her coaching clients.

Her personal life events add to her ability to empathize with her clients and see them through difficult situations. She has been blessed with a gift of deep insight which she shares with individuals and groups all over the world coaching one on one, small groups, in her authorship experiences, and speaking at large stage events.

Through her coaching and reiki practice, Courtney is known as a gateway to activating her clients' greatest dreams and igniting their passions.

When you are ready to wake up your hidden potential, accelerate your journey toward fulfillment, and live your dream life, make Courtney your next connection!

www.crystalclaritylifecoaching.com

Instagram @crystalclaritycoaching

Facebook @crystalclaritylifecoaching

LinkedIn @courtney-dematteo

Kathy White

33

~ Grace ~

The Goddess of Grace, with her gentle embrace, empowers hearts to
release the weight of guilt, granting the strength to forgive themselves
and embrace the boundless possibilities that lie ahead.

You Have To Forgive Yourself To Move Forward

by Kathy White

Monday morning, and the week starts with the school drop-off. At 7:30 a.m. I drop both kids off at school and head to work. When I arrive, I set myself up for the day ahead. Coffee – check. Water – check. Headset – on and working. I log on to the computer and into Google Messaging. (Instant messaging was a new technology to us back then. It was fun to get these messages so quickly but distracting as well.)

The message box on the bottom right corner of my screen lights up, telling me I have a message.

It is a weird-looking smiley face from the guy I work with, and I have no idea what he wants.

The only thing I do know is that the smiley face looks creepy, kind of like the devil. I reply and ask him if he needs anything. He asks me a few work questions that I respond to. I go about my day until work ends. I drive to get the kids from school and head home. On the weekends my husband Mike and I normally had Saturday training at the office and Sunday was church. This was the normal routine.

Monday morning, and the routine starts again. I drop the kids off at school and head to work. As soon as I log on to Google Chat, the evil smiley face appears. But this time it's different. My heart and hands start to tingle. In my mind I'm asking myself, "What is wrong with me?" I feel like a schoolgirl with her first crush. Brian asks me work-related questions again and I reply with work-related answers. This goes into a repeat pattern for months: evil smiley face followed by "Hey… business question". I start to wonder why he keeps asking me questions he already knows. Does he have butterflies whenever my face pops up when I log on to the computer?

I knew what the Bible stated about divorce and adultery. It's an abomination in the eyes of the Lord, and you will go to hell for it.

Yet, with every message, my heart would flutter. Kathy, you are married. Quit entertaining these feelings. I knew my marriage wasn't the happiest, but that seemed to be the norm with every other relationship I knew. Our business had crashed during the financial crisis of 2008 and left both me and Mike in a state of despair and depression. I had to get this separate job to make sure our bills were being paid. Household tensions were high with both of us. We didn't have money to pay our mortgage. We had to get state assistance to buy groceries to feed the kids — one thing I told myself I would never do.

Work was my happy place. I didn't like working for my boss at all, but that paled in comparison to how I felt when I went to work to find Brian was there. He made me feel different. I had never felt this way about someone before. Why was he sent to me? Was this a test? My heart was bound by law to one and bound by emotion to another.

I would respond to his questions and ask him about his life. This wasn't what someone in a committed relationship should be doing but I felt I had gone too far down the hole. It was as though we had this emotional connection that I couldn't explain. People get upset when you have a physical affair but what about an emotional affair? Was that what this was? Where in the Bible is this wrong? Intuitively, I knew.

It was now a routine. I couldn't wait to get to work. I'd log on to my computer and then into Google Chat. Brian's evil smiley face popped up. He knew I was married. He even asked here and there about Mike and the kids. I wondered what was going through his mind. I was naïve and just thought he was being friendly. I was the one who had illicit feelings for him… or so I thought.

Mike would come home angry at the world. Depressed. I struggled with wanting to be around him. We had gone to numerous counselors over the 17 years of our marriage. The tools they taught us worked for a while and then we were right back to where we started. The day came when I'd had enough and asked Mike for a divorce. He didn't see it coming. Our life as we knew it was crumbling down and I was to blame.

I could hear the Bible verses in my head being repeated over and over. If I followed through with the divorce, then I was going to hell. What kind of loving God was this I believed in? I had these thoughts racing through my head: "How bad is hell? What is hell?" I started researching other people who had got divorced and their lives turned out OK. Are they going to hell? Well, if they are, then I will be hanging out with them. My life wasn't what I'd imagined it to be when I was a young girl in love, yearning to spend the rest of my life with him. For me to ask for a divorce was something I honestly didn't know I had in me.

Of course, my daily chats with Brian at work kept up. He knew exactly what I was going through. We decided to go on a hike one day during the separation. While on the hike, neither one of us could keep our hands off each other. It was as if the handcuffs had been unlocked. I went to work the next day not feeling the best about myself. Then the guilt set in; I wasn't legally divorced yet and the shame I felt was too much to bear.

Mike and I decided to work on our relationship and get back together for the kids. This was a hard decision because my heart was torn in two different places: life with my kids and Mike or life with my soulmate, Brian.

I knew I had to tell Mike about Brian and what had happened if we were to move forward with our relationship. I still remember it vividly. We went for a walk at the local park and were looking at a flower garden. I told him I had something to tell him and proceeded to tell him that I'd had sexual relations with Brian during our separation. It was by far one of the hardest things I have ever had to do and the look in Mike's eyes is one I can never forget. It was full of hurt, anger, jealousy, and despair.

We tried for a year to make our marriage work and one day I'd had enough. I packed my stuff and went to my sister's. I just couldn't do it anymore. Whether I went to hell because the Bible said I would; whether Mike hated me because he already did and could never forgive me; whether the kids were disappointed in me for leaving, I wasn't happy and I had tried for years. Our daughter, Kienna, was happy when we told her we were getting divorced. Our son, Lawson, was heartbroken. I couldn't be a good mom if I was unhappy. I'd seen it in my mom and didn't want to repeat this pattern. My kids deserved a happy mom. Our divorce was finalized in 2011.

Nothing ever happened with me and Brian after my divorce. It was a heartache that healed itself over time. I went through intense emotions with Brian — from the fierce emotional electricity whenever we were in each other's presence, to the heart-wrenching pain of having to mourn a relationship which came to me at the wrong time in my life. I curled up in a ball for numerous days, crying the pain away.

Relationships, good or bad, are always 50/50. Each person involved is as much to blame for the faults in the relationship, and as much to praise for the harmony in a relationship. The stuff with Brian happened, but honestly, I would have divorced Mike even without it. It just took another to show me how much pain I truly was in. I talked to each of the kids and told them how I felt. I told them how broken and unhappy I was on the inside and why I'd asked Dad their dad for a divorce.

Is the world as disappointed in me as I am in myself? I saw my life as a failure. My heart was tied up in knots trying to do the right thing, failing at being perfect. I was in so much emotional pain, it felt like a tornado wreaking destruction within its path. I didn't feel worthy of love. I didn't feel worthy of forgiveness. More than anything, I didn't feel worthy of grace.

Why, Grace, do you hate me so? Your embrace of forgiveness, love, and compassion eludes me, but not others. You see the hurt in my heart, yet don't care. You see the guilt I'm carrying for hurting another, yet you hold your arms of loving embrace for others and not for me. I am hurting. I am struggling. I am crying with despair.

My counselor said I needed to take time to mourn my marriage — something I never thought I would have to do. Honestly, I was mourning two deaths: one being my marriage and the other not being with my soul mate. I thought I was a failure. Who would love me after committing adultery and being divorced? I was destined to be single the rest of my life. I had to let myself mourn the person I wanted to be with. I had to mourn the expectations I'd had for my life. This was giving myself grace. What is grace? "Grace is about more than mercy, and it requires actions of love that go beyond forgiveness. It is a gift that not only forgets our past wrongs but also makes us whole, no matter our current or future imperfections."

In my book, "Unleash the Warrior Within" I quote Paul Coelho: "Tears are words that need to be written." The sting of death of my marriage healed with time. I had to give myself grace to take the time to mourn and cry. Crying is good for the soul. It's tears that need to flow. Crying relieves mental stress and soothes your emotional state.

I still had a lot of anger in my soul. Studies show that suppressed anger could be a precursor to cancer. I was diagnosed with breast cancer a few years later. Karma? Possibly. Life? Possibly. Looking back, this was the best thing that could have happened to me. Although it was a difficult time, it allowed me to slow down my life; reflect on who I wanted to be as a person; and led me on a healing journey to where I am today.

It took years before I could look at myself in a mirror and be proud of the woman I had become — and love that woman unconditionally. My heart was still shattered from things that have happened throughout my entire life. I had been on antidepressants for most of my life and wanted to get off them. I met a shaman who changed my life. I did a healing ceremony with him in which we allowed my shattered heart to become whole again.

During one of the ceremonies, the song in the background was the Hawaiian song, "Ho'oponopono" – a beautiful Hawaiian teaching about forgiveness. People who struggle with the concept of forgiveness – both for themselves and for others — often find comfort in this deep healing age-old practice. Accordingly, chanting this phrase over and over is a powerful way to cleanse the body of guilt, shame, haunting memories, ill will, or bad feelings that keep the mind fixated on negative thoughts.

During this healing ceremony and song, it was a beautiful time of forgiveness where I was able to forgive Mike and forgive myself.

- Step 1: Repentance – Just say: I'm sorry

- Step 2: Ask for forgiveness – Say: Please forgive me

- Step 3: Gratitude – Say: Thank you

- Step 4: Love – Say: I love you

I had to forgive and give myself grace for the version of me that was doing actions I wouldn't necessarily want to repeat. I had to forgive that version of me that was in pain. I wouldn't do these actions again and have imposed strict rules on myself. I took the time over the next few weeks to journal my feelings about my marriage, both the good and bad.

I said and thought these things to myself constantly for months: "I'm sorry for the actions I did. Please forgive me and thank you for the woman who got me through 17 years of marriage and started my life with my kids. I'm grateful to her. I love you and I let that version of you go."

It brings tears to my eyes thinking about it. The love I had for myself blossomed and has grown every day since. I had loved being single. I felt like I could fly. I could now be my own person and find who I truly am. What I missed most was the companionship in a relationship. I met my knight in shining armor, Jeff, in 2014. In him I had somebody who was ready to be with the version of me I'd spent so long creating and healing. It was as if Jeff knew exactly what I needed and was incredibly patient waiting for me to heal until I was ready for a relationship. Me, my kids, and my family adore him. He has been a godsend to my family.

I now have my happily ever after. I had to go through the pain of growing into the person I am today so I could find my prince. He has always known about these things that I had kept from others, and he's always loved me fully and completely. I believe that is grace.

Rumi states, "The wound is where the light enters you." Grace comes to forgive and forgive again. Life is a balance of holding on and letting go. The only way is to go through the pain and feel it. You have to keep breaking your heart until it opens. Yet don't get lost in your pain, because one day your pain will become your cure. You have to heal the pain in order to cure it. It is a mirror for you to reflect and once you heal the pain, you will heal yourself. Pain will teach you to become a better version of yourself.

You've seen my descent. Now watch my rising.

Prayer for Grace

by Kathy White

Divine Goddess of Grace, hear my heartfelt plea, I humbly beseech your healing energy. Wrap your loving arms around those in need, with tender mercy, let your light intercede.

Goddess of Grace, in your gentle embrace, Bring solace and comfort to every wounded place. With your sacred touch, mend broken hearts, and guide us through life's most intricate parts.

With each breath we take, let your blessings flow, renew our spirits, let your healing essence bestow. Grant us strength to rise from depths of despair, And the courage to face life's burdens with care.

Goddess of Grace, with your gracefulness divine, illuminate our paths, like stars that brightly shine. In times of darkness, be our guiding light, lead us to healing, and make our troubles take flight.

May your soothing presence fill every space, Reviving our souls with your divine embrace. Restore our bodies, minds, and souls anew, with your boundless love, make us whole and true.

Goddess of Grace, we offer this prayer, with unwavering faith, trusting that you are near. We thank you for your divine healing might, and for the blessings you bring, both day and night.

In your sacred name, this prayer we send, knowing that your healing grace will never end. Forever and always, may we be embraced, By your love, your light, and your infinite grace.

Kathy White

Kathy White, a Utah native residing in Murray, is a true embodiment of success and personal growth. With a Bachelor's degree in accounting from the University of Utah and extensive experience managing Accounts Payable departments at industry-leading companies like Overstock.com and Ultradent Products, Kathy has established herself as a corporate powerhouse.

Driven by an insatiable thirst for knowledge and personal development, Kathy has immersed herself in transformative programs by Bob Proctor and received mentorship from renowned figures like John Assaraf and Niurka. As an International Best-Selling Author, her work has garnered acclaim, earning the honor of having a foreword penned by the influential motivational speaker Les Brown.

Kathy's spirit knows no bounds when it comes to adventure. From snowshoeing to skydiving and swimming with sharks, she fearlessly embraces thrilling experiences. In a testament to her resilience, Kathy even encountered a mountain airlift in Kauai.

Continuing her quest for personal and professional growth, Kathy is an ambassador coach in training with the esteemed Napoleon Hill Institute. Her dedication to empowering others is a testament to her character and unwavering commitment to uplifting those around her.

Kathy White's inspiring journey showcases the convergence of determination, resilience, and a hunger for personal growth.

Through her expertise, motivational writing, and adventurous spirit, she captivates audiences, serving as a beacon of limitless possibilities for all who have the privilege of crossing paths with her.

Kathy loves to help people transform their lives through coaching. She believes that everyone has the potential to be happy and fulfilled, and she uses her skills to help people identify their strengths, overcome their challenges, and create a life that they love. As an agent of change, she is committed to helping people create a more positive and sustainable world. She uses her coaching skills to help people develop the skills and confidence they need to make a difference in the world.

www.coachkathywhite.com

Social Media @coachkathywhite

coachkathywhite@gmail.com

Closing

As I come to the end of this incredible journey, I am filled with a deep sense of gratitude and awe for the 33 gods and goddesses who have graced these pages.

Their stories have touched my heart in ways that I never thought possible. I have been moved by their courage, inspired by their wisdom, and humbled by their power.

Each of these divine beings has taught me something invaluable about life, love, and the human experience. They have reminded me of the beauty and mystery that lies at the heart of all existence.

As I close this book, I carry with me the lessons and blessings of these 33 gods and goddesses. They have become a part of me, and I will forever be grateful for their presence in my life.

May their stories continue to inspire and uplift all those who read them, and may their divine essence shine forth in the world for all eternity.

I am reminded that the journey never truly ends. There are countless deities out there, waiting to be discovered and embraced.

And so, I embark on a new journey, one that will take me into the depths of this century, in search of the brave ones who have chosen to become "player one" in their own lives. The ones who have chosen faith over fear, love over hate, and who embody the qualities that we all aspire to.

I am excited to discover the deities of this century, to learn from their stories and teachings, and to share their wisdom with the world. I know that this journey will be filled with challenges and obstacles, but I am ready to face them with an open heart and an open mind.

May the lessons and blessings of the 33 gods and goddesses who have graced these pages be my guide, as I continue this journey of discovery, growth, and transformation.

I am grateful for the opportunity to have shared this journey with you, and I look forward to the adventures that lie ahead.

It's Only the Beginning...

Made in the USA
Columbia, SC
20 July 2024

40fa717f-39e0-414c-a27e-e0ef876797cdR04